The Soviet Union and the Construction of the Global Market

Oscar Sanchez-Sibony reveals the origins of our current era in the dissolution of the institutions that governed the architecture of energy and finance during the Bretton Woods era. He shows how, in the second half of the 1960s, the Soviet Union sought to dismantle the compartmentalized nature of Bretton Woods in order to escape its material ostracism and pave a path to global finance and exchange that the United States had vetoed during the 1950s and 1960s. Through the construction of a set of pipelines that helped Europe's energy regime change from coal to oil and gas, the Soviet Union succeeded in developing market relations and a relationship with Western capital as durable as the pipelines themselves. He shows how a history of the development of capitalism needs to integrate the socialist world in bringing about the new form of capitalism that regiments our lives today.

Oscar Sanchez-Sibony is Associate Professor at the University of Hong Kong. He is author of *Red Globalization. The Political Economy of the Soviet Cold War from Stalin to Khrushchev* (2014).

The Soviet Union and the Construction of the Global Market

Energy and the Ascent of Finance in Cold War Europe, 1964–1971

Oscar Sanchez-Sibony

The University of Hong Kong

CAMBRIDGE
UNIVERSITY PRESS

CAMBRIDGE
UNIVERSITY PRESS

Shaftesbury Road, Cambridge CB2 8EA, United Kingdom

One Liberty Plaza, 20th Floor, New York, NY 10006, USA

477 Williamstown Road, Port Melbourne, VIC 3207, Australia

314–321, 3rd Floor, Plot 3, Splendor Forum, Jasola District Centre, New Delhi – 110025, India

103 Penang Road, #05–06/07, Visioncrest Commercial, Singapore 238467

Cambridge University Press is part of Cambridge University Press & Assessment, a department of the University of Cambridge.

We share the University's mission to contribute to society through the pursuit of education, learning and research at the highest international levels of excellence.

www.cambridge.org
Information on this title: www.cambridge.org/9781108834544

DOI: 10.1017/9781108993555

First published 2023

A catalogue record for this publication is available from the British Library.

Library of Congress Cataloging-in-Publication Data
Names: Sanchez-Sibony, Oscar, 1977- author.
Title: The Soviet Union and the construction of the global market : energy and the ascent of finance in cold war Europe, 1964-1971 / Oscar Sanchez-Sibony, The University of Hong Kong.
Description: New York, NY : Cambridge University Press, [2023] | Includes bibliographical references and index.
Identifiers: LCCN 2022044741 (print) | LCCN 2022044742 (ebook) | ISBN 9781108834544 (hardback) | ISBN 9781108995184 (paperback) | ISBN 9781108993555 (epub)
Subjects: LCSH : Finance–Soviet Union–History. | Soviet Union–Commerce–History. | Soviet Union–Foreign economic relations–History.
Classification: LCC HG186.S55 S254 2023 (print) | LCC HG186.S55 (ebook) | DDC 332.0947–dc23/eng/20221116
LC record available at https://lccn.loc.gov/2022044741
LC ebook record available at https://lccn.loc.gov/2022044742

ISBN 978-1-108-83454-4 Hardback

Contents

Figures

Acknowledgments

This volume was mostly written up in the quiet and withdrawn circumstances of Covid seclusion in Hong Kong. As Hong Kong shut itself away from the rest of the world, conferences, workshops, and other usual venues of intellectual interaction were shut away as well. One positive outcome, alas, was the mass peregrination of this kind of exchange to recorded videos on the internet, which had the effect of bringing conversations to those of us who are far from the centers of discussion in our fields. Intellectual debts have become more anonymous even as they become more diffuse among disciplines, and I hope I have done a creditable job citing these. Before this state of affairs descended on us, I did manage to workshop some of the ideas in this book in a more traditional manner, and I'd like to thank Andrew Sloin, Alexandra Oberländer, Patrick Neveling, Aleksei Popov, Brian Porter-Szücs, Felix Wemheuer, Anna Krylova, Arturo Zoffmann Rodríguez, Karl Gerth, Stefan Link, and all the participants at the germinal conference "Global Capitalism and the Worlds of Socialism" that I had planned for a long time to take place in Hong Kong, but had to move online in 2021 – because hope took a long time failing.

The write-up in times of covid followed a fairly long period of preparation and research in archives in Moscow. This documentary accumulation would have been impossible without the several generous grants that afforded both the resources for the annual trips to Russia as well as the time off teaching necessary for the write-up. I thank the University of Hong Kong for its seed funding as well as Hong Kong's Research Grants Council, which supported this research (HKU17600817). My departmental colleagues at the University of Hong Kong, especially David Pomfret, Charles Schencking, John Carroll, Peter Cunich and Robert Peckham also rendered crucial practical support, for which I am very grateful. I'd like to thank Metropol Verlag for permission to reprint as part of Chapter 4 the text they translated in "Energie, die Sowjetunion und der Kampf um Kapital nach dem Zusammenbruch des Bretton-Woods-Systems," *Jahrbuch für Historische Kommunismusforschung* (2020):

193–208. I feel particular gratitude to the archivists of the different Russian state archives where I worked every summer since 2014 until the world shut down, and especially to Nadezhda Mikhailovna Kostrikova, whose professionalism and good cheer under trying circumstances never failed to make me feel welcome and grateful to be working on the questions and ambiguities of political economy.

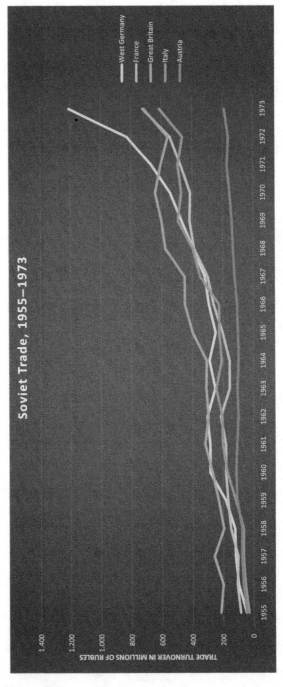

Figure 0.1 Soviet imports and exports, 1955–1970 (in millions of rubles)

Introduction

Lorenzo finally heeded his mother's entreaties to come back to Spain. She had visited him only once in Paris, where Lorenzo had landed after he was jailed for anti-Francoist agitation and banned from all of Spain's universities for two years. He had grown weary of Europe's Communist parties as well as the socialist states in Eastern Europe that he felt had betrayed the cause in Spain. Like so much movement toward greater democracy in history, the one in Spain had been led by miners fighting regime violence for freedom of assembly and the right to unionize. Miners' power of economic sabotage, so prevalent and effective during the struggles for greater democracy in the first half of the twentieth century, would soon wane as the industrialized world moved to petroleum-based economies. Unlike the previous mineral regime, hydrocarbon energy was a form whose production could be outsourced to undemocratic geographies and whose fluid materiality was ultimately difficult to sabotage in the cause of making democratic claims. Before that energy regime change, however, the actually existing socialist world had offered its mineral resources to the West, even when it meant undermining budding political struggles against enemy regimes, even when it meant fighting actually existing fascism, even when it meant danger and penury for foot soldiers like Lorenzo fighting for democracy and socialism. Lorenzo came home defeated not by Franco and his machinery of oppression, but by the socialist world – the undemocratic, caudillo style of Communist Party management in Spain and the economic ambitions of their patrons to the East.

Before exiling himself to France to continue the fight for an end to Franco and for socialism, the bright Lorenzo had started a degree in engineering at the Engineering School of Roads, Canals, and Ports in Madrid, an institution more than a century and a half old that took in the country's brightest sons. He did so in the face of a notoriously discouraging academic culture that thought nothing of summarily failing whole cohorts of students. Lorenzo was one of five to get a passing grade in the first year. Engineers were the technocratic heroes of the European postwar miracle, and for that matter the miracles of growth evident in the 1960s throughout Eastern Europe as well. Years later, Lorenzo's neighbors to his own future middle-class apartment in Madrid would be a married couple with a particular past: Both were Spanish children rescued by the Soviet Union during Spain's Civil War, given an education in engineering and medicine respectively and welcomed back to the new social regime in Spain as full participants in the emergent middle class of the country. A socialist gift to fascist Spain. Lorenzo's own path to that apartment, however, would not pass through engineering. Just as the future was starting to look bright for young Lorenzo, he was struck down by a kidney stone that, at that time, required a crude open surgery to take out. During the months-long convalescence in his Castilian village, Espinosa de Henares, Lorenzo's interest migrated to economics. He was coaxed in that direction by an odd confluence: the advice of the parish priest that first introduced the discipline to him, and the discovery of a recently published book, *The Economic Structure of Spain* (*Estructura económica de España*) by the then Marxist economist Ramón Tamames. The book explained precisely that: a structure of industrial exploitation, latifundist agrarian organization, and the deep historical roots of Spain's unreconstructed inequalities. It had quickly become a touchstone of left political identity in Spain, read by academics, students, and workers alike. Tamames' book ushered Lorenzo to the economics faculty of the Complutense University of Madrid, but the encounter that subsequently formed him there was with José Luis Sampedro, a charismatic economist, playwright, novelist, general Renaissance man, and author of the introduction to Tamames' book. Sampedro had fought for the Spanish Republic Franco had mutinied against, before being taken prisoner and conscripted to fight for Franco's nationalists. After the Civil War, he graduated in 1947 in the very first cohort of a new discipline in Spain, economics, and became a professor at the Complutense, where Lorenzo met him. Sampedro remained a socialist throughout his career, suffering a purge at the university and exile before returning to his academic seat and as advisor to the Banco Exterior de España in a country still suffering from a dearth of educated technocrats – the same country that would welcome Lorenzo's future, Soviet-educated neighbors. In the late 1970s, Sampedro even briefly became a socialist senator in the first democratically elected parliament in Spain. The two economists who had changed Lorenzo's course developed quite differently. From the 1980s Tamames became ever more conservative, to the point of flirting with Spain's present-day Francoist party in his old age, even as his colleague Sampedro inspired the 2011 anti-austerity protests in Spain that gave rise to the left-wing Podemos Party and stimulated occupy movements around the world. Neoclassical economics is a broad enough ship. It took Lorenzo out to sea, and he never built one bridge.

After his decision to change careers, Lorenzo came to know torture, Marx, exile, and disillusion, in that order, the last three in France. Three years later, he was back at the Complutense to finish his economics degree under the tutelage of Marx-inflected economists in Francoist Spain. He graduated into a job under another economist, Antonio Pulido, who supplemented his meager wage as an economics professor at the Complutense by helping Franco's government put together the indicative five-year plans under which Spain was growing, from 1959, into a middle-income country. From there Lorenzo moved to Gallup, Inc., an American company known for its political polling. Spain's authoritarian regime had little use for such surveys, but desperately needed a different kind of statistical analysis. Lorenzo, with his knowledge of statistical planning techniques, was the kind of scarce young professional the company could use to develop its consulting business on market analysis in Spain. Engineers and technocrats built Spain's material infrastructure, but it was the steadily empowering field of economics, with an esoteric knowledge and language of quasi-ecclesiastical qualities, that never stopped accumulating social power.

Over the course of his budding career as an economist, Lorenzo had developed a set of skills that made him exceptional in the impoverished social landscape Franco had built in the postwar period. This perhaps explains the tolerance the regime evinced toward economists, whatever their political loyalties. In the late 1960s, Lorenzo gained entrance to the Chamber of Commerce, which offered him a choice of several posts abroad: Greece, Italy, Colombia, Angola. To the surprise of his colleagues, he chose the African destination. They did not know of Lorenzo's revolutionary past, and that fire yet flickered. He wanted to experience for himself the truth behind another one of his formative touchstones, Frantz Fanon's *Wretched of the Earth*. He was sent to Angola just as the Civil War was heating up. It did not take long for regime officials at the Chamber of Commerce to learn they had sent a fellow traveler of the liberation effort there; Spain's government preferred to travel with the neighboring dictatorship that had held Angola in an imperialist clutch well after European states had given up on empire – or at least on empire in that form. It took an incident for the notoriously incompetent ruling brass back in Madrid to realize who Lorenzo had been.

It went like this. Joselito was a former child actor and singer, wildly famous during the 1950s and early 60s in Spain and abroad. As he approached his thirties, Spain had moved on. After his last failed film in 1969, Joselito, destitute and broken, asked his Portuguese distributor to help him move to Angola, where he spent his time hunting and touring an imperial geography in which his fame still shimmered. When the brother of his local drummer ran into trouble with the Portuguese imperial police, Joselito made the decent choice of helping him escape, depositing him in a village far from the capital, whereupon his drummer's brother joined the guerrillas seeking to liberate the territory from Portuguese imperial rule. Joselito's drummer, however, fell into the clutches of the Portuguese intelligence services, and under torture, he denounced Joselito as co-conspirator. Lorenzo had met Joselito and been to his parties in his short time in Luanda, Angola's capital, and when he heard that Joselito had been jailed, he tried to get the Spanish ambassador in Angola to intercede. It is only then that the regime rediscovered who Lorenzo had been, and quickly recalled him to Madrid. But what awaited him there was not Joselito's fate; the Franco regime met him with a stern warning, and a promotion.

The warning was the obvious outcome of a certain socialist past, easily understood through the many dramatic retellings of Cold War confrontation. But his promotion was the outcome of another socialist genealogy. This one lacks the epic narrative Cold War histories relish but proved to be of more consequence to Lorenzo's life. It is a genealogy that harked back to his apprenticeship with the socialist economist Sampedro. Among his many lives, Sampedro had been part of the group of Spanish professors in the late 1950s to work out for the first time ever a set of national accounts for Spain, using output-input techniques with the help of a room-sized computer in Rome. The Harvard Professor Wassily Leontief would receive a Nobel Prize in 1973 for the development of these accounting techniques, but its roots lie in his country of origin, in Russia. There, while Leontief was working toward his degree in economics at the beginning of the 1920s, the utopian science fiction writer, physician, and Marxist theoretician Alexander Bogdanov first worked out notions of sectoral interrelationships. This would form the foundation of input-output analysis, contributing both to the development of Soviet planning at the end of the 1920s, and the development of national accounting (leading to the invention of the Gross National Product, GNP) in the West at the end of the 1930s – for which the Soviet Union had served as one of its first analytical targets because of the large trove of statistical data the Soviets had elaborated over the previous two decades.[1] The professional expertise Sampedro bequeathed young

---

[1] A. A. Belykh, "A Note on the Origins of Input-Output Analysis and the Contribution of the Early Soviet Economists: Chayanov, Bogdanov and Kritsman," *Soviet Studies* 41:3 (1989): 426–429. Bogdanov's ideas were later elaborated by Lev Kritsman. Leontief

Lorenzo, and the appeal it held for social improvement that drew Lorenzo to Sampedro, had direct roots in the transformations wrought by the Russian Revolution. Sampedro spent a professional lifetime in academia expanding on that legacy as an admirer and student of Yugoslavia's socialist self-management, and as a participant in East–West–South dialogues on development economics, many of which exchanges of ideas were linked to Latin America and the Spanish-speaking world.[2] Lorenzo transformed that bequest into a promotion to director of the international department at Spain's Chamber of Commerce. The regime needed Lorenzo, despite all his faults as a true-believing democrat, to teach a new cohort of officials the esoteric arts of indicative planning and market analysis in order to promote Spanish consumer goods around the world.

His final reward was a secondment to Taiwan in the mid-1970s. Lorenzo used the generous salary of that secondment to pay off his new apartment and join the ranks of the country's burgeoning middle class, right beside his red-educated neighbors.[3] He had been sent to Taiwan after Spain's Chinese mission moved irrevocably to Beijing in the aftermath of the United States' own move from Taipei to Beijing. More importantly – or they might not have sent an economist – he had been sent to oversee the exponentially growing trade of the region. What he observed and helped govern there were the rising tigers beginning to reweight the global balance of power and capital on a point much further East than the purported socialist domain that had failed Lorenzo in his youth. These were the globalizing forces that had foreclosed venues of revolution that Lorenzo had tried to open in the early 1960s. These forces would, in time, restrict labor organizations in Spain while

always denied any Bolshevik influence on his intellectual innovations, having left the Soviet Union in 1925, and ascribed to it Walrasian roots. Most historians of Russian economic thought now discount Leontief's denials. See also D. L. Clark, "Planning and the Real Origins of Input-Output Analysis," *Journal of Contemporary Asia* 14:4 (1984): 408–429.

[2] On the transnationalism of the epistemic community of neoclassical economics, with special reference to the socialist East, see Johanna Bockman, *Markets in the Name of Socialism. The Left-Wing Origins of Neoliberalism* (Stanford: Stanford University Press, 2011). For the anti-authoritarian dialogue on socialism carried out transnationally among socialists in Yugoslavia, Chile and Peru see Johanna Bockman, "Democratic Socialism in Chile and Peru: Revisiting the 'Chicago Boys' as the Origin of Neoliberalism," *Comparative Studies in Society and History* 61:3 (2019): 654–679.

[3] This was with the related but distinct High Council of the Chambers of Commerce, Industry and Shipping (*Consejo Superior de Cámaras de Comercio, Industria y Navegación* de España), which while nominally a private sector organ, was in fact fully integrated into the state. The pay was three to four times higher than had he remained in Madrid, so he was able to quickly pay off a modest apartment that was already quite affordable to any young professional at the time, a situation that has now radically changed.

changing the structure of its industry and labor force. And yet these very forces furnished Lorenzo, armed with an economics expertise of rare value in Spain, with access to a middle-class lifestyle for himself and his new family that his past revolutionary self had never especially aspired to.

Lorenzo certainly made the most of a transnational development of knowledge and expertise that had little use for Cold War boundaries. But knowledge alone does not drive social organization, or history for that matter. In the 1940s and 1950s, Sampedro and Tamames themselves, titans of Spanish economics, could only operationalize that knowledge within the shabby academic structures of a nascent dictatorial regime. And many of their earlier students could only find recruitment as bureaucrats developing the administration of taxes for a state whose main area of expertise had heretofore lain in mass killings and the theft of the country's cultural capital (later in life, Sampedro liked to joke that the education of an army of tax officials, many of whom became cabinet ministers, was his great professional sin). A poor, underinstitutionalized country, a country like 1940s Spain, had little use for economists. Knowledge can only ever be operationalized within extant social structures and institution building. And under capitalism, the drive for capital accumulation realizes this potential in a feedback developmental loop. American power, in its crassest form of geopolitical anti-communism, had supported Franco's vision for Spain, and quite directly. But it had enabled another kind of infrastructure as well that conciliated Lorenzo and the government that had incarcerated him. What organized Lorenzo's life chances, along with that conciliation, was the US dollar and the international intelligibility and accumulation it made possible through global commerce and a system of currency convertibility. In the absence of justice and democracy, a political expedience on which both Cold War sides converged, Lorenzo devoted his professional life to organizing interconnection and the growth of capital.

Interconnection and transnational capital now organizes us much more forcefully than vice versa. The increasing feeling that we live a life without agency has given rise to a significant backlash. In a world of Brexit, increased border patrolling, and any number of Great Firewall projects to filter and partition the World Wide Web, we seem to have reached some kind of political limit; interconnection looms in both the left and the right as a cascade of abstract power, a torrent of biblical proportions. And we cannot seem to know how to turn it off. It is difficult to imagine that just a generation ago, globalization required so much goading, or that it was new in the lives of people. But those people are still with us. Go ahead, ask them, you will find that it was so. Lorenzo was born in post–Civil War Spain, in a cruel victor's peace during World War II, and came of age in an era of institutionalized national compartmentalizations. The overarching architecture of those compartmentalizations was known as Bretton Woods. And overcoming it required some doing. The irony is that the doing was very attractive; it had to be, or it would not have attracted the force required to overcome it. And here lies the core of that irony: Bretton Woods was not overcome in a concerted, oppositional struggle. It was overcome under the governance of professionals like Lorenzo working away toward a middle-class lifestyle. It was overcome using tools, as Lorenzo used, forged in the aspiration for a socialist world. But what they forged at length, was a new form of capitalism.

****

That many of these tools, along with the aspirations of many of its wielders, originated in the Soviet Union is not coincidental. Neither is the outcome. Tools may or may not determine use; this is a difficult historical question, even if we historians like to pretend that nothing is ever determined – itself a deterministic heuristic that is often more honored than practiced. Whatever the case may be, these tools were developed to govern the economic life of nations more carefully. And whatever their original purpose – and certainly Bogdanov's 1908 utopian science fiction novel *Red Star* imagined a different purpose to all the tabulations of socialist economic life he was already dreaming up – they came to function under the idea that social betterment was a consequence of growth and productivity, to which end the Soviets developed a massive governing bureaucracy. By the 1950s, this growth imperative came to dictate so much of the top line initiatives emanating from the Kremlin. When speaking of it within a Cold War frame, Khrushchev called this "peaceful coexistence." Economic competition was its mainstay, and that competition, importantly, could be econometrically measured. That sentence could also be reversed; once these goals could finally be given statistical visibility, a possibility available and made widespread mostly in the post-Stalin era, they could become amenable to a discourse of comparative growth and competition – rather than the more prevalent discourse under Stalin of survival and the military protection of the revolution.[4] In fact the regime often invited its subjects to exult over

---

[4] Vladimir Kontorovich, *Reluctant Cold Warriors. Economists and National Security* (Oxford: Oxford University Press, 2019) recovers a basic truth of pre–World War II Soviet political economy, that the purpose of Stalinist economic management was militarization, rather than growth for its own sake, one already broached in Karl Polanyi, *The Great*

announcements that it had outstripped the enemy in the production of some commodity or another. This is well understood, and not really the purpose of this history. This book seeks something else: to inscribe the Soviet Union, not only as participant in the world, or merely as an alternative path to modernity, but as constitutive of the world that emerged from the 1970s. It was so of the man Lorenzo became. But not because Lorenzo remained a revolutionary; in middle age he was neither loyal to Soviet socialism, nor even to Eurocommunism when democracy was finally torn out from the dictatorship's institutions through struggles by Spaniards like him. Rather, the Soviet Union was constitutive of the structures of the international system in which Lorenzo participated in his professional life.

It could be said that the Soviet Union did not help constitute, but merely participated in the system of economic compartmentalizations we call Bretton Woods. The Soviet Union did not help design any of the institutions that governed the system, and ultimately decided not to invest any of its resources in them, monetary or political.[5] American hostility came to preclude active, invested participation anyway. But the Soviets did participate, enthusiastically, in the global US dollar economy the Bretton Woods system in time constructed. The Soviets husbanded their own reserve of dollars, borrowed and lent them when needed, and generally governed their commerce through the sorts of calculations the US dollar made possible in an ever-growing number of economic geographies. In fact the Soviet Union configured exchange within its own bloc according to the values created in the US dollar

---

Transformation. The Political and Economic Origins of Our Time (Boston: Beacon Press, 1944): 255–256. However, it is equally clear that this rationality of governance more or less lost its way with the rise of a growthist ideology under Khrushchev in the 1950s. Moreover, this change to an explicit politics of growth was global, occurring simultaneously in the industrialized countries. I documented this argument in Oscar Sanchez-Sibony, "Economic Growth in the Governance of the Cold War Divide: Mikoyan's Encounter with Japan, Summer 1961," Journal of Cold War Studies 20, no. 2 (2018): 129–154. The property of these new statistical metrics in providing new cognitive domain for governance in the postwar was global, as argued for example in Adam Tooze, "Reassessing the Moral Economy of Post-war Reconstruction: The Terms of the West German Settlement in 1952," Past & Present 210 (2011): 61–65.

[5] Soviet near-miss participation in Bretton Woods institutions has finally been given archival treatment in Vladimir O. Pechatnov, "The Soviet Union and the Bretton Woods Conference," in Giles Scott-Smith and J. Simon Rofe, eds., Global Perspectives on the Bretton Woods Conference and the Post-War World Order (London: Palgrave Macmillan, 2017). Pechatnov documents the seriousness with which the Soviet leadership considered joining the IMF and the World Bank, with Stalin's hesitant rejection coming down to the wire. Tellingly, ruble convertibility seemed always out of the question.

world.[6] These the Soviets considered more authoritative than their system's own values. Inflect the signification of "values" in those last two sentences to expand it from a synonym of "price" to its full array of meanings and you might begin to discern how the Soviets thought of their position in the world the US dollar was creating.

While the Soviet Union participated in this world, this book will argue that it actively helped to constitute the world after, our current world. Which is to say, it helped dismantle the world of Bretton Woods and reconfigure how economic life was to be directed once Bretton Woods had moved on. Unlike Bretton Woods, the post–Bretton Woods world (often called neoliberal, or post-Fordist, or even postmodern, in its more cultural hue) was not formed by committee. This book aims to contribute to an understanding of the dismantling of our previous era from the perspective of a geography that is rarely considered to have had much agency in that transformation. This exclusion results from the entrenchment of a series of binaries during the Cold War for thinking about systemic differences about capitalism and socialism.[7] While these binaries were not particularly analytically helpful, they were useful to the establishment of a Cold War politics that continues to distort how we think about the Soviet Union and the socialist bloc, and implicitly the capitalist world and ourselves, in other words, our history and our present. The stubborn perpetuation of this kind of thinking – plan vs. market, economic dysfunction vs. efficiency, irrationality vs. rationality, the collective vs. the individual, subjection vs. freedom, etc. – is a mere reflection of the power it continues to hold over the constitution of our current politics and social organization. In this respect, the Soviet Union is still very much with us, a past overcome in our pursuit for a more perfect future. But what if it was with us in a more material way? What if we could understand their choices

---

[6] A useful elucidation of the problems inherent in this organization is Francoise Lemoine, "Trading Prices within the CMEA," *Soviet and Eastern European Foreign Trade* 15:1 (1979): 21–41. And excellent archival investigation of the uneven incorporation of the CMEA into capitalist exchange is Łukasz Stanek, "Buildings for Dollars and Oil: East German and Romanian Construction Companies in Cold War Iraq," *Contemporary European History* 30:4 (2021): 544–561.

[7] While these binaries remain essential to Cold War narratives, they have been critiqued for quite a while now in other areas of studies, such as consumption and material culture, for example in David Crowley and Susan E. Reid, eds., *Pleasures in Socialism. Leisure and Luxury in the Eastern Bloc* (Evanston: Northwestern University Press, 2010); Paulina Bren and Mary Neuburger, eds., *Communism Unwrapped. Consumption in Cold War Eastern Europe* (Oxford: Oxford University Press, 2012); and Karl Gerth, *Unending Capitalism. How Consumerism Negated China's Communist Revolution* (Cambridge: Cambridge University Press, 2020). A similar development is beginning to reappear in studies of labor, see Marsha Siefert, ed., *Labor in State-Socialist Europe, 1945–1989. Contributions to a History of Work* (Budapest: Central European University Press, 2020).

because they were our own? What if they helped us construct our present? What would that say about us?

The problem with these kinds of binaries, which emanate largely from a mythical understanding of capitalism, will become obvious as this history proceeds.[8] The reader will find the traditional roles of East and West by and large reversed.[9] This evidence subverts another tenacious tendency in many of the histories on the Soviet Union, although this one dates back only three decades: Western triumphalism. In fact, what this history records is a certain kind of victory for the socialist bloc. The period covered in this book saw, quite literally, the materialization of an access to capital the Soviet state had been fighting for ever since it signed on to the gold standard back in the 1920s. That doing so came to dismantle a system that had served the Soviets well enough was neither here nor there for them. That we now know that doing away with Bretton Woods as a pegged system of currency exchange corresponded in some ways with the project of avowed neoliberals should give us some pause in how we have categorized our knowledge. At a minimum, it should allow us the space to question the usefulness of triumphal narratives of a Cold War epic in which a tally of winners and losers should not only be mapped at the international level but must also be analyzed as well at the level of domestic geographies, business organization, and the structure of labor.

We have always known that the Soviet Union and its socialist allies were present in the world economy from the 1970s and through the 1980s. They were present in trade with the Global South and capitalist West – a peculiar nomenclature that might more usefully be reversed to read the capitalist South and the global West. They borrowed massively in financial markets – so much so that some socialist countries consequently went bankrupt. And the Soviets especially were present to profit

---

[8] Problems with binary thinking have been noted often. Two articles from Anna Krylova have systematized thinking on this with reference to the Soviet Union and the master narrative of "decline" and shown the way forward: "Soviet Modernity: Stephen Kotkin and the Bolshevik Predicament," *Contemporary European History* 23:2 (2014): 167–192; and "Imagining Socialism in the Soviet Century," *Social History* 42:3 (2017): 315–341.

[9] It shares in this revisionism a critique of the self-aggrandizing narratives the West tells of itself, and the historical erasures this process creates, as in the Nuremberg trials and the development of human rights, whose complex origins Francine Hirsch has recently explored, documenting a much more productive role for the Soviet Union than the usual East/West binaries have allowed, in *Soviet Judgment at Nuremberg. A New History of the International Military Tribunal After World War II* (Oxford: Oxford University Press, 2020). The unintended consequences Hirsch records find a parallel in the larger story of socioeconomic world-making this book has begun to tell.

from the oil crises of the 1970s.[10] How and why they got there, however, remains fuzzy. The explanation that it must have been a policy innovation of the Brezhnev leadership is the conventional wisdom, even if it has never held much water. The most widespread premise involves the Soviets (and other socialist leaderships) realizing that their system was deeply flawed; in this schema, foreign trade acts as a salve. The idea of the oil crisis postponing the demise of the Soviet system, whose most successful popularizer has been Stephen Kotkin's triumphalist *Armageddon Averted*, becomes an egregious, hindsight version of this interpretation.[11] Another sometimes complementary interpretation involves a kind of moral degradation of communist belief. As discipline deteriorated in all aspects of its society and among Soviet elites, the Soviet Union's autarkic impulse could not be maintained. A more sophisticated version of an explanation for the seemingly sudden irruption of the Soviet Union in international trade was that of scholars working within the world systems paradigm. In this tradition, the Soviet Union's commercial operations were rather unexceptional, and Soviet commercial politics came wrapped in a rhetoric similar to that of capitalist nations, and operated analogously. The reason, they surmised, was that the Soviet Union ultimately operated within a capitalist world system, which compelled the former revolutionaries into adopting a parallel political economy to that of the systemic hegemons. This explanation, at least among some of its exponents, had a domestic corollary reminiscent of Trotsky's interpretive castigation of the fate of the revolution. In order to operate within this world system, the process of capital

---

[10] Cold Warrior tracks have emphasized this petroleum bounty in terms of politically neutral understanding of money and debt, including Arthur Klinghoffer, *The Soviet Union and International Oil Politics* (New York: Columbia University Press, 1977); Marshall Goldman, *The Enigma of Soviet Petroleum. Half-Full or Half-Empty?* (London: Allen & Unwin, 1980); Vladislav Zubok, *A Failed Empire. The Soviet Union in the Cold War from Stalin to Gorbachev* (Chapel Hill: The University of North Carolina Press, 2007). More detailed analyses have tended to see the oil price instability as fostering a set of crises the Soviets were ill-equipped to handle domestically, as in Thane Gustafson, *Crisis Amid Plenty. The Politics of Soviet Energy under Brezhnev and Gorbachev* (Princeton: Princeton University Press, 1989). Michael de Groot has qualified that the Soviets themselves did not see this as a bonanza, only to arrive at the same triumphalist, deterministic endpoint of a system that failed to move on to the next (natural?) stage of post-Fordist evolution, in "The Soviet Union, CMEA, and the Energy Crisis of the 1970s," *Journal of Cold War Studies* 22:4 (2020): 4–30. A more sophisticated account that interfaces energy with finance and takes price structures seriously is Marvin Jackson, "When Is a Price a Price? The Level and Patterns of Prices in the CMEA," *Soviet and Eastern European Foreign Trade* 22:1 (1986): 100–112.

[11] Stephen Kotkin, *Armageddon Averted. The Soviet Collapse, 1970–2000* (Oxford: Oxford University Press, 2001).

accumulation had been taken over by the state and managed by its apparatchiks.[12]

These approaches explain the economic engagement as a policy innovation of the Brezhnev administration. They require a policy and ideological change, which together with a generalized, systemic paralysis and a dynamic West draws the Soviets – and the socialist world – into debt. Globalization, however, was of a piece with financialization. In analyses of the capitalist system it has been well understood for a while now that you cannot talk of one without the other. In the study of socialism, however, the two are sequentially connected. The usual story is a moralizing one of liberal self-understanding: The need for Western material modernity consequent to the inefficiencies and failures of the socialist system forced irresponsible leaderships of an inevitably dying system to try and buy themselves out of their troubles – whether through Western technology or, rather less empirically grounded, consumer goods. Ideology, which had explained everything before, gives way to a material crutch that ends up in debt and moral bankruptcy, often represented in the decline of previous ideological commitment. What is missing from this materialist narrative, as happens often with stories produced within Cold War tenets, is attention to how global power is produced. The rise of finance in its capture of global profits from industry, the financialization of everyday lives globally, these things are incidental, of no concern in the context of geopolitical maneuvering. They are perhaps especially irrelevant because they are confined to geographies Cold War narratives reserve for the capitalist world, and didn't capitalist societies win? Part of the way these narratives are made to function is by ignoring any precedent before the Brezhnev leadership's presumed decision in the late 1960s to reject an autarky that is said to be deeply ingrained within socialist political economy.[13] But as has become clear from archival documentation – as should always have been clear even without it – this was not a political decision of the late 1960s, but a well-established, ideologically fixed policy going back to the 1920s. The novelty was not

---

[12] This was generally the view of the approach's founder, Immanuel Wallerstein; for example, see his collection of essays *The Capitalist World-Economy* (Cambridge: Cambridge University Press, 1979). A useful, critical survey of the subject from within world systems theory is Zeev Gorin, "Socialist Societies and World System Theory: A Critical Survey," *Science & Society* 49:3 (1985): 332–366.

[13] The imposition of a Cold War timeline on the economy means that this is often said to be part of a general détente policy with the West, summarized for example in Sara Lorenzini, "Comecon and the South in the Years of Détente: A Study on East-South Economic Relations," *European Review of History: Revue européenne d'histoire* 21:2 (2014): 183–199.

in Soviet policy, but rather in the structural changes globally that made old Soviet ambitions possible.

Since the publication of this book's prehistory, *Red Globalization*, which showed the rapid Soviet involvement in world trade in the 1950s and 1960s as the realization of a long-standing policy choice, explorations in the intellectual history of socialism have recovered a tradition of socialist international free-trade thought that paralleled and allied itself with the liberal discourse on trade, peace, and prosperity. This goes far in recovering the discursive genealogy of the empirical evidence in commercial practices uncovered in *Red Globalization*.[14] In other words, the policy is internal to a logic that had been present from the revolutionary outset, not one that was adopted or consented to because of some external compulsion. And it certainly did not arise from an internally produced analysis of obvious failure, a far-fetched and quite undocumented premise. Embarrassingly for everybody – including myself, as I spent almost a decade reinventing the wheel on the subject – André Gunder Frank had, almost half a century ago, already worked all this out from copious statements on policy, strategy, practice, and ideology that Soviet leaders had been pronouncing since the 1920s. It was also apparent to Gunder Frank from the statistical evidence and common sense that the Cold War and its bards had overthrown, a process that took on a particular zeal from the 1980s.[15]

From the film *Brazil* to analytical categories such as stagnation, the Soviet Union has usually been rendered in the popular imagination as a society caught in a time trap, even as the capitalist West moves confidently forward to the next shiny stage of capitalist development:

---

[14] Marc-William Palen, "Marx and Manchester: The Evolution of the Socialist Internationalist Free-Trade Tradition, c. 1846–1946," *The International History Review* 43:2 (2021): 381–398. IPE scholars and so-called Cold War revisionists had long ago shown that trade protectionism and autarky were in fact forms of international statecraft associated with capitalist powers, the United States being a leading example. This formed the background for the traditional adoption of free-trade positions among socialists. The Cold War reversal – and continued espousal in academia – of the perception of socialist autarky is all the more astonishing in this light, and contrary to more accurate understandings in the Global South, as recovered in Johanna Bockman, "Socialist Globalization against Capitalist Neocolonialism: The Economic Ideas behind the New International Economic Order," *Humanity* 6:1 (2015): 109–128.

[15] André Gunder Frank, "Long Live Transideological Enterprise! The Socialist Economies in the Capitalist International Division of Labor," *Review (Fernand Braudel Center)* 1:1 (1977): 91–140. It is not coincidental that another thoroughly empirical effort at correcting the myth of autarky as a Soviet ideological project, Michael R. Dohan, "Soviet Foreign Trade in the NEP Economy and Soviet Industrialization Strategy" (PhD dissertation, MIT, 1969), was equally discounted, nor that both works could appear during this late 1960s/1970s window that closed in the 1980s.

post-industrial, postmodern, post-Fordist, flexible, nimble.[16] Environmental historians tend to disagree, noting that the core of socialist economy was in effect a speeding up of time, both vis-à-vis history and in relation to cycles of reproduction and transformation in the natural world it exploited.[17] The idea of socialist torpor is equally difficult to square with the relations of exchange with the West as they emerge from Soviet archival evidence, at least at the moment of transformation in the second half of the 1960s. Here, we will find, it was the Soviet state that was the dynamic element pushing for new forms of interrelations among nations, particularly through the medium of finance and long-term material bonds. The Soviets did not use energy in the materialist key of the conventional narrative Kotkin rehearses. They did not simply want to barter energy for things. What they wanted was not Western stuff to keep the people happy, but rather a new relationship with the West, which is to say, a new relationship with the global production and circulation of capital.

The Soviets were dynamic vis-à-vis Western governments with whom they were forced to cooperate, but their ambition also incorporated them into a built capitalist environment that was live, contentious, structuring, and in flux. The Keynesian project of fettering the global flow of capital had never been meant as a means of instituting some form of socialism on the world, but rather as a means of instituting regulatory structures within which to protect what Keynes (and Karl Marx before him, as well as Joseph Schumpeter more contemporaneously) had considered to be one of capitalism's most progressive forces: capitalist competition. Already during the Bretton Woods era of dollar shortage during its first decade and a half of life, there had been a series of consolidations that produced national oligopolies. If convertibility had always been one of the key objectives of Bretton Woods, the idea was precisely to create the conditions under which international competition would prevent consolidations and keep markets dynamic. Convertibility from 1958 achieved its first purpose well enough. Competition everywhere spurred European

---

[16] "The collapse of socialism came in part from the massive rupture produced by its collision with capitalism's speedup .... My point, in short, is that the fall of socialism lies not simply in the intersection of two temporal cycles but rather in the collision of two differently constituted temporal orders," argues Katherine Verdery, *What Was Socialism, and What Comes Next?* (Princeton: Princeton University Press, 1996): 36–37.

[17] This is made particularly forcefully and often in Bathsheba Demuth, *Floating Coast. An Environmental History of the Bering Strait* (New York: W. W. Norton, 2019). Kate Brown argues the nuclear explosion at Chernobyl was the outcome of a system of temporal accelerations that characterized Soviet political economy, in *Manual for Survival. A Chernobyl Guide to the Future* (New York: W. W. Norton, 2019).

business into desperate action. It did not, however, comply with theory in preventing corporate consolidation. Soviet archives tend to corroborate Robert Brenner's stress on looking to international competition, rather than labor power, for the sharp reduction in business profit rates in the second half of the 1960s.[18] This was certainly what Western businesses worried most about in their discussions with the Soviets, a worry the Soviets leaned on gleefully with a performative discourse of market competition they repeated ad nauseam.

But even perhaps more than convertibility, it was another political decision that had thrown European business into that dynamic of competition the Soviets profited from. The 1957 Treaty of Rome that created the European Economic Community (EEC, now the European Union) set in motion a spiral of liberalization that set national firms into competition with one another within an increasingly liberalized European space.[19] Externally, it also made the start of 1970 the deadline after which economic relations between the countries of the Common Market and their Eastern neighbors, up to then carried bilaterally, would be taken over on the Western side by the EEC's European Commission.[20] Soviet officials complained endlessly about the Common Market. They worried that they would, once again, be excluded from competition and be subject to a generalized tariff discrimination. And they folded this worry into a moral discourse of Ricardian fairness. But in fact the Common Market proved to be a boon to the Soviets. As competition intensified in Europe, European businesses in turn intensified their contacts with the Soviet Union and its allies, seeking markets in the socialist world that might forestall the rapid

---

[18] As Robert Brenner shows, the zenith of labor power had occurred two decades earlier. He shows that labor organization had not been particularly effective in increasing wages toward the end of the 1960s, unlike in earlier postwar periods. However, competition for international markets from Germany and Japan had suddenly erupted from 1965, leading to a swift a decline in profits. His carefully crafted argument is directed in particular against a stubborn, politically conservative understanding of labor unions as the reason for the rise in inflation in the 1970s and the end of the postwar miracle growth. Robert Brenner, *The Economics of Global Turbulence. The Advanced Capitalist Economies from Long Boom to Long Downturn, 1945–2005* (New York: Verso, 2006).

[19] This book coincides with observations in Neil Fligstein and Alec Stone Sweet, "Institutionalizing the Treaty of Rome," in Alec Stone Sweet, Wayne Sandholtz, and Neil Fligstein, eds., *The Institutionalization of Europe* (Oxford: Oxford University Press, 2001), that the institutionalization of supranational market frameworks was driven by corporate winners against the sometimes-successful resistance of those who stood to lose from further market integration. In this ecology of corporate lobbying, the Soviet Union clearly stood for market integration and against continued market segmentation.

[20] Suvi Kansikas, *Socialist Countries Face the European Community. Soviet-Bloc Controversies over East-West Trade* (Frankfurt: Peter Lang, 2014): 68–70. Kansikas' study is best for looking at socialist bloc deliberations on its relationship with the Common Market and the European Commission that was tasked with running it out of Brussels.

decline in their rate of profit. A world without global markets, the world without global money of the dollar shortage era during the first fifteen postwar years, was a world in which the US government had fewer pressure points to press in order to exclude the socialist bloc. The Soviets understood that a proliferation of interests would enhance their negotiating reach and their ability to transact. They did not simply meet trading deals as they came. They conducted a politics of diversification and market-making that allowed them greater purchase in the world the US dollar finally began to organize in the 1960s.

But what does it mean to say that the US dollar organized global relations? How did this come about? What, ultimately, was this Bretton Woods system the Soviets triumphed over?

****

Bretton Woods was a failure built on failure and power. That it prevailed was not foreordained; rather it speaks to the sheer authority the United States was able to develop over the first decade and a half of the postwar period. Authority often has two mothers, compulsion and attraction; how these descend on the people that effect this authority is the stuff of justice and history. The development of authority has also a dialectic quality that is difficult to portray in historical narrative, but that certainly does not comport to the kind of simple rationality that, say, economics often models. Its boundaries are often sustained through violence, but it develops more readily in the everyday practices to which people and institutions dedicate most of their daily hours. Authority is developed as much in the policing of social behaviors or the physical and discursive violence visited on female ambition, as it is in the everyday transaction of a sovereign money or the material provision of differentiated social status. Authority cannot be decreed, but rather is cobbled up in the exercise of power and the infrastructures it builds or borrows in the course of that exercise. This, at least, is what the participants of that fateful conference of July 1944 at the Mount Washington Hotel in Bretton Woods, New Hampshire learned soon after approving the most thoroughgoing redesign of international relations in history.

The conference was meant to resolve the dysfunctions of the 1930s, above all the ability of governments to do what they at length did. During the 1930s, after nations had been cut off from one another in the generalized autarky, states everywhere brought themselves into the direct governance of the economic life of their citizens. Transnational governance, especially that of banks, was to become international governance, institutionalized in such a way so as to make sure that national governments maintained political control over the fiscal and financial levers that they needed to manage a new conceptual object: the economy.[21] But the Bretton Woods conference was also not some moment of creation *ex nihilo*. Rather it was the culmination of a series of attempts over the previous decade or so to arrive at the institutionalization of international economic coordination, the absence of which, Barry Eichengreen has most insistently argued, was at the root of the problems of the 1930s.[22] Less remarked upon is the fact that the most important settlement that laid the groundwork for the system that made Bretton Woods possible was not in the realm of finance, but rather in the realm of energy.

In an important rethinking of the imbrication of energy and Fordist society, economic geographer Matt Huber has described the foundational function of oil to the social settlements that were necessary for the stability and spread of Fordism during the Bretton Woods era.[23] He shows, importantly, that Fordist production was not inherently capable of the stability and growth it demonstrated in the post–World War II era. Corporate and other business-led forms of organization embodied in the construction of John D. Rockefeller's Standard Oil Trust and the international coordination of oil majors arranged in the Achnacarry Agreement of 1928 were developed to try to deal with the inherent problem of overproduction in the oil market. Oil companies were less

---

[21] On the distinction between transnational and international foreign relations, especially as related to banking, see Marcello de Cecco, "Financial Relations: Between Internationalism and Transnationalism," in Roger Morgan, Jochen Lorentzen, Anna Leander, and Stefano Guizzini, *New Diplomacy in the Post–Cold War World* (New York: St. Martin's Press, 1993). De Cecco argued, interestingly, that our usual periodizations, while meaningful, are not hard watersheds, but rather trending processes that become crystalized at particular junctures. The internationalization of transnational banking was already apparent at the turn of the century before its culmination in the 1930s, and likewise the transnationalization of financial governance was already taking root in the 1950s, before becoming such a decisive feature of international life in the 1980s. On the invention of the economy as an object of state governance see Timothy Mitchell, "Fixing the Economy," *Cultural Studies* 12:1 (1998): 82–101, and his many refinements over subsequent writings, notably "Rethinking Economy," *Geoforum* 39:3 (2008): 1116–1121. For how the new methods of accounting developed by Keynesian macroeconomists that Mitchell follows were deployed as aid, development advice, and in the discovery of inequality and the development of the abstract order of nations see Daniel Speich, "The Use of Global Abstractions: National Income Accounting in the Period of Imperial Decline," *Journal of Global History* 6:1 (2011): 7–28. The theoretical framework of both authors, which describes the creation of the epistemic regimes of political economy, owes much to the oeuvre of Bruno Latour.

[22] In conversation with Kindleberger's argument of hegemonic stability theory. On the conceptual and practical groundwork leading to the conference see Eric Helleiner, *Forgotten Foundations of Bretton Woods. International Development and the Making of the Postwar Order* (Ithaca: Cornell University Press, 2014).

[23] Matt Huber, "Fueling Capitalism: Oil, the Regulation Approach, and the Ecology of Capital," *Economic Geography* 89:2 (2013): 171–194.

interested in producing oil than in producing scarcity, in other words. Yet they failed to maintain price stability during the Great Depression, or incorporate into the system a growing number of independent producers that threatened to keep the oil market in disarray throughout the 1930s. As a consequence, from 1935 a series of regulatory bodies were instituted throughout the oil-producing geographies of the United States and at the federal level, the most famous and powerful of which was the Texas Railroad Commission. The regulation of the oil industry, along with its price, allowed a stability upon which Fordist production and its corollary, mass consumption, was organized. The consequence was the construction of a particular civilization characterized by levels of energy consumption that did not just imbue production with miraculous productivity gains, but penetrated the non-working lives of every American with the development of vehicles, roads, plastics, individual housing, and other forms of energy consumption based on the advent of novel, energy-intensive spatial rearrangements.[24] As with many areas involved in the regulation of capitalism, that settlement did not happen without a degree of structural violence against oil and gas producers deemed to be "in a state of insurrection against the conservation laws of the state." To control production, martial law had to be enforced with armed troops in Texas and Oklahoma in 1931 as part of the institutionalization of the new energy dispensation.[25] Market construction has always depended as much on design as on a level of structural violence, that is, on the institution of a relation of power.

Although Huber stops at the national borders of the United States, this book serves in part as a continuation of that story. As with other New Deal settlements, this one too was replicated abroad. The vehicle for this extension was the Marshall Plan, which was designed to do more than simply remedy the shortcomings of Bretton Woods designs. The Marshall Plan is usually thought of as eclectic in the infrastructure it financed. In fact oil from American companies was the single largest expense the plan financed – 10 percent of the total.[26] Besides this explicit subsidy to the oil majors, much of the rest concerned the infrastructure necessary for the production and consumption of petroleum energy: oil refineries, aircraft, roads, petrochemical plants, tractors, and vehicles of all sorts – which Europeans at times resisted in favor of trains, a technology that at

---

[24] Huber folds these elements into what Marxists call "wage relations," usefully incorporating what might be conceived as an energy wage into the postwar Fordist trend that leveled inequality.

[25] Matthew T. Huber, "Enforcing Scarcity: Oil, Violence, and the Making of the Market," *Annals of the Association of American Geographers*, 101:4 (2011): 816–826.

[26] David S. Painter, "The Marshall Plan and Oil," *Cold War* 9:2 (2009): 160.

least France would famously link to atomic energy. If this book insists on imbricating energy and finance as entangled elements in the sociopolitical restructurings of the twentieth century, it is because we do a certain measure of historical violence when we dissociate one from the other. Just as the reorganization of energy relations was crucial to the establishment of a particular social organization during the Bretton Woods era, its disordering would play an equally central role in the general disassembly of the Bretton Woods era and the rise of financialization.

Unlike the institutions regulating energy, however, the institutions the Bretton Woods conference decreed into existence became a well-rehearsed catalog of failed institutionalization. The International Monetary Fund (IMF) was created to institutionalize consensual changes to the exchange value of international currencies, a collective endeavor meant to forestall the competitive devaluations of the 1930s. But upon its creation, the IMF found its primary mission voided by a lack of currency convertibility. There were no currencies exchanging one for the other.[27] This void lasted for a decade and a half. The World Bank (formally the International Bank for Reconstruction and Development, IBRD) was formed to generate development loans for countries and projects that, while economically important, might not attract the attention of profit-seeking commercial banking. But this mission too saw itself superseded by the development of the Marshall Plan and the Organisation for European Economic Co-operation (OEEC, later the OECD), which took over the responsibility for the reconstruction of Europe. Meanwhile development aid remained a stubbornly national affair; in effect many former state offices engaged in the administration of overseas empire seemed to simply change the sign at the door and become development aid outfits.[28] The third pillar of Bretton Woods, the International Trade Organization (ITO), failed to form altogether, after the US Congress refused to ratify it. The organization that supplanted it, the General Agreement for Tariffs and Trade did not move the needle on trade liberalization until the Kennedy Round of the mid-1960s, well after other transnational institutions, notably the OECC and its spiritual descendant, the EEC, moved

---

[27] Relatedly, its other major prerogative was to extend short-term loans to countries having temporary problems in their balance of payments, a rare problem in a world that remained relatively autarkic for the first decade and a half, and where most trade was strictly balanced anyway.

[28] See Frederic Cooper, "Writing the History of Development," *Journal of Modern European History* 8:1 (2010): 5–23; and in the same volume Joseph M. Hodge, "British Colonial Expertise, Post-Colonial Careering and the Early History of International Development," *Journal of Modern European History* 8:1 (2010): 24–46. See also Véronique Dimier, *The Invention of a European Development Aid Bureaucracy. Recycling Empire* (Basingstoke: Palgrave Macmillan, 2014).

it first on a regional basis. All these institutions rose to prominence as vectors of power enacting the mobilization, protection, and globalization of capital only in the 1980s, after the failure of Bretton Woods – the auspice under which they were created – was complete.

It is a strange historiographical quirk that we regularly begin to tell the story of Bretton Woods by enumerating a set of institutions that took four decades to become prominent and did so only under dramatically changed circumstances and with a very different set of practical politics than those originally envisioned. And yet the Bretton Woods system persevered amid this institutional ruin. It did more than persevere; it successfully organized international economic life, if only for a while. It did so not because it was built on far-sighted economic rationality, but because it was built on the power and the authority of the United States. That authority was vested in its capacity to create a debt-making mechanism that, over time, came to create a system of international obligations and political settlements. To be part of the international community meant obliging to the US dollar's system of compulsions and attractions. How these descended on the nation-states is the stuff of history, certainly this one. Two remaining institutions are important here: the fixed exchange rate of the US dollar to gold at $35 an ounce, which lent the system a patina of gold standard credibility, and especially a system of trade and financial controls that governments could exercise in order to regulate flows of money and goods coming in and out of the country. What this meant was that governments were not beholden to the whims of international finance; governments were not made to change their politics of taxing and spending in order to pay off international investors. They remained free to cater to domestic relations of power, however they were configured.

What transpired in the aftermath of the conference was a series of stop gap measures and creative solutions that did not run through any of the institutions of the Bretton Woods system, but did comport to the spirit of the thing. The first provision in the articles of agreement of its center-piece, the IMF, tells the tale: "To promote international monetary cooperation through a permanent institution which provides the machinery for consultation and collaboration on international monetary problems." Above all, the Bretton Woods conference substantiated a culture of summits and institutionalized cooperation that began in the 1930s and only gathered force as time wore on. Soon after the conference, a dollar shortage descended on the world. This represented the very real problem European countries had in clawing dollars out of the United States through sales of products American consumers might want to buy. These problems crystallized when the US forced Great Britain to open its capital accounts in 1947 only to see remaining British financial reserves converted into US dollars in a stampede of investors anxious over the British future.[29] The United States quickly consensualized a series of ameliorative measures, most notably the Marshall Plan, which put US dollars in European hands and jumpstarted a modicum of transatlantic trade.[30] This was supplemented by arrangements like the European Payments Union that allowed for more organized and intensified barter among Western European countries, and hence savings in scarce US dollar reserves.[31] And still, the success of these improvisations may well have rested on the sharp devaluation of European currencies in September 1949 that finally rendered manageable the vast trade and current account imbalances opened up by World War II.[32]

Although the Soviet Union was largely ostracized from these initiatives, technological advancements in Europe and large military expenditures by the United States began to unlock dollars and put them in the service of international circulation by the end of the 1950s. For the Soviet Union the stability the United States proffered in Europe meant a more intensified relationship with commercial partners that can be described as lightly financialized barter. That is, trading lists would be negotiated in roughly equal value, and the goods in those lists would be traded through small, short-term loans of just enough time and capital to cover transit. In addition to continuing and expanding trade in dollars with the Soviet Union, by the late 1950s and early 1960s Western European countries along with Japan were offering the Soviets slightly longer-term loans to

---

[29] This was the final piece in an eighteen-month attempt to restore convertibility to the British pound and create a much more liberal financial order than the kind of "embedded liberalism" that ultimately obtained. It was led by bankers and their allies in government who had opposed the Bretton Woods agreements and had found themselves suddenly in a position of influence after President Roosevelt's death and Harry S. Truman's ascension to the presidency, which also had the complementary effect of isolating key architects of the Bretton Woods edifice, Harry Dexter White and Henry Morgenthau. Eric Helleiner, *States and the Reemergence of Global Finance. From Bretton Woods to the 1990s* (Ithaca: Cornell University Press, 1994): 52–58.

[30] Not because European economies were poor and sluggish, as a reading of US Secretary of State's George Marshall's speech might suggest, but because they had been growing and importing, and further growth was being sharply constrained by a lack of US dollars, as shown in Alan S. Milward, *The Reconstruction of Western Europe, 1945–51* (Berkeley: University of California Press, 1984). For the Plan not as an instrument of economic recovery, but of sociopolitical change in Europe see also William I. Hitchcock, *The Struggle for Europe. The Turbulent History of a Divided Continent, 1945–present* (New York: Doubleday, 2003): 134–141.

[31] Recently and comprehensively covered in Adrien Faudot, "The European Payments Union (1950–58): The Post-War Episode of Keynes' Clearing Union," *Review of Political Economy* 32:3 (2020): 371–389, in which he notes that City financiers in London lobbied energetically for an end to the EPU and the restoration of convertibility.

[32] Marcello de Cecco, "Origins of the Post-War Payments System," *Cambridge Journal of Economics* 3:1 (1979): 49–61.

finance targeted exchanges of industrial technology for Soviet resources like timber, coal, and limited amounts of oil. The origins of the compensation trade the Soviets insisted on in the 1970s lie in these forms of financialized barter.[33]

This, then, was the Bretton Woods context within which Soviet relations with the world began to develop. By the middle of the 1960s, a series of gas-for-pipe contracts, most notably with Italy and Germany, exponentially expanded these kinds of exchanges. The pipes at first went toward the construction of an energy system that linked Eastern Europe to Soviet oil and gas fields – a pipeline web constructed with pipes produced in the Soviet Union, Czechoslovakia, East Germany, and Western European countries. European states, meanwhile, had been in the process of transforming their energy regimes from coal power toward oil and gas. A new energy system thus began to be constructed in Europe that invited for the first time an important and escalating measure of Soviet commercial participation. As European states moved away from coal, they formed a cooperative arrangement with a socially repressive Soviet state that allowed the latter to negotiate ever better terms of finance from Europe and Japan.[34] Barter had created an energy system within the Soviet Union's sphere in East-Central Europe, and the steady prolongation in the credit terms the Soviets received culminated in the gas-for-pipe deals that began to be signed in 1968 and saw Soviet gas warming Western European houses and powering European production from 1968, first in Austria and then Germany, France, and Italy.[35]

But this sketch of commercial and financial history as it developed in the postwar period is a somewhat orphaned story. It cannot be understood without the changes in the energy regime that occurred simultaneously and in relationship with it. This is the dimension of global capitalism that will be at the center of the history this book will recount. Let's retake the story of the Soviets as they finally, perhaps even unexpectedly, opened the door into a new energy, financial, and moral order, by the early 1970s. Leading this new order, as before but changed, was the deracinated US dollar, that is, the

---

[33] Compensation trade is a form of countertrade in which the investor does not acquire a stake in the object of investment but is instead paid back in the form of the production from that object, for example, from the production of the factory the investor provided resources to construct, or, more immediately to our purposes, in the form of gas provided by the pipelines the investor financed.

[34] For more detail, see Oscar Sanchez-Sibony, *Red Globalization. The Political Economy of the Soviet Cold War from Stalin to Khrushchev* (Cambridge: Cambridge University Press, 2014): chapters 4 and 6.

[35] As thoroughly documented in the excellent Per Högselius, *Red Gas. Russia and the Origins of European Energy Dependence* (Basingstoke: Palgrave Macmillan, 2013).

Eurodollar.[36] In the pursuit of growth that had become in the postwar a bedrock of Soviet social governance, the Soviet state had long pursued technologies of production and societal regulation from countries in the West that were at the cutting edge.[37] Diplomatic approaches to governing material exchange in a compartmentalized world, especially the negotiated trade lists and long-term agreements that had come into being in the 1930s and been the basis of foreign economic policy, had made Soviet trade one of the fastest growing in the world during the era of the Bretton Woods regime. But an unexpected energy regime change in the West that shifted consumption from coal to oil – at a rate that never failed to confound predictions – changed the way capital accumulated and was managed. Among other advantages from states' perspective, the less labor-intensive, more technical extraction of oil and gas circumvented the social conflict that had historically been incited by strong, well-networked miner communities and the crippling industrial sabotage they often led: what we know as the general strike.[38] On the one hand, oil-powered capital – capital being a social category whose productivity depended on the application of energy to labor – began to discern a way of shaking free from the demands of labor on its governance.[39] Unlike coal, oil and gas are concentrated forms of energy whose materiality encourages the construction of systems that require little labor for energy production and distribution. The forms of sabotage that labor-intensive coal production had allowed in the rate of capital accumulation were circumvented by oil and gas; the politics governments could thus apply around these systems of energy administration had the social effect of concentrating formerly decentralized – and more democratic – decision-making while more effectively answering to the energy needs of their citizens.

---

[36] This refers to dollars usually held in European banks that were not subject to the regulatory controls of the United States. They could thus be lent without state control, usually at a higher interest rate. This was partly because it was not subsidized, as many kinds of export and import credits were, and partly because Eurodollars were both unregulated and without a backstop until the early 1970s, which is to say without an entity that might step in to save the market if it were to fail, for example through the provision of liquidity.

[37] The role of growth as Cold War governance of international trade is documented in Sanchez-Sibony, "Economic Growth in the Governance of the Cold War Divide." For Japan, see Scott O'Bryan, *The Growth Idea. Purpose and Prosperity in Postwar Japan* (Honolulu: University of Hawai'i Press, 2009). The classic statement on this for the United States is Charles Maier, "The Politics of Productivity: Foundations of American International Economic Policy after World War II," *International Organization* 31:4 (1977): 607–633.

[38] Timothy Mitchell, *Carbon Democracy. Political Power in the Age of Oil* (New York: Verso, 2011): 18–31.

[39] Paolo Malanima, "The Limiting Factor: Energy, Growth and Divergence, 1820–1913," *The Economic History Review* 73:2 (2020): 486–512.

This supercharged governance of energy provision worked better without the input of social constituencies. While animating less democratic forms of decision-making in the West, geological serendipity meant that European states found a ready partnership in a country that, Cold War discourse notwithstanding, was especially interested in using what mechanisms for global material exchange it could leverage to continue the economic growthism it had made such a fundamental part of its social governance. Leverage that could formerly be expended by Western social constituencies now accrued to parties that thrived in the undemocratic management of capital accumulation. Timothy Mitchell has pointed to this new energy regime as the first instance of outsourcing that eventually deindustrialized the West over the next few decades. The beneficiaries of this energy outsourcing were imperial or otherwise authoritarian polities well beyond the reach of European labor movements.[40] Mitchell had in mind Saudi Arabia, Iran, and other such autocratic Middle Eastern regimes under Western imperial sway; to these we must append the Soviet Union, more economically variegated, but similarly repressive of labor power.[41] New alliances were forged, and a new architecture for global material exchange began to materialize around the agency of these newly empowered historical actors.[42] The Soviets wanted at long last to command a global purchase that US hegemonic dominion over Cold War politics had long denied them. Decolonization from the mid-1950s had been one vector through which the Soviets had managed a measure of purchase in the world. This is partly why throughout the Global South the Soviets promoted the economic independence of countries newly liberated from imperial control that in turn, and not coincidentally, gave the Soviets an equal measure of independence from Western pressure. The other vector had been a rebalancing of accumulated capital globally, or what economists saw as successful catch-up strategies, which had the effect of breaking US-orchestrated Western discipline toward the socialist East.[43] The new energy systems now

---

[40] Mitchell's *Carbon Democracy* follows the theory of sabotage in Thorstein Veblen, *The Engineers and the Price System* (New York: B. W. Huebsch, 1921).

[41] For Saudi Arabia's repression of labor in their oil industry see Robert Vitalis, *America's Kingdom. Mythmaking on the Saudi Oil Frontier* (Stanford: Stanford University Press, 2007).

[42] Importantly, these have included powerful oil conglomerates in the West that have been so instrumental in propagating neoliberal ideas. Mitchell, *Carbon Democracy*, chapter 7. Mitchell's thesis finds support in Jane Mayer, *Dark Money. The Hidden History of the Billionaires Behind the Rise of the Radical Right* (New York: Doubleday, 2016).

[43] Barry Eichengreen, *The European Economy since 1945. Coordinated Capitalism and Beyond* (Princeton: Princeton University Press, 2007). Materially speaking, rebalancing refers to the flow of gold from the United States to Europe that served as the nominal basis for currency exchange under Bretton Woods from the immediate postwar period, when the United States held two-thirds of gold reserves, to the end of the 1950s, when the weight had

potentially available were the materialization of this politics of indiscipline.[44] In yet another instance of the paradoxes of the commercial and financial structures constructed under Bretton Woods, the Soviets used this development to command US dollars, acquiescing to a hierarchy of global value based on a currency they had no control over, one that was politically managed according to the interests of its most implacable enemy. This is not to invoke the United States generally, but rather the US state. For the fact was that acquiescing to the US dollar, the main technology of a global order managed by the United States and one of that order's two main pillars along with the military, was made easier by the fact that at the very moment the Soviets were finding greater purchase in that order, the management of the US dollar was decentralizing, and it was doing so precisely in order to create a new mode of governance that allowed the Soviet state a voice almost to the same extent as it was increasingly negating that of European citizens. The concentration oil and gas brought to political decision-making had the sociopolitical effect of bringing a reduced set of actors to the fore in the political decisions made over how capital would be accumulated and deployed in the continent. To bring this effect about, the Soviets demanded a breach to the prudential measures the US and the UK had put in place in Bretton Woods, which had until then allowed newly legitimized technocratic states everywhere greater control over categories such as employment and inflation through which they came to see some of its fundamental governing principles. The vehicle through which the Soviets finally broke through the financial dikes of Bretton Woods was the energy infrastructure it began to negotiate in 1965 with a country, Italy, that was looking for its own breakthroughs in the largely Anglo-American management of the global energy regime. The durability and economic capacity of the infrastructural bond the Soviets began with the construction of a gas pipe in the West itself necessitated an infrastructural rearrangement for the deployment of capital, and a reorganization of the East–West relationship's

---

fallen to one-half. This simply reflected the underlying socioeconomic fact that Europeans and Japanese were catching up to Americans in productivity, and their respective businesses were catching up to US business technologically. Barry Eichengreen has also laid this out concisely and lucidly in *Globalizing Capital. A History of the International Monetary System* (Princeton: Princeton University Press, 2008).

[44] In Rüdiger Graf, *Oil and Sovereignty. Petro-Knowledge and Energy Policy in the United States and Western Europe in the 1970s* (New York: Berghahn Books, 2018) the author has noted the difficulties of Western cooperation and unity in the face of the energy crisis, in which Western states each followed their respective interest rather than organize a common policy. The focus there is on relations with Middle Eastern oil producers, but a similar dynamic can be discerned, perhaps even earlier, with respect to Soviet energy. The book will show the importance of the Soviets and finance in organizing a measure of European coherence that Europe's political leaderships might not otherwise have achieved.

temporal order so as to make it more consonant with the logic of capital accumulation required by that infrastructural construction. The consequence of all these restructurings was the reemergence of finance, patronized and fortified by important allies like the Soviet Union, as the control center for global capital allocation, a position that would slowly render financiers with ever greater political control over both the allocation of capital, the mechanisms and technologies through which it would be accumulated, and ultimately the logics and values through which that accumulation would take place.

****

The periodization of the end of Bretton Woods more or less depends on what one thinks was its core as an institution. Understandings of Bretton Woods that highlight its ultimate foundation on gold will take 1971 to be the defining year in which President Richard Nixon, under pressure from domestic constituents and truculent countries like France, delinked the value of the US Dollar to gold. The epilogue to this story occurs in 1973, with the end of the patchwork Smithsonian agreements and the beginning of floating exchange rates among the main currencies. This diagnostic analysis highlights the French critique of American financial power, America's "exorbitant privilege."[45] It elevates the Triffin dilemma as well, essentially making of Bretton Woods a Greek tragedy, a death foretold. In this reading, the most widespread among scholars of international political economy (IPE) and economic historians, the contradictory design of Bretton Woods identified by Belgian economist Robert Triffin in 1959 meant that while American gold reserves underpinning the US dollar were necessarily limited, the expansion of international trade demanded ever more dollars in global circulation. Gold had a physical limit, but global trade (and the dollars it needed) could expand forever. In time, as dollars in circulation outstripped the value of the gold in US reserves backing them, the credibility of the US dollar's gold link was inevitably undermined, ushering the US and the world into global currency

---

[45] This refers to the phrase of then Finance Minister Valery Giscard D'Estaing used to refer to the many benefits the US enjoyed as a consequence of the fact that its currency was the global reserve currency. Seigniorage, persistent deficits, and lower interest rates are some of these privileges, but the one the French most resented was the extent to which, within a Bretton Woods framework, American deficits meant dollars were sent abroad for the surplus countries to absorb by printing their own currency to maintain the dollar peg. The central banks of the surplus countries ended up with reserves of dollars they had to keep (sterilize), but in doing so they expanded the money supply of their own country. The accusation was that American profligate spending created deficits and inflationary pressures the US could effectively export abroad.

system based on fiat. Scholars such as Barry Eichengreen and Jeffry Frieden have made of this contradiction a central arena of the international and domestic political struggle that played out at the end of the 1960s and beginning of the 1970s.[46] Fed up with its exorbitant privilege, America's political allies decided that enough was enough, that they would no longer accept the hegemon's international politics of inflation. In the face of this political defiance born of a structural flaw, President Nixon decided to pursue domestic priorities over the duties of international hegemony. The collapse of Bretton Woods was a failure of coordination similar to the collapse in the 1930s of the gold standard: history repeating.

Other scholars have elevated a different element of Bretton Woods as its most significant: not the gold-dollar nexus, but the regime's limits on international capital circulation.[47] These emphases are obviously not incompatible, but they shift the story and its protagonists in meaningful ways, enough to bear on issues of historical agency and the political lessons one draws from that history. Maybe the design was flawed from the beginning and the problem was compounded by excessive spending from the US government, a view shared by a wide range of observers from centrist and slightly left-of-center liberals to conservatives to neoliberals. But there are some problematic foundations to these ideas. For one, they are based on a monetarist understanding of inflation and money that was untenable well before the 2008 crisis made it absurd – featuring as the crisis did very low inflation despite the immense expansion of money supply everywhere. Inflation is a sociopolitical phenomenon, not a mechanical equation arising from profligate states and their money-printing propensities. There is also, in this rendering, an absence of power, a social absence. The narrative is amenable to analyses that give agency to great men and the ideas they might have toiled under – a subject cherished by certain academic traditions.[48] Power, the struggle for it and the backlash against it, is assumed and absent, together with the society that power begets at a domestic and international level. In its stead, this emphasis has made extensive use of another power paradigm, one that more or less gave

---

[46] Jeffry A. Frieden *Global Capitalism. Its Fall and Rise in the Twentieth Century* (New York: W. W. Norton & Company, 2006); Barry Eichengreen, *Exorbitant Privilege. The Rise and Fall of the Dollar and the Future of the International Monetary System* (Oxford: Oxford University Press, 2010).

[47] For example, Helleiner, *States and the Reemergence of Global Finance*, which makes capital controls central to both the purpose of Bretton Woods and the engine of its collapse.

[48] Broadly speaking, I mean the Cold War narrative tradition of Great Man history. While this tradition usually ignores political economy, some histories of economic policy occasionally complement Cold War paradigms, for example, Daniel Sargent, *A Superpower Transformed. The Remaking of American Foreign Relations in the 1970s* (New York: Oxford University Press, 2015).

birth to IPE as a discipline: hegemonic stability theory. According to this framework, Nixon's decision to delink the dollar from gold was an outcome of the hegemonic decline this theory prognosticated.[49] The theory did not age well. And neither did the predictions on the post–Bretton Woods fate of the US dollar, which, if anything, continued gaining authority and reach. It was no coincidence that the theory had been developed in the turbulent 1970s. It did not so much predict hegemonic decline for the United States as it was built from the assumption of that decline. What occurred subsequently was more complex, and what ultimately limited the theory was its main analytical category: the nation-state.

Reassessing the core of Bretton Woods as a regime for the control and management of the global circulation of capital recovers an important historical axiom to our understanding of the Bretton Woods system: It reminds us that the control of capital, or the "euthanasia of the rentier" as Keynes put it, was always central to the architects of the regime, very much including Keynes.[50] This book follows this understanding of Bretton Woods because the evidence points to capital controls as the main dragon the Soviets strove to slay. The story told here seeks to widen the field of power beyond the offices of Western political leaders in Paris, Bonn, London, and Washington DC. It does this not only to incorporate political centers around the world that defied that power – not least Moscow – but also to

---

[49] The theory was developed to explain the interwar time of troubles as the result of the absence of a hegemon, in Charles P. Kindleberger, *The World in Depression, 1929–1939* (Berkeley: University of California Press, 1973). The term was coined in Robert Keohane in "The Theory of Hegemonic Stability and Changes in International Economic Regimes, 1967–1977," in Ole R. Holsti, Randolph M. Siverson, and Alexander L. George, eds., *Change in the International System* (Boulder: Westview Press, 1980) and became the basis of subsequent IPE analysis by some of its leading exponents, for example Keohane, Robert O. Keohane, *After Hegemony. Cooperation and Discord in the World Political Economy* (Princeton: Princeton University Press, 1984), and the textbook codification in Robert Gilpin, *The Political Economy of International Relations* (Princeton: Princeton University Press, 1987).

[50] As argued in Matías Vernengo, "The Consolidation of Dollar Hegemony after the Collapse of Bretton Woods: Bringing Power Back in," *Review of Political Economy* 33:4 (2021): 529–551. See also James Crotty, *Keynes against Capitalism. His Economic Case for Liberal Socialism* (London: Routledge, 2019) and Harold James, "The Multiple Contexts of Bretton Woods," *Past & Present* 210 (2011): 290–308. Lilia Costabile follows a different Keynesian critique to the same end, this one from the 1920s, that the interwar financial system was already a dollar standard, a fact that remained constant for a century, and that highlights capital controls as the main variable, in "Continuity and Change in the International Monetary System: Dollar Standard and Capital Mobility," *Review of Political Economy* 34:3(2022): 585–597. Finally, for an interpretation that emphasizes the Keynesian notion of liquidity preference as a principal engine of this (and other eras') transformation, thus linking the domestic with the international much more securely than standard narratives, see Jonathan Levy, *Ages of American Capitalism. A History of the United States* (New York: Random House, 2021).

disaggregate national categories into its contending components. While Western-centric historical narratives track political leaderships and national economies in a geopolitical tussle, a view from Moscow highlights a different set of relations and scales: Rather than national economies, it follows sectoral political economy – steel corporations, banks, energy conglomerates – and rather than geopolitical struggle it underscores transnational alliances. Furthermore, the project to do away with capital controls went far beyond some ideological battle between Keynesians and Neoliberals.[51] More immediately, it concerned those who most stood to benefit from the emancipation of global money: those who could produce it, and those who could use it. Or to historicize it more precisely, those who stood to become producers and users of money only under a new system of capital circulation (bankers and the capital poor), whether because Bretton Woods marginalized them, or in the case of Keynes's rentiers, euthanized them.

The story of Bretton Woods has been, historiographically speaking, a Western story. The story tells of how the Great Depression, and more importantly the escape from it in the 1930s, brought about a reappraisal of international organization.[52] Commercial and financial dikes were put in place after the war to make compatible the realms of international exchange and the newly ascendant politics of domestic economic management. These domestic technocratic policies were geared toward the achievement of maximum growth and full employment, as well as the generation of a grand social bargain that presumably brought labor into negotiations over industrial management, states into global cooperation, and peace to the social and international disputes of the 1930s. And it brought about John Maynard Keynes' long-standing call for "the euthanasia of the rentier."[53] Through governmental techniques of capital

---

[51] Philip Mirowski finds a measure of neoliberal intellectual hegemony precisely in these binary contrasts, in "Polanyi vs Hayek?" *Globalizations* 15:7 (2018): 894–910. Timothy Mitchell also argued against binary thinking, with special reference to concepts of the material/immaterial in "Metaphors of Power," *Theory and Society* 19:5 (1990): 545–577.

[52] The Bretton Woods regime has been most thoroughly examined in the field of IPE, which has largely emphasized the Anglo-American nexus, starting with as far back as Richard N. Gardner, *Sterling-Dollar Diplomacy. Anglo-American Collaboration in the Reconstruction of Multilateral Trade* (Oxford: Clarendon Press, 1956). The conference's fifty-year anniversary volume, gathering leading IPE scholars and Keynesian international economists continued this tradition, Peter B. Kenen, ed., *Managing the World Economy. Fifty Years after Bretton Woods* (Washington DC: Institute for International Economics, 1994). And the major IPE textbook, Frieden, *Global Capitalism*, maintains that broad exclusion, separating the Global South into its own, self-contained chapter. Historians have followed suit, for example, Sargent, *A Superpower Transformed.*

[53] From the perspective of the 1970s, Marcello de Cecco assessed even this attempt of Keynes as a failure, as the New York banking community defeated the attempt to ban short-term international lending, which became the loophole that in time and through constant pressure

controls and licensing systems for imports and exports, a renovated, coordinated global capitalism with the national economy as its basic political unit was set to manage economic policies freed from the pressures of international finance and responsive instead to national constituents. The results of these massive reorganizations seemed to surpass all expectations, ushering almost three decades of economic growth in the industrialized world unparalleled in its history. Bretton Woods was accorded the main credit for the various economic miracles around Europe and Japan and came to constitute a normative baseline for the (positive) valorization of Western capitalism as an economic system.[54] Bretton Woods' pull on today's political imaginary remains strong and explains the periodic calls for a Bretton Woods–like sociopolitical settlement every time economic crisis stalks the globe.[55]

Since the 1990s, the critique of Western centrism has successfully been overpowering earlier historiographical traditions in the many fields of the historical profession, instituting a new common sense on the diversified drivers and proper protagonists of history. The story of Bretton Woods, however, continues to resist this general trend.[56] The resistance may have to do with the subject matter; cultural approaches have often proved rather diffident in contesting the prerogative of those fields – especially economics – that claim the study of the material, the very subject against

became the tear in the fabric that grew into a hole (one example being the Eurodollar) and at length rent it apart. In Marcello de Cecco, "International Financial Markets and US Domestic Policy since 1945," *International Affairs* 52:3 (1976): 381–399. The euthanasia was not as thoroughgoing as advertised, although this book will follow a different genealogy than de Cecco did toward that rending of the Keynesian fabric.

[54] This normative baseline was particularly true of economists, and constituted the main target of criticism in Thomas Piketty, *Capital in the 21st Century* (Cambridge: Harvard University Press, 2014). It is worth noting that, since then, and under very different contexts of international political economy, other countries have managed the same feat, most notably China and India, further undermining the idea that the Bretton Woods order was the sine qua non of this miracle growth.

[55] This point is Adam Tooze's, "Everything You Know About Global Order Is Wrong," Foreign Policy, January 30, 2019, https://foreignpolicy.com/2019/01/30/everything-you-know-about-global-order-is-wrong/, retrieved September 10, 2021. As examples, Tooze records two such cases right on the dot, a 2008 UN report headed by Joseph Stiglitz, and a 2019 manifesto by Klaus Schwab, founder of the World Economic Forum, timed for that year's annual meeting at Davos.

[56] Two notable exceptions are Helleiner, *Forgotten Foundations of Bretton Woods*, and the edited volume by Giles Scott-Smith and J. Simon Rofe, eds., *Global Perspectives on the Bretton Woods Conference and the Post-War World Order* (Cham: Palgrave Macmillan, 2017), both of which deal mostly with the Bretton Woods conference itself. A more recent and thoroughgoing effort at decentering the West in the construction of global economic governance is Christy Thornton, *Revolution in Development. Mexico and the Governance of the Global Economy* (Berkeley: University of California Press, 2021).

which many poststructuralist approaches have defined themselves.[57] And yet there is also a certain propriety to this state of affairs. The institutional reconfigurations under scrutiny were derived from political decisions made in the powerful institutions of the West, a West that had itself come to dominate much of the world, whether in the form of empire, economic preponderance, or both. There is a certain symmetry to focusing on the countries of the West that, after all, capitalized Bretton Woods institutions like the IMF and the World Bank, and whose currencies were the primary targets for the eventual convertibility that was the overarching aim of the regime.

This book represents the uneasy tension that a study of capital generates between West-centrism and the provincialization of the West. West-centrism is of course an old academic original sin. And yet this book not only concerns Europe almost exclusively, but also argues that the dynamics it uncovers there, particularly those of a financial nature, might well be applicable to experiences elsewhere in the world. The book takes seriously the centrality of Europe as the site for the transformation of capitalism in the late 1960s and 1970s. The parallel supremacy of the US dollar means minimizing the United States would make a nonsense of the 1980s and the debt crises, the denouement of the history I tell here. Any history that takes political economy seriously, quickly finds the bounds delimiting the project to decenter the West. Global environmental history, for example, makes a very simple calculation to measure the weight of Western productive and accumulative hegemony: The advanced capitalist countries of the North, encompassing 16.6 percent of the population, were responsible for 77.1 percent of the CO_2 pumped into the atmosphere from 1850 to the year 2000. Scholar of human ecology Andreas Malm asks, who lit this fire?[58] The West, surely. Those limits have become apparent, for example, when historicizing China's global imprint. We have spent the last decade or so rewriting history to provide China with an unearned protagonism in global affairs. No doubt the rise of the concept of Chimerica and Niall Ferguson's insistent promotion of the notion convinced some to endorse a

---

[57] Timothy Mitchell, *Rule of Experts. Egypt, Techno-Politics, Modernity* (Berkeley: University of California Press, 2002): 1–8. Mitchell himself was part of a turn of the century cohort that have since institutionalized that contestation through journals such as the *Journal of Cultural Economy*, founded appropriately in 2008, with an especial emphasis on ideas of the performativity of economics of French sociologists Michel Callon and Bruno Latour. Contestations in the fields of economic sociology and anthropology are older, but these approaches have been slow in migrating to the field of history.

[58] Andreas Malm, "Who Lit This Fire? Approaching the History of the Fossil Economy," *Critical Historical Studies* 3:2 (2016): 215–248.

retroactive position to China of globe-straddling proportions. For years even after the 2008 global financial crisis we continued to worry about what would happen at the end of the unsustainable relationship that was Chimerica. But as Adam Tooze has argued, this fixation with China blinded us to the fact that it was imbalances and decades-long practices of the North Atlantic Rim that generated the economic sinkhole at the end of the first decade of the new millennium.[59] Although nothing here aims to eliminate China's considerable importance, the search for the origins of financialization and transformation of the post–Bretton Woods global order will still require an emphasis on the North Atlantic World, and a recovery, as scholars are increasingly noting, of the "central structural role" of European banks and European states.[60]

Financialization, however, is only one facet of the wide-ranging changes that occurred at this time and have collectively come under the rubric of neoliberalism, whose very multidimensionality went on to generate a broad and constructive discussion, and still does. And though its historical effect must necessarily give protagonism to the geographies of capital accumulation, its agents and allies, this study proposes, may be found across the world. Moreover, it finds historical effect in practice, rather than in the realm of ideas. This story of financialization is not that of the "valiant fellow" who "had the idea that men were drowned in water only because they were possessed with the idea of gravity."[61] As some are noting, the components of neoliberalism were not simply a successful intellectual and political project in the West; important elements were produced elsewhere as measures to overcome historically situated problems in the system of postwar international political economy as part of a revamped development strategy.[62] Historians are finding neoliberalism's generative sources in the peripheries of the capitalist system, imbricated with the export of New Deal developmental programs and with

---

[59] Adam Tooze, *Crashed. How a Decade of Financial Crises Changed the World* (New York: Penguin Books, 2018).

[60] Iain Hardie and Helen Thompson, "Taking Europe Seriously: European Financialization and US Monetary Power," *Review of International Political Economy* 28:4 (2021): 775–793.

[61] Karl Marx and Frederick Engels, C. J. Arthur, ed., *The German Ideology* (London: Lawrence & Wishart, 1974): 37.

[62] Raewyn Connell and Nour Dados, "Where in the World does Neoliberalism Come From? The Market Agenda in Southern Perspective," *Theory and Society* 43:2 (2014): 117–138. A similar critique more specific to the socialist bloc is made in the introduction of James Mark, Bogdan C. Iacob, Tobias Rupprecht and Ljubica Spaskovska, *1989. A Global History of Eastern Europe* (Cambridge: Cambridge University Press, 2019), although it is often contradicted elsewhere in more conventional, West-triumphalist narrative sections in the book, especially and unsurprisingly those pertaining to political economy.

decolonization.[63] These findings ultimately replicate a key argument of Kim Phillips-Fein's study of New York in the 1970s: that the rise of finance amid the restructuring of New York's budgetary crisis did not follow the adoption of new economic models or intellectual fashions, but was the outcome of hard-nosed business negotiations and spatial reorganizations.[64] The political consultations that attended these changes did not refer to academic papers, nor even economists. Where the Soviet Union was concerned, decision-making flowed from productivist compulsions, institutional organization, geological serendipities, geopolitical constraints, and a political and ideational commitment to commerce that had been deeply rooted within Soviet political economy since the revolution took its first steps toward state-building in the New Economic Policy of the 1920s.[65]

The concern here is that West-centrism, however justified in the study of institutional power centers, has also encouraged a certain degree of artifice in how we understand the Bretton Woods regime and the history of capitalism that are at the base of this story. This artifice is particularly visible at the regime's end at the turn of the 1970s, the focus of this study. The transformation's apparent suddenness and speed very quickly displaced early emphases on social dynamics that were offered in real time.[66] The rise of Ronald Reagan and Margaret Thatcher lent the

---

[63] Respectively, Amy C. Offner, *Sorting Out the Mixed Economy. The Rise and Fall of Welfare and Developmental States in the Americas* (Princeton: Princeton University Press, 2019), and Vanessa Ogle, "Archipelago Capitalism: Tax Havens, Offshore Money, and the State, 1950s–1970s," *American Historical Review* 122:5 (2017): 1431–1458. Meanwhile, in a broad series of articles, Patrick Neveling has been constructing an excellent investigation of the role of Export Processing Zones as incubators of some of the most important elements of neoliberal capitalism, an excellent example of which is "The Global Spread of Export Processing Zones and the 1970s as a Decade of Consolidation," in Knud Andersen and Stefan Müller, eds., *Contesting Deregulation. Debates, Practices and Developments in the West since the 1970s* (Oxford: Berghahn Books, 2017): 23–40.

[64] Kim Phillips-Fein, *Fear City. New York's Fiscal Crisis and the Rise of Austerity Politics* (New York: Metropolitan Books, 2017). In a similar vein, see Jack Copley's explanation for James Callaghan and Margaret Thatcher's liberalization of capital controls as the outcome of a political attempt at supporting industrial exporters rather than a commitment to neoliberal thought, in "Why Were Capital Controls Abandoned? The Case of Britain's Abolition of Exchange Controls, 1977–1979," *The British Journal of Politics and International Relations* 21:2 (2019): 403–420. On the intellectual leadership of business leaders and gurus rather than economists in terms of the changes that were wrought through business practices see Louis Hyman, *Temp. How American Work, American Business, and the American Dream Became Temporary* (New York: Penguin Books, 2018).

[65] Oscar Sanchez-Sibony, "Global Money and Bolshevik Authority: The NEP as the First Socialist Project," *Slavic Review* 78:3 (2019): 694–716.

[66] Daniel Bell, *The Cultural Contradictions of Capitalism* (New York: Basic Books, 1976); Fred Block, *The Origins of International Disorder. A Study of United States International Monetary Policy from World War II to the Present* (Berkeley: University of California Press,

appearance of a purposeful, designed and coordinated attack on the old regime; as with all great (wo)man histories, the ideologies these great leaders represented acquired explanatory currency; conventional understandings came to seek the grand neoliberal transformation in the political location of authoritative thought that hastened the end of an earlier form of capitalist organization and gave rise to a new form, sometimes called neoliberal to stress the apparent primacy of markets over an earlier one of the state.[67] Inevitably, these contributions to our knowledge of the end of Bretton Woods and the era more generally involved Western characters, entities and dynamics.[68]

Another kind of critical assessment has insistently made the Global South a victim of northern hegemony; having been written out of Bretton Woods' historical core in Europe and the United States, the South appears as a terrain of neoliberal experimentation and depredation. And closer to the geographical vehicle of this article, the socialist world – still functioning under the Cold War metanarrative of three worlds and categorized in its antagonistic, or at best liminal, second-world guise – continues to be written as if on the other side of the woods, a geography in pursuit of interests largely formed of ideological proclivities inimical to those of the capitalist West. Its historical role is often alleged to go even further; the bloc on the other side of the Iron Curtain not only refused to participate in the historically miraculous system devised by Westerners but it also helped organize it only by providing the anti-politics necessary to overcome myriad obstacles of domestic and international conflict within the West.[69]

1977); David Harvey, *The Condition of Postmodernity. An Enquiry into the Origins of Cultural Change* (Oxford: Basil Blackwell, 1989).

[67] David Harvey exemplifies this arch, with *A Brief History of Neoliberalism* (Oxford: Oxford University Press, 2005), which did not reject earlier emphases on the social dimension but embraced ideological explanations. More recent interventions in intellectual history have rejected the state/market binary as the locus of neoliberal thinking, most foundationally in the work of Philip Mirowski, for example Philip Mirowski and Dieter Plehwe, eds., *The Road from Mont Pelerin. The Making of the Neoliberal Thought Collective* (Cambridge: Harvard University Press, 2009); see also Loïc Wacquant, "Three Steps to a Historical Anthropology of Actually Existing Neoliberalism," *Social Anthropology/Anthropologie Sociale* 20:1 (2012): 66–79. For a critique more broadly of the postmodern turn as a sublimation of the totalizing and intellectually paralyzing subordination to the values generated by the universal market system, as evinced by the striking parallels in how we conceived of postmodernism and globalization as analytical categories and historical eras in the 1990s and 2000s, see David Graeber, *Toward an Anthropological Theory of Value* (New York: Palgrave, 2001).

[68] A unique exception is Johanna Bockman, *Markets in the Name of Socialism*, which turns the development of neoclassical economic thinking into an East–West conversation.

[69] In the literature of political economy, this is usually the work of a citation; for a recent example see Barry Eichengreen, "Bretton Woods After 50," *Review of Political Economy* 33:4 (2021): 553, citation 4.

The borders created by Bretton Woods and attendant political systems, such as the Cold War, were real in certain ways, but illusory and obfuscating in others. This book will show how the Soviets searched for allies and mechanisms through which to disrupt an ostracism from capitalist exchange that was part and parcel of a politics organized from Washington DC – possible by and large while the US government's control over the US dollar was absolute. But the Soviet Union here is meant to represent a wider exercise in enlarging the cast of characters involved in the story of the birth of our world at the end of Bretton Woods, one that can be reproduced from other economic geographies. The alliances and associations detailed here were repeated across the world, all aimed at the attenuation of power emanating from political centers in Europe and the US. However, this history also calls attention to the particularities and importance of the Soviet Union in the construction of the material and financial infrastructures that capitalized the disassembly of the 1930s institutions upon which Bretton Woods itself was established.

Observing this pan-European effort to dismantle Bretton Woods from Moscow is both illuminating and efficient. The effective state monopoly of foreign trade in the Soviet Union meant that all foreign business had to be done in Moscow. European firms, banks, and state officials all conducted their business in the capital, even when their final suppliers or clients were a continent away. The bureaucracies that attended to them – Gosplan, the Ministry of Foreign Trade and its departments, the Bank for Foreign Trade under the State Bank, and the Ministry of Foreign Affairs – all left behind the documents these visits generated in an equally concentrated manner. Any equivalent study in Europe involving these many characters in the business, financial, and political world would entail researching a prohibitive plurality of archival funds in too many languages for the average scholar to master successfully. Choosing to plumb the Soviet archives deeply rather than spread the research thinly across many sites allows a measure of contrast among European countries that I have made a feature of in this book. The Soviet archives clarify a contrast of European approaches that may have been difficult to discern otherwise. There are two absences in this text that perhaps should have received some treatment together with the European countries the book spotlights: Finland and Japan. They are absent in the sense of the research carried out here, but they are, the reader will find, quite present, hovering like specters in talks, reports, and the thought of the protagonists of this story. These two countries were clearly generative of Soviet thinking and approaches to the construction of markets, financing, and exchange. They were arguably as important as the central characters here: Italy, Great Britain, Austria, West Germany, France, and the United States. The contrast they represent in the Soviet Union's foreign relations and the historical development of capitalism will continue to enrich our understanding of the world we live in.

The book will argue that the Soviet Union found empowerment and purchase in the West with the formation of international markets; and it found leverage and access to capital with the construction of an energy infrastructure that in time came to supply up to a quarter of energy consumption in Europe.[70] Global capital, in other words, was finding the political allies and technopolitical means to shake free from its Bretton Woods bonds well before the oil crisis and petrodollar recycling that is often foregrounded in the literature on international political economy, or in a more critical key, the literature on neoliberalism.[71] Using archival documents from the different departments of the Soviet Union responsible for its commercial and financial exchanges, this book will start with a historical vignette of the problem of US power facing the Soviets at a moment of crisis in 1963, after a series of crop failures forced them into the ignominy of grain imports in a world without ready global markets. It will then document the means of its escape from the constraints of Bretton Woods that had allowed the United States such structural power over Soviet international relations to begin with. That this liberation turned out to be a Faustian bargain by the 1980s has little to do with any Western-generated neoliberal plan, and everything to do with the enduring power, attraction, and dysfunctions of liberal constructions of capitalism, and their compatibility with a politics built on economic growth and capital accumulation that found allies among any number of undemocratic regimes, very much including the Soviet Union.

The archival material gathered here offers insights into Soviet political economy that readers will readily understand to go against the grain of what we have thought were basic tenets of Soviet governance and

---

[70] An important caveat is that the Soviets did not pursue market liberalization at home. Market-like systems were an important part of the reforms the Soviets pursued concurrently to this history, but of a much more constrained nature than the encompassing liberalization they sought from the West. However, recent research is making clear that socialist bloc countries were otherwise very much engaged in the global reorganization of economy toward more flexible production and the disciplining of the cost of labor. See James Allen Nealy, Jr., "Making Socialism Work: The Shchekino Method and the Drive to Modernize Soviet Industry" (PhD dissertation, Duke University, 2022); and Alina-Sandra Cucu, "Going West: Socialist Flexibility in the Long 1970s," *Journal of Global History* (forthcoming).

[71] One study was able to discern from the German archives one of the key arguments of this book: the deliberate politics of a construction of interdependence inherent in Brezhnev's energy politics with Europe. Frank Bösch, "West Germany, The Soviet Union and the Oil Crises of the 1970s," *Historical Special Research/Historische Sozialforschung* 39:4 (2014): 165–185.

international relations. The apparent socialist economic emergence in the world of the 1970s was not a Brezhnev innovation or an outcome of détente; market organization was far from antithetical to Soviet politics; systemic failure did not motivate the Soviet Union's global economic participation. So it goes. Many past assessments were premised on binary contrasts that view capitalist and socialist economic systems in a static standoff of ideal forms.[72] When both are viewed as systems in continuous transformation, however, we can begin to discern the ways in which each constituted the other, even if they did not do so just as they pleased. Within the power structures of a world in flux, the Soviet leadership made choices that, like Lorenzo's, would make the world we live in. Like the antebellum American South in the historiography of a decade ago, socialist geographies do not feature much in our understanding of the creation of our current capitalist era.[73] This book makes an argument for why they should. Soviet agency clarifies the actors and logics that pushed the world toward greater liberalization and financialization. To take one example, Nancy Fraser writes of the United States, *tout court*, as the power organizing the transformation of capitalism. "In overseeing the transition to the new regime, the US also prolonged its hegemony .... Despite considerable loss of moral authority and a shift in its status from creditor to a debtor nation, the US still serves as capital's global enabler and enforcer, resorting alternatively to the force of arms, the cudgel of debt, and the blandishments of trade as it pushes to globalize and liberalize the world economy, now enlarged to include the ex-communist sphere."[74] There is no disputing the importance of power and institutions emanating from the United States, but what Fraser and many others agglomerate and distill, this study seeks to disaggregate and multiply. What results is a more systemic panorama of global capitalism shaped by contradictory impulses from unexpected places.

The "communist sphere" was there all along, and it was not victim of a US-led transformation of capitalism; it perpetrated the very actions Fraser ascribes mainly to that unwieldy aggregate, the United States.

---

[72] This follows on Kate Brown's critique. Brown shows instead striking similarities at the root of both US and Soviet governmentalities of city construction, in "Gridded Lives: Why Kazakhstan and Montana Are Nearly the Same Place," *American Historical Review* 106:1 (2001): 17–48; and again in *Plutopia. Nuclear Families, Atomic Cities, and the Great Soviet and American Plutonium Disasters* (Oxford: Oxford University Press, 2013).

[73] The corrective literature on the subject is now too vast to enumerate, but a useful sample of that literature can be found in Sven Beckert and Seth Rockman, eds., *Slavery's Capitalism. A New History of American Economic Development* (Philadelphia: University of Pennsylvania Press, 2016).

[74] Nancy Fraser, "Legitimation Crisis? On the Political Contradictions of Financialized Capitalism," *Critical Historical Studies* 2:2 (2015): 176–177.

Committed to a logic of governance built on the accumulation and expansion of infrastructure, production capacity, and commodity consumption, they helped liberate finance and construct market environments that could constrain a set of (US government-led) politics arrayed against them. They picked up allies along the way, allies as committed to capital accumulation as the Soviets were. Like other capital-constrained countries around the world, the Soviet Union did not seek access to finance because of greed or to ease a failing governance; in fact they did not just seek access to finance. The archives show that they sought to change relations of capital allocation globally within a very specific, historically situated moment in the development of capitalism. And more uniquely than many like-minded countries, the Soviet Union had the means, not to dictate, but at least to push for terms. That the push succeeded may owe much or very little to the Soviet Union – that is an assessment that requires more research – but understanding why, how, and the power relations that arbitrated that political endeavor compels us to incorporate the socialist world as a constituent agent of a history of capitalism.

Prologue
The Grain Crisis, 1963

Khrushchev's Presidium did not wait to deal with the onrushing grain crisis. As soon as the first harvests started coming in in the late summer of 1963, the top leaders rescinded most commitments to export grain that year.[1] They mobilized their ambassadors all over the bloc to convey the news of the bad harvest and lower their allies' expectations on purchases of Soviet grain over the coming year. The Soviet leadership's own expectations to get through the crisis through economizing grain resources rather than turning to outside sellers were likewise quickly dashed. Despite a stubborn Western conventional wisdom on the matter, the Soviets had consistently refused to use their gold reserves to fulfill imports, but in August they acceded to doing just that. And they threw in all their hard currency savings in the bargain, even as they began renouncing planned imports of different industrial goods.[2] Khrushchev would eventually be widely blamed for the harvest failure of 1963; denouncements of his harebrained agricultural reform schemes would play a significant role in his ouster a year later, and they continue to constitute the received wisdom of his historical legacy.[3] But the truth is that crop

---

[1] Much of the following is taken from N. Iu. Pivovarov, "Zernovoi krizis 1963 g. v SSSR i vneshnetorgovye kollizii ego razresheniia [The Grain Crisis of 1963 in the Soviet Union and Foreign Trade Collisions of Its Resolution]," *Gumanitarnye nauki v Sibiri* 26:1 (2019): 28–33. The suddenness was also noted in the USA, where Secretary of Agriculture Orville L. Freeman observed that when he last spoke with Khrushchev at the end of July the Soviets thought the harvest would be normal. Summary Record of the National Security Council Meeting, October 1, 1963, US Department of State, *Foreign Relations of the United States* (hereinafter FRUS), 1961–63, Vol. V, Soviet Union (Washington, DC: US Government Printing Office, 1998): 778.

[2] Although an initiative from the Ministry of Foreign Trade to sell 120 tons of platinum was not supported by the Ministry of Finance. Pivovarov, "Zernovoi krizis 1963 g. v SSSR," 29.

[3] These included wide-ranging administrative reorganizations that did away with traditional ministries, causing administrative havoc and deep-seated resentment among the apparatchiks and managerial class, as well as an ill-thought virgin lands campaign that brought the virgin steppe lands under cultivation, which at first yielded bumper harvests followed by erosion, soil degradation, and ultimately harvest failure. A more than

failure occurred all over Eastern Europe, much of it driven by adverse weather that also had the effect of halting all growth in Western European agricultural production.[4] In fact Khrushchev's corn campaign may have attenuated the disaster, as it was designed to do, and may have helped Soviet agriculture weather earlier global crop failures in 1961/62.[5] We might consider instead that as his last year proceeded, it may be that Khrushchev's authority diminished in exact inverse relationship to the steady rise in agricultural products the communist bloc now had to import rather than export – a process rather than a shock. For another fact is that 1964 was the first time in more than a decade that the trend toward lower global average prices for agricultural products was reversed, regaining more than a third of the 22 percent decline in its purchasing power against manufactured products.[6] That decline had gone unbroken since 1951, after the shock of the Korean War to commodity prices began to wane. In fact, the comparative decline of agriculture had reinforced a postwar, postcolonial critique that castigated the injustice of the capitalist international economic system for slowly impoverishing the agriculturally oriented Global South as prices for what they produced failed to keep up with prices for the manufactured goods produced in the north.[7] Now, in one fell swoop, the communist world had reversed the trend, undermining one of the main pillars of dependency theory and the ideas behind the import substitution industrialization practiced by their erstwhile allies in the South. To deepen the irony, the largest beneficiaries of the rise in

complete panoply of Khrushchev's failures is showcased in William Taubman, *Khrushchev. The Man and His Era* (New York: W. W. Norton, 2003).

[4] Food and Agricultural Organization of the United Nations (FAO), *The State of Food and Agriculture 1964* (Rome: FAO, 1963): 21.

[5] A rare and excellent reassessment of Khrushchev's agricultural policies is Aaron Hale-Dorrell, *Corn Crusade. Khrushchev's Farming Revolution in the Post-Stalin Soviet Union* (Oxford: Oxford University Press, 2018). The continuum of crises in the last years of Khrushchev's leadership were not so much a treadmill of reforms as a dialectic from crisis to reform to crisis, to the point where eggs came to sporadically replace the ruble in the Soviet countryside, a story pieced together in an outstanding investigation by Alexandra Oberländer, "Hatching Money: The Political Economy of Eggs in the 1960s," *Cahiers du monde russe* 61:1–2 (2020): 231–256. Oberländer's dates for the recurring practice in the countryside of turning eggs into money are suspiciously coincidental with harvest failures and subsequent mass imports of grain the following year.

[6] FAO, *The State of Food and Agriculture 1964*, 5.

[7] This refers to Engel's Law, which posits that the proportion of spending on food declines as income increases, and its successor the Prebisch-Singer thesis developed in the late 1940s by the Argentine Raúl Prebisch, later secretary general of the United Nations Conference on Trade and Development (UNCTAD) and main economic theorist of dependency theory, and the British heterodox economist Hans Singer. An excavation of the thesis is in John Toye and Richard Toye, "The Origins and Interpretation of the Prebisch-Singer Thesis," *History of Political Economy* 35:3 (2003): 437–467.

agricultural prices turned out to be the rich capitalists of the Anglo-Saxon countries of recent settlement: Canada, Australia, and the United States.

It is true that all agricultural products benefitted in this inflation. According to the UN's Food and Agricultural Organization (FAO) report of 1964, prices were pushed up by a 4 percent increase in the volume of international trade in agricultural goods to its highest ever markup to that point.[8] However as the report pointed out, the main driver was the trade in wheat going to the Soviet Union. The Soviets, in turn, ended up having to help their suffering allies in the Eastern Bloc by acting as buyers and intermediaries of grain imports.[9] Incidentally, the other driver that the FAO's report pointed to was the steep rise in the price of sugar, which serendipitously owed to the latest socialist revolution, that in Cuba – the main cause being the Kennedy administration's embargo of the island, which brought about a dislocation in the production and distribution of Cuban sugar and led to that steep rise in 1963 and sugar price volatility more generally.[10] The Soviets, with the weight of the Eastern Bloc on their shoulders, had to send a procurer out to Canada, where they secured almost seven million tons of grain.[11] Together with some 1.7 million tons from Australia, this went much of the way in making up for the more than ten million ton shortfall in grain deliveries from Soviet farms they suffered compared to the year before.[12] But not before enduring a number of setbacks and indignities during the negotiations: The initial three-year credit proffered early on turned into one for a year and a half; the 10 percent down payment of the cost of the grain turned into 25 percent with further 25 percent tranches scheduled every six months for those eighteen months, which to add insult to injury had to be made in cash; and most painful of all, the grain price offered by the Canadians suddenly skyrocketed when they received forecasts of the poor Western European harvests and then learned the US Congress was mulling a law to impose taxes on loans to other countries made by American banks – which were set to finance the whole deal in the first place. Oh, and they had to forswear any re-exports to Cuba, a small but sore point considering how much more rational it was to send the grain

---

[8] FAO, *The State of Food and Agriculture 1964*, 5.

[9] Pivovarov, "Zernovoi krizis 1963 g. v SSSR," 29–30.

[10] Which in turn locked the Soviets into overpayments for years to come, Oscar Sanchez-Sibony, "Cuba, Soviet Oil, and the Sanctions That Never Were: An Archival Investigation of Socialist Relations," *Journal of Latin American Studies* 54:4 (2022): 593–616.

[11] Pivovarov, "Zernovoi krizis 1963 g. v SSSR," 31.

[12] FAO, *The State of Food and Agriculture 1964*, 21.

to Cuba directly from Canada, rather than sending Soviet grain and flour from Soviet ports.[13]

These politicized, arbitrary negotiations continued in the US, where the Soviets hoped to pick up another three million tons of grain to supply their allies. The White House's approach was of a Cold War logic that would not have been amiss in the contemporaneous absurdist movie *Dr. Strangelove*; it rehearses again the Cold War as the grand American domestic and global project that it was.[14] The US government still held the reins of world commerce in its hands, and subjected it to a political calculus that American officials and academics projected for decades on the Soviets.[15] The "pros and cons" laid out by Acting Secretary of State George W. Ball at a National Security Council meeting after the deal with Canada had gone through could only have been dreamed up in the labyrinth of the shared fixations of the adults in that room:

1. "The purchase by the USSR of large amounts of wheat can be portrayed as a failure of Communism. The Soviet system is unable to provide sufficient food for its citizens and has to come to the West in order to meet its food needs.
2. The purchase of US wheat diverts Soviet resources from arms to food. Soviet monetary reserves are not unlimited. In order to pay for the wheat, the USSR would have to use gold, which costs the Soviets about $65 an ounce to produce and is worth only $35 an ounce on the world market.
3. We have a long tradition of helping the Russian people in periods of famine. Mr. Harriman recalls comments by Russians made to him during World War II about the Hoover food relief campaign of World War I. If we turned down the Soviet deal, we would be breaking this tradition.
4. During the months it would take to deliver the wheat to the Soviet Union, the Soviet Government would be prompted to maintain a status quo lest the wheat delivery be halted."[16]

---

[13] Pivovarov, "Zernovoi krizis 1963 g. v SSSR," 30.

[14] Anders Stephanson has long argued for this position, which Soviet documents only strengthen. A good exposition of it is Anders Stephanson, "Cold War Degree Zero," in Joel Isaac and Duncan Bell, *Uncertain Empire. American History and the Idea of the Cold War* (Oxford: Oxford University Press, 2012).

[15] The projection of American attitudes, impulses, and barbarity has long been a mainstay of US political leadership. For example, the excellent recent book by Greg Grandin, *The End of the Myth. From the Frontier to the Border Wall in the Mind of America* (New York: Metropolitan Books, 2019) can easily be read as a succession of barbarous expansionism that proceeded to project America's own brutality upon its victims, whether Mexican, Black, or Native American, a point the author makes well and often.

[16] Summary Record of the National Security Council Meeting, October 1, 1963, in *FRUS*, 1961–63, Vol. V, Soviet Union, 775.

Those, of course, were all pros. The cons were rather bloodless, the most fanciful of which was that the US might somehow lose the moral authority to continue to prevail on "underdeveloped nations" to avoid trade with the Soviets – or, in the hysterical parlance that passed for common wisdom of the day, to prevail on those nations "to avoid becoming economically dependent on the USSR."[17] More politically pressing, however, was the fact that the deal, which most in the administration supported after all, would directly contravene the congressionally imposed Latta amendment to the 1961 Agricultural Act stating that agricultural commodities could only be sold to friendly nations. The administration decided to proceed timorously; they would respond positively to requests from more politically palatable Czechoslovakia for export licenses and would then wait to see how, or whether, Congress reacted. A week later President John F. Kennedy felt better about congressional support after sounding out various key Senators; the announcement that the US government would not prohibit sales of grain to the Soviets, and that "the Soviet Union will be treated like any other cash customer in the world market who is willing and able to strike a bargain with private American merchants" required the spectacle of a presidential news conference.[18]

As soon as they sat down to negotiate the grain exchange, the two superpowers ran into a fundamental quandary: Neither had had any postwar experience trading with the other on anything like the volume the Soviets had been exchanging with America's allies for a decade and a half now. In the words of Deputy Minister of Foreign Trade Sergei A. Borisov, who led the Soviet delegation in both Canada and the US, "they did not have any normal international trade practice with the US"[19] The Soviets had hoped to simply reproduce the Canadian deal and asked the Americans whether this could serve as a blueprint. But the Canadian institutions that had facilitated the deal were mostly absent in

---

[17] Ibid., 776.

[18] On October 9, 1963, in John F. Kennedy, *Public Papers of the Presidents of the United States: John F. Kennedy; containing the public messages, speeches, and statements of the president, January 20 to November 22, 1963* (Washington, DC: US Government Printing Office, 1964): 767–775. The stress was on the benefit to "our balance of payments and gold reserves," as it had been once upon a time when Franklin D. Roosevelt acceded to recognizing the Soviet Union diplomatically thirty years earlier. On President Kennedy's deep anxiety about the US balance of payments and gold reserves see Francis J. Gavin, *Gold, Dollars, and Power. The Politics of International Monetary Relations, 1958–1971* (Chapel Hill: University of North Carolina Press, 2004). An even better, earlier treatment, without archival documentation, is David P. Calleo, *The Imperious Economy* (Cambridge: Harvard University Press, 1982).

[19] Memorandum of Conversation, October 23, 1963, in *FRUS*, 1961–63, Vol. V, Soviet Union, 797.

the US. For example, the US had no equivalent to the Canadian Wheat Board, which could negotiate a common price on behalf of its farmers so that all that was left for the Soviet delegation to do with Canadian farmers was to negotiate quantities and individual commissions. The US government rather limited itself to the provision of export licenses, but also to the obligation for the deal to use US shipping, which turned out to be the main complication for Soviet officials and US farmers alike. Here was a complex mix of market principle, power, and state diktat that did not conform to any of the binaries used to construct the ideological struggle much of the literature of the Cold War sees as foundational. At first blush, it might seem that US insistence on having the Soviets negotiate directly with US farmers, rather than with state intermediating as the Canadians had done, accorded to the core principles of the US worldview, a view US officials never failed to highlight.[20] In fact, the wheat they would be selling the Soviets would have to be released from the country's grain reserves, a technology of government put in place to forestall market abundance, create scarcity, and subsidize US farmers. Meanwhile, labor regulations in shipping had made US shipping chronically uncompetitive. The Soviets – understanding the limits of what they could push for with the preponderant Americans – suggested that they be allowed to use more market-oriented, competitive shipping from US companies that used flags of convenience from Panama and Liberia. These, of course, had been created to evade labor laws and labor union pressures.[21] The lower prices this labor exploitation constituted is what attracted the Soviets to Liberia, whose registry as a flag of convenience had been set up as a private company run by Edward Reilly Stettinius Jr. and his friends in finance – on a profit-sharing agreement with the Liberian government – only three years after leaving his previous job as Franklin D. Roosevelt's Secretary of State.[22] Come Roosevelt officials or the Communist Revolution, the thrust of capital to circumvent obstacles

[20] See for example Secretary of Agriculture Freeman's memo of his July 1963 tour of the Soviet Union, in which he triumphantly proclaims that he appeared on Soviet television and was able to "get in a plug for American agriculture and our system of private ownership and individual initiative," in Shane Hamilton and Sarah Phillips, eds., *The Kitchen Debate and Cold War Consumer Politics. A Brief History with Documents* (Boston: Bedford/St. Martin's, 2014): 146–148. Never mind that these were far from the salient qualities of an American system that aimed chiefly at regulating abundance and forestalling market dynamics.

[21] The evasion of taxes and insurance was also an important attraction for organizing shipping in this way. See Laleh Khalili, *Sinews of War and Trade. Shipping and Capitalism in the Arabian Peninsula* (New York: Verso, 2020): 233–241.

[22] Stettinius is distinguished only in being such a high ranking official. Officials in decolonizing European empires regularly took their wealth from the colonies and also deposited it in the developing geography of tax havens arising in the postwar period, and

to its accumulation, especially those thrown up by labor in its own battle for a say over its purpose and governance, claimed even labor's ideological allies through the simple virtue of operating within the material and ideological field of profit maximization. Capitalism here, in this historically situated instance, operated as a possibility of practice that drew different sets of actors into its substantiation and cumulative construction through the sheer prospect of resolving tasks both mundane and extraordinary to which those actors were committed. Capitalism draws its power from these material and ideological sources and draws its agents from all over the world. Capitalism as a social system never needed for its reproduction an ideational precommitment to it, but it did need actors, biological and institutional, with the power and material resources to mobilize values toward the accumulation of capital. The Soviet Union was just such an actor.

Which is why Borisov and Soviet Ambassador Anatolii Dobrynin had told Kennedy administration officials that they were not against using American ships to take the grain loads back to the Soviet Union, only they "had no intention to pay anyone for 'their blue eyes.'"[23] It was not surprising, then, that after the Soviets convinced the Kennedy administration to use some Soviet-flagged ships for the transaction, they met with difficulties in getting independent American dockworker unions to handle Soviet ships – a confrontation the unions had often undertaken against American owners of ships sailing under flags of convenience, and which, the administration was swift to convey, went expressly against government policy and would seek to mediate.[24] In fact, the contradictions of the extreme Cold War politics emanating from Washington DC and the absence of a state design that could routinely organize and direct agglomerated business interests meant, as Borisov noted, that the characteristic that distinguished US commercial practice with the Soviet Union from that of other countries was not, pace American self-representations, its highly marketized nature, but rather that "in no other country did he have to settle commercial matters with a State

---

solidifying during the money panic and capital flight from the Global South that decolonization and the end there of white supremacy occasioned, documented in Vanessa Ogle, "'Funk Money': The End of Empires, the Expansion of Tax Havens, and Decolonization as an Economic and Financial Event," *Past & Present* 249 (2020): 213–249.

[23] Memorandum of Conversation, October 23, 1963, in *FRUS*, 1961–63, Vol. V, Soviet Union, 799.

[24] Pivovarov, "Zernovoi krizis 1963 g. v SSSR," 32, and Memorandum of Conversation, November 6, 1963, in *FRUS*, 1961–63, Vol. V, Soviet Union, 807.

Department or Ministry of Foreign Affairs."[25] It had ever been so for the United States in the Cold War Bretton Woods order that obtained since the war. And given the difficulties with the American unions, which included threats in the press that Soviet ships would be picketed should they attempt to load wheat, Borisov was not complaining exactly. In fact what resulted from that November meeting between superpower officials was a minor conspiracy; the Soviets sought and obtained a US government guarantee of aid and good will for the transaction but promised, at the insistence of the Americans, to keep it quiet so that "the US government could influence the trade unions better."[26]

The problems with the high cost of US shipping would drag on, driven, as Secretary of Commerce Luther Hodges explained, by the higher wages and cost of unionized labor. "You will have to pay higher rates on shipping in American vessels," he told Borisov in a follow-up meeting. "There is no way to get around that, and will be no way."[27] The other reason for this, of course, was the capricious government injunction on the Soviets for 50 percent of the transportation to be done on American ships. In fact, the Americans had at first insisted – the insistence was said to be the president's – that all American wheat had to be transported on American ships, an arbitrary condition they gave up on only when they realized the Soviets were packing their suitcases to go home.[28] The wilful nature of this requirement was discussed months later, when the possibility of a Soviet purchase of 1.5 million tons in the spring of 1964 was deliberated within what was by then the Johnson administration. Wheat exporters, obviously interested in the deal, were in full confrontation with US shippers, and seeking help from the government to circumvent US-flagged ships altogether in order to get the Soviet Union's business. Furthermore, imposing this obligation on a Soviet Union no longer conditioned by a desperate hunt for grain was unlikely

[25] Memorandum of Conversation, November 6, 1963, in *FRUS*, 1961–63, Vol. V, Soviet Union, 807. "He thought that the State Department would have enough to do with problems of its own without getting involved in commercial matters," the memo records Borisov declaring.

[26] Ibid., 808–810.

[27] Memorandum of Conversation, November 14, 1963, in *FRUS*, 1961–63, Vol. V, Soviet Union, 826.

[28] Pivovarov, "Zernovoi krizis 1963 g. v SSSR," 32. Interestingly, the FRUS documents sidestep this whole affair, which came very close to putting paid to all negotiations and no doubt reflect badly on a haphazard Kennedy administration. It jumps two weeks from the initial talks on October 23 to the conversation on November 6 that got the deal back on track. Researchers using only FRUS would be forgiven for scratching their heads at Borisov's comment in the latter meeting that he would stop his grain negotiators from leaving, as he had earlier instructed them to do, in Memorandum of Conversation, November 6, 1963, in *FRUS*, 1961–63, Vol. V, Soviet Union, 808.

to succeed. In the end, the Soviets had only been induced into purchasing 1.7 million tons, far below the 4 million they had floated at the beginning and the 2.5 million they had agreed ultimately to purchase.[29] National Security Advisor McGeorge Bundy read the situation correctly when he reported to President Lyndon B. Johnson that "the Soviets found their last trade with us difficult and unrewarding, and will certainly not put us first in their list of possible sources."[30] Indeed they did not. For another decade.

The story of the grain crisis of 1963 more or less ends there, at least in its international dimension. Its aftermath, however, reverberated faintly in two respects. Most immediately and directly, the sudden need for grain crowded out more established exchanges with other countries. Suddenly, grain went from barely figuring on import tables to comprising first 3 percent in 1963 and then 6 to 7 percent of the value of all imports over the next few years.[31] Coupled with a softening in both global and Soviet economic growth in 1963, this sudden dislocation in material exchange meant a temporary stagnation in commerce with their traditional partners in Europe and elsewhere, which itself prompted proclamations of mutually beneficial friendship, of the rightness of commerce, and the need to redouble efforts all around. This small, generalized blip on rising commercial momentum, observable in the momentarily anxious discussions around economic ties throughout 1964 (before the startling triumph of trade and finance everywhere in the second half of the 1960s), serves as the chronological starting point of this book.

A second, more subtle reverberation relates to the hopeful discussion Borisov entertained with Kennedy administration officials on November 8 after the two sides dotted their i's and crossed their t's and declared – only slightly prematurely – that "the wheat question could be considered to be completed."[32] The grain crisis in the Soviet Union had brought the two superpowers to a negotiating table, even if it was a humble commercial one, and neither side wanted to get up before they had at least made some effort to discuss some of the broader problems impeding the kind of relationship of political economy the Soviets had developed with America's allies across either ocean. Ambassador Llewellyn E. Thompson Jr., until recently the US ambassador in Moscow and during many years

---

[29] Ministry of Foreign Trade, *Vneshniaia torgovlia SSSR za 1964 god. Statisticheskii obzor* (Moscow: Vneshtorgizdat, 1965): 292.

[30] Notes of a Meeting, January 23, 1964, in *FRUS*, 1964–68, Vol. XIV, Soviet Union, 17, note 5.

[31] *Vneshniaia torgovlia SSSR za 1964 god*, 37.

[32] Memorandum of Conversation, November 8, 1963, in *FRUS*, 1961–63, Vol. V, Soviet Union, 812.

ambassador-at-large for Soviet affairs opened by noting that "the principal problem pertaining to increased trade between the US and USSR ... was primarily a question of credit."[33] What he meant is that the US refused to offer the Soviets any or allow its banks to offer anything but the shortest, most discreet type of credit. The hang-up, ostensibly, was that there were unpaid, unreturned Lend-Lease deliveries left over from World War II, which the Americans insisted the Soviets should settle outright, without, say, the debt restructuring and serial postwar lending that in essence allowed Great Britain to settle its Lend-Lease tab. In the immediate postwar years, the Soviets too had expected to start their repayments after the provision of a postwar loan the US had almost followed through on, but it never came.[34] In the world of Bretton Woods in which the US restricted the Soviet Union's ability to earn US dollars, a task the Soviet economy was ill-equipped to carry out even without implacable US hostility, settling Lend-Lease would have meant payments in gold. So the issue was never settled, and in 1963, the discussion continued to revolve around what should come first: the loan that would make repayments easy (the Soviet stance), or the repayment that would open the doors to normalized relations and therefore loans (the US stance). By 1963 there was a patent willingness to resolve these problems on both sides. But they had two organized political systems pushing against this reconciliation. The first is what we call the Cold War, a political and cultural logic operating most powerfully in the United States that reduced the executive's political space to maneuver at every turn, as the Kennedy administration's deliberations over the Soviet grain crisis showed. The second is the Bretton Woods system, which generated certain forms of material politics while restricting others, all whirling and eddying around the US dollar. In the 1960s, as the monopoly over the atomic bomb had done two decades earlier, it also rendered the US preponderant, and thus narrowed the parameters for the kinds of solutions it sought to international problems. Both systems were two aspects of a whole that would change a decade later with radically different outcomes.

For now, if the problem was one of credit, as Ambassador Thompson had helpfully pointed out, then it was rather strictly an American problem. What Thompson wanted was not to resolve a problem of the Bretton Woods system, but rather to obtain Soviet cooperation in an uncertain attempt at attenuating the Cold War system of American domestic politics. When Borisov and Under Secretary of State George W. Ball both coincided in exploring the conclusion of a broad trade

[33] Ibid.   [34] This episode is covered in Sanchez-Sibony, *Red Globalization*, 59–64.

agreement, Ambassador Thompson called them to attention; he "did not think it would be useful to either side to be unrealistic as to the practical problems of congressional attitudes to any trade agreement with the Soviet Union. Such congressional attitude would be governed by overall relations between the two countries. It was therefore necessary to take steps to develop a climate which would tend to remove such obstacles."[35]

Hence the path through Lend-Lease the administration proposed, as others had before it. The Soviets had held for almost two decades now that they would be happy to first tabulate what was owed – which was not entirely clear since the "debt" related to the value of war materiel that had not been returned – and then pay it. What they needed was a loan guaranteed by the US government and a trade agreement that would facilitate the necessary earnings of US dollars and end the politics of a relentless trade discrimination in place since 1947 – and a rather effective commercial ostracism globally, whose force we saw President Kennedy was concerned might be enfeebled if they acceded to the grain deal in the same commercially minded manner the Canadians had taken.[36] And it seemed for a moment that day in November that a resolution would not have had to wait. Borisov told his American interlocutors that the USSR was even then ready to make orders on fertilizer plants they were anyway purchasing elsewhere. Trade was no longer what it had been in the 1940s and 1950s, where discreet amounts of goods were exchanged back and forth. "[I]n Europe and in Japan the Soviet Union had obtained terms long enough to permit the setting up and developing of production of such plants, that is 6 to 7 years," Borisov explained.[37] He agreed with Thompson about the problem but disagreed on the gradual approach Thompson had expressed. The structure of global trade, with an increasing emphasis on larger capital investments, was making such an approach archaic. All of this Under Secretary of State Ball enthused, "offered a basis for serious discussions" that could be taken up by Ambassadors Thompson and Dobrynin and formalized in Moscow or Washington.

It seemed for a moment that day in November ... And then, in just over two weeks Kennedy would be dead and the next day Borisov was ordered back to Moscow.[38]

---

[35] Memorandum of Conversation, November 8, 1963, in *FRUS*, 1961–63, Vol. V, Soviet Union, 814–815.

[36] Ibid., 812–814.   [37] Ibid., 815–816.

[38] Pivovarov, "Zernovoi krizis 1963 g. v SSSR," 32. The speculation that at least President Kennedy was considering an attenuation of US discipline vis-à-vis the Soviet Union through the liberalization of trade is not altogether idle. Ian Jackson has documented the extent of Kennedy's disagreement with the more careful members of his administration

If the question was credit, the Kennedy administration was seeking a resolution to it through the Cold War system, an American project only Americans could resolve. Borisov, however, pointed to a different, more diffuse resolution the Soviets would come in time and at length to pursue. The memorandum of that November conversation notes that he wanted to clarify his position before leaving:

"Actually, any significant volume of trade with the US had been discontinued long ago. It was evident that the Soviet Union would have practical difficulties, though he emphasized that this would not be impossible, to pay all at once for everything that it wanted to buy in the US. Therefore, it would be necessary to begin rehabilitating their relations with American firms. During the past seven to ten years the Soviet Union had purchased capital equipment on the world market on credit terms. Assuming that the trade agreement could be concluded once again, it would be primarily concerned with purchases of capital equipment. The Soviet Union would want to obtain the same terms here as were available elsewhere. Being exporters of capital equipment themselves, they too sold on credit, for if they did not do so, no one would buy from them. It was a well-known fact that in developing countries American and Western firms were competing with the Soviet Union in selling equipment, and it was natural that whoever sold for less and on better terms got the business. Therefore, their interest in credit was quite logical. Actually, it did not mean the introduction of anything new into international trade. This, then, was the Soviet proposal on a settlement of outstanding Lend-Lease claims."[39]

Here was the path to capital the Soviets had been seeking since 1917, a goal they only sporadically reached at punctuated moments at the end of the 1920s and again during World War II. The ineluctability of homo economicus, the recourse to a discourse of market competition, the necessity for an infrastructure to govern these ontological categories of economic life and protect them from American Cold War preponderance – these were the seeds to the resolution the Soviets would pursue. The system the Soviets sought to change in this pursuit was not the Cold War, but Bretton Woods. If the grain crisis is the recurring chronological starting moment for this book, the disentangling of the means through which the Soviets helped reorder the Bretton Woods world is the substance of its narrative.

---

who advocated for policy continuation, in *The Economic Cold War. America, Britain and East-West Trade, 1948–63* (New York: Palgrave, 2001): 171–173.

[39] Memorandum of Conversation, November 8, 1963, in *FRUS*, 1961–63, Vol. V, Soviet Union, 819.

1   Italy, Cold War Maverick

In 1964 trade with Italy had stagnated. Khrushchev's economic crises had dampened Soviet export capacity, and the later crisis in agriculture had deviated many purchases away from industrial goods in Europe and toward the purchase of grain, much of it in the Americas. In Italy this was felt as a blip in a relationship that had always been special to both Soviets and Italians (see Figure 1.1). More than any other relationship, this one embodied what the Soviets repeated ad nauseam about trade thriving on relations both parties found profitable. Italy had consistently served the Soviets to break Western European taboos about what could and could not be traded with the East. And Italy had consistently used the Soviet Union to undermine established monopolies – especially in energy – and to outflank more competitive companies elsewhere in Europe.[1] Italy, in other words, had made the most of the Bretton Woods segmentations of European economic life, and its government and business community had done surpassingly well in coordinating and administering economic relations with the Socialist Bloc.[2]

---

[1] Much of this is covered up to 1964 in Oscar Sanchez-Sibony, *Red Globalization*. The Political Economy *of the* Soviet *Cold War* from Stalin to Khrushchev (Cambridge: Cambridge University Press, 2014). Its success in international trade is further underscored by Italy's lack of competitiveness in its leading industries, especially the petrochemical industry that so successfully interfaced with the Soviet Union, as argued in Francesca Fauri, "The 'Economic Miracle' and Italy's Chemical Industry, 1950–1965: A Missed Opportunity," *Enterprise & Society* 1:2 (2000): 279–314.

[2] This is somewhat in contrast with the memoirs of Piero Savoretti, founder of Novasider and an important intermediary between Italian business and the Soviets. Savoretti represents the relation as having been built on the herculean work of Italian industrialists and despite the inertia and intermittent hostility of the Italian state. Soviet documents certainly attest to the efforts of industrialists in building those ties, but also give little support to Savoretti's representations, as they show Italian state officials to have been comparatively early and assiduous lobbyists of Italian industry working in tandem with Italian industrialists. Of course, it may be that they did not work assiduously enough to Savoretti's satisfaction. Savoretti's historical agency has been usefully presented in Valentina Fava, "Between Business Interests and Ideological Marketing: The USSR and the Cold War in Fiat Corporate Strategy, 1957–1972," *Journal of Cold War Studies* 20:4 (2018): 47–52. This does

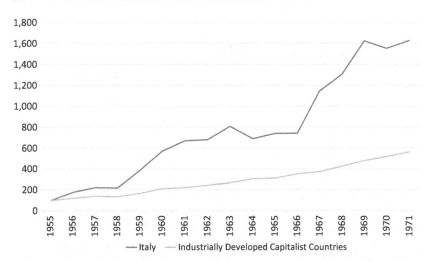

Figure 1.1 Trade growth (1955 = 100)[3]

The Italians had established a clearing payments mechanism for barter trade as early as 1948 and regularized annual trade with the Soviets through trade lists in 1952.[4] It is only a slight overestimation to say that the Soviets had learned to trade in the new Cold War world with the Italians – learned, that is, to circumvent the structural power of US dollar exclusion.[5] By the end of the 1950s, these forms of barter exchange with the Italians yielded another innovation: large-scale importation of Soviet oil through a pipes-for-oil deal. In an ominous turn, half of exports to Italy in 1962 were oil; much of the rest coal and timber.[6] This had the effect of putting the Italian state energy conglomerate – Ente Nazionale Idrocarburi (ENI) – on the

not exclude the occasional dragging of feet, as, for example, the Italian government's delay in October 1967 in insuring Fiat's contracts with the Soviets; see RGAE, f. 7590, op. 17, d. 262, l. 93. Savoretti's complaints do not seem proportional with these occasions and seem to take little account of the Italian state's efforts, concessions, and general coordinating role documented here.

[3] Constructed from the the *Vneshniaia torgovlia SSSR za ... Statisticheskii obzor* series for each year published in Moscow by *Vneshtorgizdat*.

[4] Italy's special economic partnership predates the Cold War. It was the only rich country to have quoted in its foreign exchange markets the interwar-era Soviet currency, the chervonets; see Yurii Goland, "Currency Regulation in the NEP Period," *Europe-Asia Studies* 46:8 (1994): 1259; Michael Ellman, "Money, Prices, and Payments in Planned Economies," in Stefano Battilossi, Youssef Cassis, and Kazuhiko Yago, eds., *Handbook of the History of Money and Currency* (Singapore: Springer, 2020): 478.

[5] Mikhail Lipkin has also noted the singular place of Italy in Soviet foreign economic relations, in *Sovetskii Soiuz i integratsionnye protsessy v. Evrope: seredina 1940-kh – Konets 1960-kh godov* [The Soviet Union and the Integration Processes in Europe: The Mid-1940s – the End of the 1960s] (Moscow: Ruskii fond sodeistviia obrazovaniiu i nauke, 2016).

[6] As per a January 1964 report on Soviet–Italian trade in RGAE, f. 413, op. 31, d. 284, l. 6.

map internationally. ENI's head, Enrico Mattei, had long sought to bypass the transnational monopoly power of the Seven Sisters – the seven US and UK oil companies that controlled international pricing, production, and distribution.[7] ENI's insurgent temperament was well recognized at the time: India's Oil and Natural Gas Commission (ONGC), the country's state-owned energy company and site of some of its counterhegemonic projects for Indian self-sufficiency and sovereignty, was deliberately modeled after ENI in the 1950s.[8] The Oil Majors' loss of control would in time occasion the biggest crisis of the postwar era. Some of the first steps to the oil crisis of 1973 that rearranged energy and capital flows were taken by Mattei, hand in hand with the Soviets.

Although it is often said that the Soviets were driven to export only so they may import deficit goods, the relationship with Italy clearly showed the opposite. Breakthroughs in energy exports were driving imports of all sorts of Italian industrial goods. Especially expedient were the imports of machinery and equipment at a moment when Khrushchev was driving the "chemicalization" of the Soviet economy – meaning mainly the development of fertilizers and synthetic materials through new uses of hydrocarbons.[9] The Italian relationship, then, was in various important ways the formative arena within which the Soviets nurtured their eventual relationship to the rest of Western Europe. They leaned on their energy reserves, exchanging it for technology that aimed to resolve myriad social problems of Soviet economic life and aspirations, especially in food and consumer goods. And well before the United States became anxious in the 1960s and through the 1970s about Western Europe's dependency on Communist energy, Italy had become the first Western European country to allow the Soviets a significant weight in their energy balance, up to 14 percent by 1965.[10]

---

[7] This is recounted in Sanchez-Sibony, *Red Globalization*, 184–188. The year 1962 was also the year Mattei died in a plane crash under mysterious circumstances.

[8] Matthew Shutzer, "Oil, Money and Decolonization in South Asia," *Past & Present* 258 (2023): 212–245.

[9] As Adam Hanieh has argued, while the petroleum energy regime at the production site, and as fuel, has lately been extensively revised and theorized in works such as Timothy Mitchell, *Carbon Democracy. Political Power in the Age of Oil* (New York: Verso, 2011), and Robert Vitalis, *Oilcraft. The Myths of Scarcity and Security That Haunts US Energy Policy* (Stanford: Stanford University Press, 2020), this other side energy regime has been much less studied; see Adam Hanieh, "Petrochemical Empire: The Geo-Politics of Fossil-Fuelled Production," *New Left Review* 130 (July/August 2021): 25–51.

[10] RGAE, f. 413, op. 31, d. 284, l. 8. On American anxieties over a Soviet energy relation with Europe, the classic text is Bruce W. Jentleson, *Pipeline Politics. The Complex Political Economy of East–West Trade* (Ithaca: Cornell University Press, 1986). A more recent reiteration, written in an STS key, is Roberto Cantoni, "What's in a Pipe? NATO's Confrontation on the 1962 Large-Diameter Pipe Embargo," *Technology and Culture* 58:1 (2017): 67–96. A quick, orthodox overview is Elisabetta Bini, "A Challenge to Cold War Energy Politics? The US and Italy's Relations with the Soviet Union, 1958–1969," in

These pioneering interactions in energy between the two polities could not have happened without bold advances in Italy's financial offers to the Soviets. As early as 1957, the Italians had made the switch away from clearing exchanges and toward Lira-based exchanges one year before the Lira even became a fully convertible currency. The four-year trade agreement they negotiated at the same time, covering 1958–1961, aimed to double their bilateral trade turnover; it tripled instead.[11] The possibility of controlled imbalances in trade would become a frequent point of discussion throughout the 1960s, especially as the Italians accepted a perennial deficit through which they negotiated ever greater exports (see Figure 1.2).[12] Seen from their perspective, the more primary commodities they bought from the Soviets, the more they could demand to sell to them while maintaining a moral discourse involving trustworthiness, flexibility – because they accepted deficits that had to be covered with state-subsidized credit – and good will.[13] This, at least, was generally the tenor of diplomatic exchanges between each country's ministers of trade, which were very different from the small tensions and contention deficits often occasioned with ministers of other European countries, especially in the relatively stagnating years of the Soviet economic and grain crises at the end of Khrushchev's tenure. On February 1964, for example, Minister of Foreign Trade Nikolai Patolichev was surprised by the Italian request to know in advance what other European countries offer in order to anticipate what the state subsidies might have to be in Italy. This prompted a response of equal parts pride, ideological grandstanding, and hypocrisy from Patolichev: "We don't ask for preferential conditions of credit and want only that they correspond to world practices."[14]

And yet, the Italians were not above using the stick to promote exports to the Soviets, as per the pressure they poured that summer through the

Jeronim Perović, ed., *Cold War Energy. A Transnational History of Soviet Oil and Gas* (Cham: Palgrave Macmillan, 2017).

[11] RGAE, f. 413, op. 31, d. 284, ll. 4–5.

[12] Noted already in June 1964 in an information document for administrative use as a frequent topic of Italian "solicitude," in RGAE, f. 413, op. 31, d. 284, ll. 192–205.

[13] On the readiness of the Italian state to support credit from private firms to the Soviet Union, see Italian Minister of International Commerce Bernardo Mattarella's meeting with his Soviet counterpart Patolichev on October 15, 1964, RGAE f. 413, op. 31, d. 82, ll. 91–93.

[14] In talks between the two ministers of foreign trade, Patolichev and Matarella, on February 4, 1964, in RGAE, f. 413, op. 31, d. 284, ll. 25–29. Later that year, the head of the Soviet foreign trade bank (VTB) was asking for precisely that, noting that the Italian government should pick up the tab in covering an interest rate below the 7 percent of domestic Italian markets at the time, in RGAE, f. 7590, op. 17, d. 262, l. 75. The twin issues of trade balance and Italian financial largess were also the basis of the October state-to-state meetings that same year, summarized in RGAE, f. 413, op. 31, d. 82, l. 101.

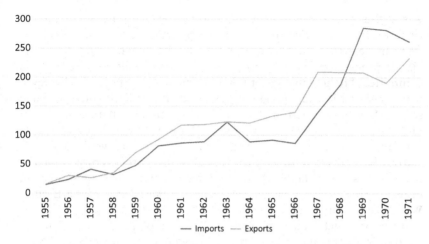

Figure 1.2 Soviet trade with Italy (in millions of rubles)[15]

licensing system while angling for more sales to the Soviets. The Italian economic miracle had peaked in 1963, and as growth slowed over the next year, current account deficits began to threaten Italy's import plans. The state responded with its licensing system – the primary Bretton Woods tool of state control. To the exasperation of the Soviets, import licenses were denied to companies that had signed contracts with the Soviets, or they were told to make counter sales of their own equipment in order to get import licenses.[16] As the pressure on Italy's balance of payments eased toward the end of the summer, officials like Italy's trade representative in Moscow made the link explicit: "If the volume of Soviet–Italian commerce continued to grow, and mutual deliveries of goods were balanced, then many issues in relation to the tendering of import licenses to Italy for Soviet goods over and above the contingents provided by prevailing agreements would be much easier to resolve."[17]

The Italian business community nurtured the relationship as assiduously as its state, if at times a bit more disingenuously. In the midst of this blip in Italy's economic miracle in the summer of 1964, an important delegation of Italian businessmen, including fifty-five company bosses, visited Moscow.[18] They were met both by Kosygin and Patolichev, but it

---

[15] Constructed from the *Vneshniaia torgovlia SSSR za … Statisticheskii obzor* series for each year published in Moscow by *Vneshtorgizdat*.

[16] RGAE, f. 413, op. 31, d. 284, ll. 186–188.

[17] Ibid., l. 271, in a meeting between the Soviet trade representative in Italy and an official of Italy's Ministry of International Commerce from August 25, 1964.

[18] RGAE, f. 413, op. 31, d. 284, ll. 90–91.

was at their more prosaic meeting with the heads of the Soviet foreign trade organizations that the Italian delegation's leader raised eyebrows when he "expressed confidence that the Soviet Union would defeat the US in peaceful economic competition. Italian industry is ready," he committed, "to help the Soviet Union in that competition."[19] This upon being told that Italian equipment was not competitive! It could be made so, the Soviets asserted, as long as Italy continued offering long-term financing.[20] Italian solicitousness paid off toward the end of the decade with a surge of exports of the large-diameter pipe that would soon knit Europe back together again. That technopolitical process owed much to the Italian state's willingness to coordinate the country's resources in order to prod at the political and economic boundaries of the Bretton Woods settlement.

It was predictably that embodiment of Italian political economy under Bretton Woods – the state-owned petrochemical conglomerate ENI – that simultaneously exemplified and propelled the relationship with the Soviet Union. It innovated for the West the five-year-long agreements that would govern Soviet/capitalist relations over the next two decades. It first signed a 1960–1965 barter agreement for twelve million tons of oil in exchange for pipe, equipment, and synthetic rubber. In 1963, it signed another five-year agreement covering 1965–1970 for twenty-five million tons of oil.[21] This last one was negotiated in parallel with state-to-state negotiations over a substantial expansion of trade as well as its extension covering the next Soviet five-year plan to the end of the 1960s.[22] Both were signed concurrently in November. Before machinery contracts, before negotiations over timber, oil rendered material a prospective relationship that both sides continued to underestimate.

This material flow, the physical substantiation of political decisions yet to cohere, also galvanized new and longer-term financial flows, credits to finance rather undetermined machinery exports to the Soviet Union to pay for the energy. They took longer to put together, though Italian bankers never seemed to doubt that they would be proffered.[23] The problem, a managing director from the Banco di Roma explained, was the economic crisis in Italy, which not only weakened the country's

---

[19] Ibid., l. 219.   [20] Ibid., ll. 218–223.

[21] RGAE, f. 413, op. 31, d. 284, l. 196. In ibid., ll. 16–17, in a January 1964 meeting, in exchange ENI committed the Soviets to buying from ENI up to 60 percent of the value of ENI oil purchases from the Soviet Union. This is almost a nation-size balancing of payments unto its own.

[22] The negotiations took place from September to November 1963. See RGAE, f. 413, op. 31, d. 284, ll. 193–194.

[23] Ibid., ll. 279–280.

reserves but was also characterized by high inflation after a decade of economic growth as miraculous as the more celebrated ones in Germany and Japan. The Bank of Italy implemented financial repression measures to lower debt levels to foreign banks and to grow currency reserves. In other words, the large, long-term loan that had been the subject of so much speculation for over a year had to wait for liquidity to return to the Italian financial system.[24] As the situation turned in the last quarter of 1964, the Soviets began to ratchet up the pressure, announcing the preparation of large orders in Italy over the next five-year plan if only the Italians would create the right financial conditions.[25] The agreement finally came in February 1965, somewhat below initial expectations – just over half the amount initially discussed.[26] Nevertheless, it allowed the Italians not only to balance the suddenly growing imports of oil but also to create the surplus they had long sought, as the Soviets binged on Italian industrial products.[27] Their trade agreement for the latter half of the 1960s had expected an impressive 50 percent increase in trade turnover over five years.[28] It doubled instead.

These then were the sorties against the energetic and financial environments that had made Bretton Woods possible, and which the very stability of Bretton Woods itself would undermine. In June 1965, the final, prolonged assault would commence. That was the month in which the insurrectionary Italians made two proposals that would evolve into two of the largest transnational European projects of the 1960s, one likely the most famous East–West cooperative endeavor, the other certainly the

---

[24] Ibid. This meeting between the Soviet trade representative in Italy and a managing director of the Banco di Roma dates from September 1964. The Italian banker expected the situation to improve in a couple of months, when both sides might finally negotiate the loan.

[25] Ibid., ll. 287–288 and ll. 289–291, in talks by the Soviet trade representative in Italy in October 1964.

[26] Although given its success in prompting exports to the USSR, as early as 1966, the Italians were looking to increase it to the 100 million rubles originally discussed. See the Italian ambassador's unprompted suggestion in RGAE, f. 413, op. 31, d. 1129, ll. 1–3. The credit as the main stimulating factor is also the ambassador's assessment.

[27] They had hoped to reach this balance by 1965, but had in fact to wait three more years. See the talks between Matarella and Patolichev on October 15, 1964, in which Matarella leans on a moral discourse of trade, reminding his counterpart that Italy was not only the first Western country to buy oil from the Soviets but also the first to maintain a tendency toward greater trade. In RGAE, f. 413, op. 31, d. 284, ll. 294–296. In this routine exchange, both make clear their particular concerns of political economy. While Matarella pledges to be especially attentive to the financial needs of companies that export to the Soviet Union, since that stimulates Italian industry, Patolichev asserts that "although we can produce many goods ourselves, we are for a rational international division of labor."

[28] RGAE, f. 413, op. 31, d. 568, ll. 108–110.

most important. Fiat's president made his initial pitch for a factory in the Soviet Union on June 28, eleven days after ENI had made a rather more ambitious pitch: a gas pipe to puncture the iron curtain.[29] Both would require large outlays of credit, but the pipeline alone would anchor a pioneering practice in East–West relations. The proposal was new enough that the Soviets found themselves a bit confused. They had not done this before, they told ENI, and any pipe would have to go through Hungary, Austria, and Yugoslavia – countries that would demand some of the gas flowing through them. Who would pay for all this? ENI offered to lay the pipe, and the Soviets could pay it back in gas deliveries.[30]

★★★★★★★★★★

Perhaps no consumer product has defined and embodied the modern age like the car. Although the meat industry innovated the assembly line in the American Midwest, it was its use in car production that opened new potentialities in industrial imaginaries. The car reshaped rural and urban geographies and continuously defined and redefined sociocultural norms of work and leisure over the ensuing decades.[31] Perhaps it was the social weight with which it had been invested everywhere that produced the fascination that followed the deal between the Soviets and the most upwardly mobile of car manufacturers at the time, Fiat. The deal occasioned a flurry of diplomatic activity between the two countries in 1966, making the Italian Ambassador in Moscow, Federico Sensi, a regular visitor to the ministries of Soviet trade and economic management – proliferating business between the two countries, after all, meant proliferating complications for the ambassador to deal with.[32] A measure of that proliferation is the fact that by the time the cooperation ended, some 2,500 Italians had worked in Fiat's Tolyatti plant – mirrored by a similar number of Soviets who visited Italy for training and other work.[33] It was

---

[29] These are to be found in RGAE, f. 413, op. 31, d. 595, ll. 53–56 and ll. 64–67, respectively.

[30] Ibid.

[31] An excellent case for its multilayered social impact in the socialist world is made in Lewis H. Siegelbaum, ed., *The Socialist Car. Automobility in the Eastern Bloc* (Ithaca: Cornell University Press, 2011).

[32] RGAE, f. 413, op. 31, d. 1129, ll. 1–3 for any number of issues arising from counter purchases, delivery schedules, business representation in Moscow, etc., as discussed in a January 19, 1966, meeting Sensi had with Foreign Trade Deputy Minister I. F. Semichastnov.

[33] Philip Hanson, *Trade and Technology in Soviet–Western Relations* (London: Macmillan Press, 1981): 109. Hanson helpfully contrasts this with a 1964 turnkey contract for a polyester fiber plant, which was large enough at about a third of the price of the deal with Fiat, but involved a fraction of the number of specialists moving across borders.

clear before negotiations even started that if the Fiat deal went through, both sides would have to think on forms of credit other than the ones that had been the norm until then.[34] These had generally involved comparatively small and at best medium-term bank-to-(Soviet) bank loans. The sheer volume of the Fiat deal necessarily involved a much bigger loan than had ever been contemplated. The semi-public Istituto Mobiliare Italiano (IMI) was tasked with sourcing the US$ 300 million credit at a low interest, which the bank managed by combining efforts with a private bank before bank consortia became standard financial practice. To address the inescapably global nature of the technological transfer to the East, IMI also committed itself to getting credit from banking systems in the countries selling the necessary technology. Insofar as much of the technology was American, the Soviets very much welcomed this indirect line of transfer of American technology that put the responsibility of acquisition – and its financing – on the Italians.

These financial innovations moved forward the largest single turnkey project to date for the Soviets. But the project proved to be the crowning achievement of a world that would soon move on. The deal took less than a year to come together, which would prove to be rather fast compared to the original energy deal ENI proposed that June. This was still longer than usual, but not by much, as the Fiat contract was not qualitatively different from any number of turnkey deals the Soviets had negotiated over the previous decade or so.[35] Industrialists had put together a one-time project requiring the erection of a particular financial scaffolding.[36] It is important that the financial scaffolding remained particular and did not become a model of future business practices. When finance emancipated itself in the 1970s, it did not do so through discreet transnational deals between

---

[34] As per Sensi's own statement in a meeting at the Ministry of Foreign Trade on February 12, 1966, in RGAE, f. 413, op. 31, d. 1129, ll. 16–18. Sensi was here passing along Fiat President Vittorio Valletta's own suggestion. To this end, Valletta further suggested that a Soviet delegation visiting Turin – then planned for February 1966 to make some preliminary assessments on possible cooperation with Fiat – should include representatives from Soviet financial organs, as conveyed by Sensi in a meeting with the deputy head of the State Committee for Science and Technology (GKNT), Dzhermen Gvishiani, on February 9, in RGAE, f. 413, op. 31, d. 1129, ll. 11–13.

[35] The deal was signed in May 1966. The social history of the resulting AvtoVAZ plant is in Lewis H. Siegelbaum, *Cars for Comrades. The Life of the Soviet Automobile* (Ithaca: Cornell University Press, 2008): 80–124.

[36] This is not to disagree with Valentina Fava's argument that Valletta had pursued a deal with the Soviets not because of its inherent profitability, which in fact proved elusive, but in order to become an important supplier of machinery not necessarily related to its automobile business. But it is to note that despite the commitment, these kinds of deals remained vulnerable to economic crisis and discontinuity that was radically different from the energy bond.

national banks, as with the deal with Fiat. It did so on the basis of a global reordering of energy – its flows, sources, materiality, and sociopolitical consequences. And part of the groundwork for it was laid by ENI.

ENI had gotten to Moscow only a week and a half before Fiat on that fateful June month of 1965. But the company had been building trust with the Soviets for seven years by then and through the kind of long-term, plannable exchange practices the Soviets had long desired from the West. The commodity exchanged – oil – helped the cause, as did the vast transformations then occurring in the energetic base of European prosperity as it changed from dirty and socially unruly coal to more socially manageable, and more calorific, petroleum. This historic change – which, Timothy Mitchell has convincingly argued, helped assemble neo-liberal governance from the 1970s, and to the detriment of Europe's labor unions and worker interests – was in large part produced with the enthusiastic cooperation of the Soviet Union.

But it was first spearheaded in Europe by the United States and its Marshall Plan. It was the market position in energy the Marshall Plan built for US companies in Europe that ENI wanted to destabilize. This included the generous lending that Italy's private petrochemical companies had received from the Americans, amounting to as high as 6.1 percent of Marshall Plan funds.[37] Part of the purpose of the establishment of ENI as a public company was to forestall the monopolization of the industry by the biggest beneficiaries of this American largess, Montecatini and Anic.[38] And more specifically as it concerned the Soviets, ENI's representative in Moscow, Pasquale Landolfi, explained that what ENI wanted from its deal with the Soviets was to escape the necessity of extending yet another contract for gas to the American oil corporation Esso, with which they had recently signed a contract to bring 10 billion cubic meters (bcm) of gas from Libya per year. As the switch out of coal the Americans had initiated in the 1940s continued apace, ENI found it would need to add another 6 bcm of gas to the energy haul from abroad.[39] The decision, Landolfi urged the Soviets, would have to be made soon, as ENI "was already forced to buy 3 billion cubic meters of gas in Libya," and the contract would be for twenty years.[40]

The Soviets very quickly maximized the counterproposal, proposing that they may import gas pipe equipment deliveries large enough in order to prepare for the export of 20 bcm of gas a year to Italy. ENI balked, for two reasons. Italian industry, Landolfi said, could not produce that much

---

[37] Fauri, "The 'Economic Miracle,'" 287.   [38] Ibid., 289.
[39] RGAE, f. 413, op. 31, d. 1129, ll. 24–27, in a meeting on February 21, 1966, at GKNT.
[40] Ibid., ll. 28–30, in a meeting the next day at the Ministry of Foreign Trade.

equipment. And, more importantly for the Italian government, the bigger the pipe project, the greater the repayment period would be.[41] They proposed instead to help build an export capacity of 10 bcm a year, six of which would go to Italy, and the remaining four could be sold in the countries through which the gas flowed. At this point, February 1966, the Italians were envisioning yet another modest push on the financial boundaries of the era. If they signed the deal in 1966, the Italians would take two years to deliver and lay the pipe and equipment. The cost would be repaid in gas over the next seven years.[42] The credit, in other words, would be for nine years, a mere half year longer than Fiat's special arrangement.

The Soviets were only certain about the kind of financial deal they wanted to extract from this new kind of gas-for-pipe contract. They were less certain about where the gas might come from and spent the next half year cooling ENI off a little and figuring out the feasibility of bringing the gas directly from their new monster fields in western Siberia.[43] By the time ENI Director General Raffaele Girotti visited Moscow in August, the Soviets were ready. Their strategy was to slow everything down, which meant lengthening the loan out. Deputy Foreign Trade Minister Nikolai Osipov, who would lead most energy-related negotiations with Western European countries, laid it out.[44] Italian equipment deliveries would begin only in 1967, and they would continue until 1970. The gas that would pay back these deliveries would only flow into Italy from 1971, when they would deliver 2 bcm of gas. The Soviets would add 1 bcm every year until reaching 6–7 bcm annually by 1975 – a rate that would ensure a longer repayment period. The contract, Osipov offered, could be for fifteen to twenty years; the prices would adjust themselves to world prices; the interest rate on the credit should not exceed 5 percent. In February, ENI had asked for a quicker resolution and a smaller, more financially manageable project. Half a year later, the Soviets had come back with a much larger project than the one the Italians had rejected in February.

The two partners were envisioning this quite differently. ENI had in mind an already enormous project that would strain its financial and productive capacity to the limit. It wanted to bring gas in from Ukraine – and through Hungary and Yugoslavia. The Soviets had altogether something else in mind: They would use this opportunity to get the Italians to fund the connection of the West Siberian gas fields to the gas pipe networks of

---

[41] Ibid., 25–26.   [42] Ibid., 29.
[43] Ibid., ll. 87–88, as a deputy minister of foreign trade told Landolfi on May 20, 1966.
[44] Ibid., ll. 115–118, in a meeting on August 4, 1966, to which the rest of the paragraph refers.

European Russia and Eastern Europe.[45] This is in effect how they presented the deal to other participants like Czechoslovakia, to whose Gosplan they communicated that they "will build a gas pipeline from Tyumen to the western part of the Soviet Union (about 5,000 km) so that a certain amount of gas from the western fields could be released for export. At the same time, the Italians are to finance the construction of this pipeline by providing us with a loan."[46] Complementarily, they wanted to use the occasion to mark a new financial precedent they could use elsewhere as they continued creating a market for subsidized capital for themselves in the industrially advanced world.[47] Predictably, nothing with Italy was agreed on, except that the first round of negotiations should take place in September or October.

Coming into the negotiations in October with everything left to negotiate, the Italians anticipated Soviet financial requests they knew were coming by warning that their government's credit resources were already stretched by the Fiat deal. The main issue for them, they said, was price. The Soviet Union had a different concern; the "principal question" for them was making sure that gas would serve as "payment for all costs of pipe and equipment, which will be delivered on credit."[48] And more, they expected the interest rate on it to be lower than that of the Fiat deal.[49] The deal's main goal, in other words, was for a long-term credit arrangement to go with a long-term material bond with Western Europe.[50] And although price was a secondary concern, its task was also made clear from the beginning: The price "should be mutually beneficial, with which we can materialize a project for the delivery of gas from Tyumen."[51] From early on in the process, Italy ascertained that Austria and France would also be in on the deal in some capacity, which would have the added benefit of

---

[45] Ibid., ll. 117–118. Osipov insisted that there was no question of exports of gas from Ukraine without building a network of gas pipes in the northern fields, as "deliveries of gas from Ukraine are tied to the delivery of gas from Siberia to the center." Meanwhile, the Soviets told ENI that pipe outside of Soviet territory would have to be negotiated directly with the countries hosting the pipeline, though they were happy to help the process along.

[46] RGAE, f. 413, op. 31, d. 2294, l. 1.

[47] Ibid., l. 3. They had clearly decided on this in that 1966 hiatus, declaring to their Czechoslovak allies that autumn: "We mean to conclude an agreement for at least 15 to 20 years."

[48] RGAE, f. 413, op. 31, d. 1129, l. 143. This first protocol meeting of the first round of negotiations started October 11, 1966.

[49] Ibid., ll. 145–46. As they made clear the next day in the first financial working group meeting.

[50] As, for example, Patolichev kept insisting after the deal laid moribund a half year later, in RGAE, f. 413, op. 31, d. 1699, ll. 145–146.

[51] In the working group for pricing, in ll. 147–148. Starting negotiating positions were quite wide, with the Italians offering $8 per 1,000 cubic meters, and the Soviets offering that amount at $14, RGAE, f. 413, op. 31, d. 1129, ll. 150–151.

satisfying the Soviet Union's demand for the kind of large deal the Soviets had laid out earlier.[52]

As negotiations ground on, it became apparent that ENI would not deliver the kind of generous, long-term loan the Soviets were hoping for. Still Italy moved its price higher, and its credit repayment schedule forward, while France and Austria piled on; by the end of 1966, at the moment when the Italians had hoped the deal would be closing, Soviet horizons began to expand for the gas deal, from a bilateral deal in a typical Bretton Woods mold to a continental one. And with that, negotiations with Italy as the grand mediator withered on the vine. Italy had opened the door through which capital could now enter. This was a technopolitical effort necessitating the lifting of the pipe embargo in November 1966, a result Landolfi attributed to Italian efforts.[53] But the Soviets were happy to wait for the assembly of the kind of coalition that could offer capital on the kinds of terms and volume they had envisioned – and the technology to match. The Soviets were waiting for West Germany.

The Germans had made unofficial noises over joining the deal in November 1966, and the Soviets were ever less motivated to lower their demands in any of the parameters under discussion, whether in credit volume and length, gas price, pipe technological specifications, or pipe delivery schedules. Everything slowed down, to the frustration of the Italians. ENI and the Italian government still did not cherish the idea of financing the Soviet Union's domestic pipeline construction, and credits to the Soviets had flowed freely on deals with Fiat, the tire and rubber products manufacturer Pirelli, and the office machines producer Olivetti. The only thing that put them at ease, Foreign Trade Minister Giusto Tolloy confessed, was that "the Soviet Union is the most solvent country" – a quality he compared rather favorably with Argentina, where Italy had also much invested.[54]

The first mention in Soviet–Italian talks of German – really Bavarian – involvement, and the first the Soviets heard of it, was in early February 1967.[55] ENI's Landolfi reported that the Austrians were having financial difficulties and were now proposing to run the pipeline through Bavaria in Germany and Tyrol in Austria before reaching Italy. This new

---

[52] Ibid., l. 144. This would be for 7 bcm annually, four of which would go to Italy, two billion to France would and one billion to Austria.

[53] Ibid., l. 194.

[54] RGAE, f. 413, op. 31, d. 1699, ll. 191–193, in a meeting in March 1967 with the Soviet ambassador in Italy, to whom he brought the good news that the Kennedy round of GATT was likely to bring further liberalization to trade with the Soviet bloc.

[55] Ibid., ll. 216–219. In talks between Landolfi and Osipov on February 3.

proposal, Landolfi explained, would allow the Austrians to tap private Bavarian firms for finance, although it would also mean that perhaps up to 2.5 bcm of gas would have to stay in the region – a prospect the Italians presented as a negative development, although the Soviets would hardly have thought so. The Italians were against the proposal, and against German participation generally. The reason they gave was whimsical: They feared "German terrorists" around the regions where the pipe would be laid, they said. They wanted to delay German involvement altogether until after the ink dried on the 10 bcm gas deal to Italy.[56]

A further round of negotiations in June 1967, however, made it clear that the Italians would not get their quick resolution. And as the Bretton Woods structures concerning the gold value of the dollar began to be uncertain, the Soviets added a gold proviso to the list of points to be negotiated, to guard against the risk of US dollar devaluation. This was a rather new practice in long-term international agreements; currency uncertainty seemed a thing of generations past. Indeed the kind of twenty-year-long energy relation sealed in cement and steel that proliferated in the 1960s was new in itself; risks could be many over twenty years, and in 1967 the US dollar revealed itself as one of them.[57]

While talks continued through that summer, the Soviets went back to lobbying Italy to further liberalize its trade, which they complained to date had only opened about 300,000 rubles worth of exports for the Soviets.[58] State approval for each deal with the Soviets was slow and cumbersome, and the Soviets encouraged the Italians to deregulate trade flows.[59] In December the Soviets even suggested to do away with annual trading protocols if only the Italian state liberalized the import of Soviet goods, a suggestion the Italians rejected, arguing that any liberalization would be slow and in stages.[60] The Soviets found Italian assurances of their goodwill toward the import of Soviet goods empty, noting that Italy had asked the common market to implement additional import duties for socialist pork and sunflower oil.[61]

In May 1967, Alitalia inaugurated the first regular flight to Moscow.[62] Despite the delays on the gas deal, the fact was that the mid-decade stagnation in Soviet–Italian trade came to an end that year. It did so on the old standby: oil for industrial goods. The engine behind the

---

[56] Ibid., l. 218.
[57] Ibid., ll. 96–97. As per a memo of various conversations, this one on July 14, 1967.
[58] Ibid., 115–118.
[59] A point they made often, for example, to an Italian business delegation in May, RGAE, f. 413, op. 31, d. 1699, ll. 158–159, to Foreign Trade Minister Tolloy in July, ibid., l. 94, and to Fiat's Gianni Agnelli in October, ibid., l. 42.
[60] RGAE, f. 413, op. 31, d. 1699, l. 6.   [61] Ibid.   [62] Ibid., 158–159.

breakthrough was finance, again. A new level in the volume of Soviet oil exports, the prospect of a secure, infrastructural relation, and the large Fiat deal all contributed to the loosening of financial flows eastward – with a debt closing already on the $1 billion mark.[63] Oil broke the impasse; finance finally turned Italian trade deficits into trade surpluses at the end of the 1960s. And all the while the gas deal languished. Patolichev had been around long enough to know why: Italy and the Soviet Union had even recently had no problem arranging for immense deals like the Fiat factory and assorted oil deals with ENI; a pipeline connection was a very different kind of bond, however, and new to the Soviets.[64] They were not going to get this wrong.

---

[63] In ibid., l. 91 in talks in July and ibid., ll. 191–193 in talks in March, more than 500 billion lira – more than $800 million US dollars – was the number Trade Minister Tolloy bandied about Moscow.

[64] Ibid., ll. 4–6, in conversation with the Italian ambassador to Moscow, December 16, 1967.

2   Great Britain
Bretton Woods and the Financial Fix

The British minded the gap. Great Britain bought more from the Soviet Union than it sold, and this trade gap had to be balanced, argued Douglas Jay, president of the British Board of Trade – as the ministry of trade was called in Great Britain – in Moscow in October 1964.[1] This was an old problem (see Figure 2.1), and the Soviet counter was equally old: The Soviet Union spent the pound sterling it earned from its trade surplus with Great Britain in the sterling zone, and that money eventually circled round to Great Britain as the Global South recipients of Soviet purchases in the zone turned around and bought things in Great Britain. As far as the Soviets were concerned, the accounts balanced. Or as they told Jay two years later in what became a ritual of British–Soviet interactions, the problem "did not exist."[2]

The result was a chronic British deficit with the Soviets that no amount of British cajoling ever repaired. British sterling exceptionalism, predicated in part during the postwar period on the fact that the buying and selling of Iranian oil was conducted in British currency, meant the British had little recourse other than imposing import quotas or some other hardline measure to obstruct Soviet trade.[3] That and an entirely ineffective discourse of probity. As Jay told the Soviets, the problem was a moral one, since he was under the impression that Soviet leaders had promised to close the gap, and moreover the British went against the wishes of many friends in offering long-term credit to the USSR and expanding trade relations.[4] The reply that October day, expressed many times in many forms throughout the 1960s, cut to the nub of British economic woes in the postwar era: British firms were not competitive with those in continental Europe, the Soviets retorted, and that is why they were losing Soviet business to their European allies; moreover they had encountered

---

[1] RGAE, f. 413, op. 31, d. 59, ll. 121–125.   [2] RGAE, f. 413, op. 31, d. 1106, l. 35.
[3] For a threat – ultimately empty – to impose quotas if British exports do not exceed fifty million pounds in 1965, for example, see RGAE, f. 413, op. 31, d. 59, ll. 148–152.
[4] RGAE, f. 413, op. 31, d. 59, ll. 121–125.

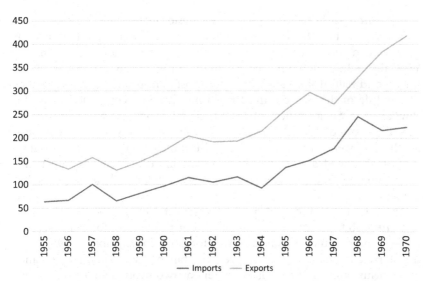

Figure 2.1 Soviet trade with Great Britain (in millions of rubles)[8]

problems with British equipment, which had turned out to be of low quality.[5] Or, as they told the British Embassy's trade advisor a few months later, the British often would not deliver a product because it was made under a US license.[6] Episodes recalling previous British indiscretions in the country's commitment to commercial liberalism were dredged up often as well. For example, when in February 1965 a British trade delegation tried to sell ships to the Soviets, the delegation's pitch started with an acknowledgment of previous wrong, when the British government banned the sale of British ships to Communist countries. The Soviets rarely missed a chance to express the consequences of that failure of liberal conviction, however, and in that meeting explained that they had established relationships with shipyards in Finland, Sweden, Denmark, and especially Japan in the aftermath of that 1950s British recalcitrance, and they were simply not interested in damaging those relationships. And in a twist of the knife: Even the British buy ships abroad for well-known reasons, they added.[7]

---

[5] Ibid.
[6] RGAE, f. 413, op. 31, d. 574, ll. 185–186. The meeting dates from February 4, 1964.
[7] Ibid., ll. 182–183, in a meeting on February 25, 1964.
[8] Constructed from the the *Vneshniaia torgovlia SSSR za ... Statisticheskii obzor* series for each year published in Moscow by *Vneshtorgizdat*.

If Japanese ships had the edge in price and quality, the British argued defensively, at least British financing was more competitive.[9] This indeed may explain why Great Britain was the top Soviet trade partner in the West throughout the 1960s as a whole, and especially through most of the second half of the 1960s. As with most European countries around the middle of the decade, the British had become concerned with the slowdown in Soviet orders of their national goods. As with the others, they understood that the Soviet grain crisis of 1963 was a major reason for this and were willing to forbear.[10] But unlike their fellow Europeans, the British alone feared they were losing out in the deepening competitive environment of international exchange. And the face of that fear was the Soviet Union.

The Soviets liked to confirm these fears, and often: "Some proposals from English firms are not competitive. For this reason, for example, the Soviet Union could not place orders for ships in England in 1963 and transferred them to Japanese, French, Italian, Swedish, Finnish, and other firms, and in 1964 a large order for two caprolactam production plants [for the production of nylon] was transferred to a Dutch firm. Often English firms cannot deliver goods in the right quantity, for example high-pressure polyethylene [plastic], pipes, staple fiber, high-strength cable, etc., or refuse to supply individual goods to the USSR."[11] The British objection that the nylon plants were lost because the Dutch had their own patents badly missed the Soviet point: Soviet market behavior was unsentimental, and the British were increasingly playing in an international terrain of intensifying market competition.[12] The Dutch had their own patent, and technology transfer was progressively less subjected to Cold War economics. The market was inevitable, the Soviets argued consistently, and the British were meeting it in the mid-1960s with an uncompetitive industrial base. The Soviets could attest that the British lost orders worth about 140 million rubles through 1964 to the first months of 1965. By way of an implicit contrast, they informed the British that the increase in imports from West Germany was linked to their timely fulfillment of earlier orders delivered in 1964 and early 1965, and the rapid rise in imports from Japan had to

---

[9] RGAE, f. 413, op. 31, d. 574, ll. 182–183.

[10] Ibid., ll. 155–163. In a meeting between a British trade delegation and the head of the department for trade with Western countries Aleksei N. Manzhulo on May 24, 1965.

[11] Ibid., l. 161. These same issues, even these same examples, were too often the subject of commercial conversations. See, for example, Soviet Foreign Trade Minister Patolichev's conversation with England's Minister of Technology Frank Cousins on February 23, 1966 in RGAE, f. 413, op. 31, d. 1106, ll. 9–12.

[12] RGAE, f. 413, op. 31, d. 574, l. 161.

do with the energetic initiative of Japanese firms and their remarkably competitive goods.[13]

If the British no longer had a competitive industrial base, British imperial legacy left behind a geographically extensive and institutionally deep capital market. It is this particular quality of British commerce, its adjacent financial component, that might explain the conundrum posed by economist Michael Kaser, who argued that in fact the Soviets purchased more British machinery than its qualitative competitiveness in global trade could justify.[14] A report from the Soviet trade representation in London explained the attraction of England not just for the Soviet Union, but for the whole of the socialist bloc this way: "Currently, the socialist countries are also showing interest in trade with England, as the English market is the largest market where they are getting the hard currency they need."[15]

****

It is perhaps this contrast of attractive financing, which drew the socialists to the British Isles, even if its industry generated so much complaint. Examples of British incompetence and lack of competitiveness were repeated year after year. They became the stock answer to British complaints about the import/export gap.[16] In effect, the Soviets felt compelled time and again to teach the representatives of the birthplace of liberalism lessons in Ricardian philosophy and capitalist competition. The lecturing preambles on Soviet commercial politics mark these out as a performative politics. The goal was to nudge the rich countries into generating a competitive, integrated, liberal world economy the Soviets could engage with free of political pressures, whether they be pressures of a Cold War type (CoCom lists or more direct, capricious forms of American veto power) or those pertaining to the moral discourse that prevailed in the compartmentalized, Bretton Woods world of capital controls. "The Soviet Union has everything and can do everything," one such illustration went, "but it would be a mistake to be locked within our own boundaries. Now no country does everything on its own.

---

[13] Ibid.

[14] Michael Kaser, "Trade Relations: Patterns and Prospects," in Alex Pravda and Peter J. S. Duncan, *Soviet–British Relations since the 1970s* (Cambridge: Cambridge University Press, 1990): 201.

[15] RGAE, f. 413, op. 31, d. 641, l. 67.

[16] The British in turn used the gap to rebuff Soviet requests to liberalize the import of Soviet consumer goods, for which the British still had quotas. For the justification for the maintenance of the quotas for as long as the gap continued see RGAE, f. 413, op. 31, d. 1106, l. 82.

The situation is the same in the Soviet Union. We believe that doing everything on our own is irrational. In every country there is something better than the others. For this, contacts between the 'captains' of industry of both countries are important, as well as contacts with traders."[17] This was Patolichev in 1967 talking to a delegation of English manufacturers, all captains of industry. He followed his lecture by (mis)illustrating it with a warning – he used the term "example" according to the memorandum that recovered this episode. Patolichev recalled the "purchase of a pulp mill that went to Finland instead of France, when the French firms, having decided that the purchase of this plant was secured for them (since the purchase of the plant was provided for in the agreement), seriously overestimated prices. They believed that the Soviet Union was bound to buy this plant and asked for a price of over $80 million. Soviet organizations refused to purchase this plant in France and bought the same plant in Finland for $36 million."[18]

In recounting this miscalculation by the French, Patolichev meant to illustrate the inevitable disciplining mechanisms the Soviets merely represented. Of course, where these did not exist, the Soviets represented them discursively. In the context of a larger – and more liberalized – area of exchange, the Soviets sought to discipline their trade partners by making recourse to a discourse of market discipline and a practice of fundamentally undermining the authority of the trade lists that had once so effectively overseen the administration of exchange. The Soviets made a point of this in their talks with the British Minister of State at the Board of Trade Roy Mason, who was in Moscow in May 1966 hawking British ships: "The placement of orders by Soviet organizations for ships on the world market depends on the needs of the national economy of our country, as well as on the competitiveness of the proposals received, and not on whether ships are included in the trade agreements with the USSR that exist with other countries."[19] The victims of market competition here were the Danes, who lost orders to Dutch shipyards despite the fact that trade lists with

---

[17] RGAE, f. 413, op. 31, d. 1677, l. 30. Quotation marks are in the original document. From a meeting on April 25, 1967.

[18] Ibid., ll. 30–31.

[19] RGAE, f. 413, op. 31, d. 1106, l. 22. A few weeks later, they repeated this point to Mason's boss Douglas Jay, in ibid., l. 36: "Inclusion of ships in trade list agreements is not the decisive factor in placing orders. We can give many examples ... Commercial conditions remain decisive." A similar situation, documented in in RGAE, f. 413, op. 31, d. 574, l. 162, had caused Simon Carves Engineering company to lose an order the year before, according to Manzhulo, having given too high a quote expecting that the Soviets were committed to buying from England regardless.

Denmark specified ship purchases.[20] The Soviets fine-tuned their market discourse according to the possibilities available, and the best "commercial conditions" (i.e., finance) were what was available in Great Britain.

Or there was the moral story with a valuable lesson at the end that Patolichev told the 1967 delegation of English industrialists. This story involved Imperial Chemical Industries (ICI), the largest industrial concern in Great Britain at the time. Patolichev recounted how the slow-moving corporation had failed to put in a bid for a turnkey factory after the Soviets had invited it to do so. This meant that the purchase of two polyethylene plastic plants went to the West German chemical manufacturing company Zschimmer & Schwarz. ICI managed to miss another opportunity for two more plants a bit later. When ICI finally decided to join the market fray, Patolichev reported triumphantly, they took home contracts for six plants.[21] Because this was a business meeting, rather than one between government officials, Patolichev ended with an appeal for these English businessmen to prevail upon their government to give quick approvals to these kinds of deals. It might be that rejecting these deals has some kind of meaning for the English, Patolichev ironized, but if Soviet trade organizations do not buy the factories in England, they will buy them somewhere else, and the Soviet market will be lost to the English.[22] Patolichev was no humorless apparatchik – few at the top were. He understood irony and knew when to employ it: There are goods in the lists of forbidden exports to the Soviet Union that the Soviets could sell to the British, he observed. Ultimately this appeal had a precise end point: They would need a factory for the production of rubber products with a capacity of 40,000 tons a year; they were carrying out negotiations with the Italians, but they could just as well buy it in England "under certain favorable conditions."[23]

Goading the business community into becoming lobbyists for Soviet interests was a useful if limited strategy, one British officials at least outwardly dismissed when pursuing the ethical line they in turn used as ineffectively on the Soviets. When ICI chairman Paul Chambers publicly

---

[20] See also RGAE, f. 413, op. 31, d. 1106, l. 36, in that May meeting with Douglas Jay, where this message is repeated, with the addition that in fact the Soviets were at that moment negotiating the purchase of three dredgers, and that ultimately when it came to ships like tankers and dry cargo ships, even the English admitted they were not competitive, or so alleged Deputy Minister of Foreign Trade Mikhail Kuz'min. The objective to all this, as ever, was to goad the British into making a competitive offer, even though ships had not made it in the trade lists the Soviets drew up with Great Britain.

[21] RGAE, f. 413, op. 31, d. 1677, ll. 30–31. Patolichev continues with examples: two plants for the production of polyester went to Krupp after ICI allied with DuPont refused to put in a bid, and the nylon factories purchase that went to Holland.

[22] Ibid., l. 32.   [23] Ibid.

endorsed Soviet arguments on understanding British trade deficits within the larger sphere of the sterling zone, Minister of Technology Frank Cousins dismissed him in private talks with Patolichev: "Private businessmen, Chambers in particular, can't speak for the English government," he sniffed.[24] To the Americans, however, British governments from the Macmillan ministry on had been reporting an intense lobbying campaign from British business to liberalize trade with the East.[25]

Despite anxious American displeasure, the statistics showed a clear trend in commercial engagement, and the Soviets referenced it liberally. After all, along with insistent lectures on the nylon case, which the Soviets continued to use for at least three years, they could also point out that in 1965, for instance, they increased imports from Great Britain by an astonishing 50 percent.[26] There was also the issue of British re-exports of Soviet goods like diamonds and grain, which Patolichev quoted at some fifty million rubles-worth and argued that they should not be counted as part of the bilateral gap, since in that trade the English were acting as mere intermediaries.[27] Patolichev also gestured to other invisible earnings, like freight costs and insurance fees, as elements that went some way in balancing accounts, a position later supported by British economists.[28] The Soviets, in other words, coupled a discursive insistence on British international failure of competitiveness with a repetitive discourse of market integrity and punctuated success, skillfully maintaining a current account gap against an equally insistent – but rather less effective – British drive to close it.

★★★★★★★★★★

This is an odd set of contradictions. No other country's industry was subject to so much disparaging commentary from Soviet trade officials than British industry. And yet the British were, on the whole, the most important economic partners the Soviets had in the West through the 1960s. A report on the then recent history of British economic relations with the Soviet bloc put together by the Soviet trade representation in London at the beginning of 1965 explains the reasons behind this paradox: the undeniable success of Soviet–British economic relations thriving in the light of a uniquely reproachful Soviet strategy of pontifications on the nature of markets.[29]

---

[24] RGAE, f. 413, op. 31, d. 1106, l. 10.   [25] Jackson, *The Economic Cold War*, 173–177.

[26] RGAE, f. 413, op. 31, d. 1106, l. 9.

[27] Ibid., l. 11. All these arguments were rehearsed again almost to the letter for a British official four months later in ibid., ll. 21–25.

[28] Michael Kaser, "Trade Relations," 201.   [29] RGAE, f. 413, op. 31, d. 641, ll. 66–80.

Although reports of this sort were often drawn up to inform Soviet dignitaries about to visit the country in question, this particular report seems to have circulated only within the Ministry of Foreign Trade, and mainly among the deputy ministers and heads of ministry departments. Its purpose, in other words, seems to have been the production of the ministerial and party line, that is, of precisely the arguments these men went on to repeat so relentlessly in meetings with British officials and businessmen. We find here a precise accounting of the difficulties that were compelling Great Britain to expand trade with the socialist bloc. The postwar growth of industry had been sluggish: 2.9 percent annually compared to 7 percent in France, 8 percent in West Germany, 9.3 percent in Italy and 14.4 percent in Japan. The growth of British industrial export was one-half that of its competitors. And the decline of both its competitiveness and empire was increasingly causing the sterling to yield its position as an international currency to the US dollar.[30] What is more, the British were surprised to see themselves vetoed by Charles de Gaulle from the European Economic Community in 1963. Feeling increasingly isolated, the report contended, Great Britain turned to the East, with a particular eye on Khrushchev's – and then Brezhnev's – program to expand the chemical industry. Two observations seem to have been behind the faint trace of British desperation the Soviets were reporting. First the eager turn East was bipartisan, the report noted, supported both by the Labour Party and the Conservatives. Second, unlike the Germans, the British serially defied pressure from the US and NATO to reduce credit to five years for their exports to socialist countries. The British also failed to submit to American demands to ban the export of large-diameter pipe to the Soviet Union in 1963, and, in another instance, went through with a sale of buses to Cuba in 1964.[31] "All of this speaks to the fact that in its commercial relationship with the Soviet Union and other socialist countries," the report declared, "the

---

[30] Ibid., l. 67.

[31] Ibid., ll. 68–69, 72. It is in fact uncanny the extent to which this report anticipated the narrative of US–British tensions over East–West trade of Ian Jackson, *The Economic Cold War*, drawn from a close reading of British and US archives, even down to the examples used. Evanthis Hatzivassiliou details the tensions further and extends Jackson's analysis to the mid-60s in "Commerce as a British Cold War 'Heresy:' The Intra-NATO Debate on Trade with the Soviet Bloc, 1962–5," in John Fisher, Effie G. H. Pedalu and Richard Smith, eds., *The Foreign Office, Commerce and British Foreign Policy in the Twentieth Century* (London: Palgrave Macmillan, 2016). A wider historical and geographical perspective of this US–British tensions over East–West trade is given by Alan Dobson, "When Strategic Foreign Policy Considerations Did Not Trump Economics: British Cold War Policies on East–West Trade," in the same volume.

English government maintains a more realistic and independent policy than its NATO allies."[32]

None of this meant that the British stood to liberalize their trade with socialist countries, however. The Soviets were cognizant of the fact that the British did not want to become dependent on socialist countries for essential supplies of any sort. The British government was perfectly at home with the commercial and financial controls upon which Bretton Woods was predicated, and frequently made active use of the licensing system to regulate their relationship with the socialist bloc. This affected the Soviet Union's allies rather more stringently than it affected the Soviets, as 95 percent of Soviet export receipts – largely from raw materials – fell outside the black lists the British maintained. These mostly restricted industrial equipment from coming into the country through a series of quotas that had to be individually negotiated.[33] The British government used the controls Bretton Woods afforded it to leverage any further liberalization of its trade to its advantage; in 1964, when it approached the governments of Bulgaria, Hungary, Czechoslovakia, Poland, and Romania with the possibility of scratching this quota system, the British government made a series of demands that some of the bloc allies found just profitable enough to accept. The quota system was, for the British, a disciplinary technique whose cancelation, always on a case-by-case basis, was conditional on the continued delimitation of global market competition. Some of these conditions were fair enough: anti-dumping provisions, for example. But the two most salient were an ultimately unrequited stipulation that British goods will not be imported under less favorable conditions than those of other countries, and the assurance that sales from the liberalization of quota goods will be automatically offset by purchases of equal value in Great Britain. The gain was nevertheless important: 40–50 percent of the goods Soviet allies exported had formerly been in the blacklists, but could now be more freely, if still individually, licensed for sale in Great Britain.[34]

The one primary commodity the Soviets could not get the British to buy was oil, despite the fact, the report noted, that before the war the Soviet Union provided 10–12 percent of the petroleum consumed in England. In fact this ban on Soviet petroleum was if anything tightened, expanding in 1964 to cover the granting of licenses for refined fuel oil, of which England had imported 150,000 tons annually until then. The

---

[32] RGAE, f. 413, op. 31, d. 641, l. 69.   [33] Ibid., l. 70.

[34] Ibid., 70–71. Romania and Bulgaria rejected the conditions, quite likely because they did not stand to gain much in the liberalization of largely industrial products. East Germany did not even participate in any negotiations.

Soviets even offered to buy British ships – the perennial request from a British government eager to save the country's shipyards – in exchange for oil, and the British still refused.[35] In April 1964 the British offered the Soviets the same deal they had offered their socialist allies, which the Soviets "categorically rejected" making use of an ethical discourse to denounce the conditions' "unilateral character." Earlier, in the 1959 negotiations to diminish trade discrimination against the Soviet bloc, the British had linked the closing of the import/export gap with the issue of long-term credit. The Soviets had agreed to the principle "in consideration of the importance of obtaining those credits," which the Soviets could then routinely use to demand longer terms from other Western European countries.[36] Half a decade later, and after consistent effort from British officials, the gap remained.

This then was the context of a market discourse that seemed more insistent than elsewhere. The Soviets had sensed a stepped-up campaign to close the gap, and so they too stepped up a performative practice aimed at blunting the British diplomatically while trying to encourage more competitive offers from an industrial culture rapidly growing obsolete by the very forces the Soviets discursively supported. Importantly, although the Soviets were active organizers and participants in the international industrial exhibit circuit, they did not have the structural power to create market institutions where market discourses could be yoked to the practice of buying and selling, directing with every deal made the flow of finance toward the sociopolitical constructions of their own making. In the absence of institutions of the sort, the financial community in London would become the best vector in the creation of a practice that had been curtailed by Western state design. Financiers would be the bearers of the political transformation the Soviets sought and strove for in the world economy.

★★★★★★★★★★

Against the generalized assessment that the Kosygin reforms failed to change the stubbornly failing practices of socialist organization, economist Philip Hanson argued that the second half of the 1960s saw sweeping changes in the Soviet approach to the introduction of technological innovation at the planning and managerial levels, as well as in the organization of science and labor.[37] Central to this change was the expansion of

---

[35] RGAE, f. 413, op. 31, d. 1106, l. 82.   [36] RGAE, f. 413, op. 31, d. 641, l. 72.
[37] Hanson, *Trade and Technology in Soviet–Western Relations*, chapter 6. An influential, contemporaneous argument about the stubborn, unchanging nature of the Soviet

technology imports from the West in volume, spread, and technical complexity. Here he followed J. P. Hardt and G. Holliday, who argued that the Soviets had enacted an important policy change with respect to technology transfer.[38] He quibbled, however, on the dating of this change. Unlike Hardt and Holliday, he thought it was not the Fiat deal that had spurred this change, but rather a British turnkey polyester plant in Mogilev, Belarus, that was most significant. Hanson was interested in dating the change back to 1964 in order to argue for policy continuity between the Khrushchev and Brezhnev leaderships.[39] Time and archives have shown this to be a safe instinct. But the Soviets did not see it this way. It was not a question of Soviet leadership, but rather a question of financial possibility and Western readiness, and it is hard to argue against this proposition, expressed internally and in real time in the report on British–Soviet relations we encountered earlier, and externally in virtually every meeting in which they were given an opening to express it.

The Soviet report, written four months before Fiat approached the Soviets with a turnkey deal, fully validates Hanson's argument that the polyester plant deal was trailblazing. But the trail being blazed, according to the Soviets, had less to do with the number of man-months of personal contact with Western experts, or the quality of the institutional cooperation between East and West. The blaze was financial: "For the first time in the history of our foreign economic relations with capitalist countries, we obtained long-term bank loans for important amounts. At the same time, we received these loans on more favorable terms than ever before in the entire history of credit relations between the Soviet Union and England."[40] This was not an aim in itself, but merely a step closer to the global market integration of Soviet desires: "The procurement of long-term bank loans in England in 1964 greatly facilitated the possibility of obtaining such loans in other capitalist countries, which significantly improved the competitive position of Soviet foreign trade organizations in the most profitable placement of orders on terms of long-term financial credit, making it possible to organize competition between firms from different capitalist countries."[41] The Soviets had long lobbied Western

system is Alec Nove, *The Soviet Economic System* (London: George Allen & Unwin, 1977): chapter 4. Unfortunately for the field, it is Nove's arguments and sentiment that prevails today, usually transmogrified into an implicit transhistorical understanding of an ever-existing Soviet economic essentialism, when in fact the transformation of economic life was as constant in the East as in the West.

[38] John P. Hardt and George D. Holliday, "Technology Transfer and Change in the Soviet Economic System," in Frederic A. Fleron, Jr., ed., *Technology and Communist Culture. The Socio-Cultural Impact of Technology under Socialism* (New York: Praeger, 1977).

[39] Hanson, *Trade and Technology in Soviet–Western Relations*, 108–109.

[40] RGAE, f. 413, op. 31, d. 641, l. 76.   [41] Ibid., 77.

European countries to liberalize the Bretton Woods institutions of trade regulation and extend favored nation status to the socialist world, with little to show for it; they would now wager on finance as the agent of international market integration.[42] And that wager was first placed in London.

In extending their capital resources to the socialist world, the British were being intransigent, and not just against the discipline of American Cold War prescript, although that too. As the Soviet London office explained, it was also a contravention of the Berne Union, which like other institutions of the 1930s, had helped govern international commercial credit by reconfiguring the market power of private banking interests. Launched in 1934, one of the main functions of the Berne Union was to forestall market competition among trade export lenders by establishing limits on the duration of credit to three years, which in the late 1950s was lengthened to five years.[43] This was meant to prevent export subsidies and a possible competitive dynamic that might once again create international tension, as the mixture of trade subsidies and tariffs had done during the Great Depression. Like so much of the policy-making arising from the 1930s, the Berne Union was to provide information, a forum for discussion and ultimately coordination. And like other realms of the international political economy established in the 1930s, its time was up. Just as the Soviets would help Italy's ENI erode the coordinated power of the oil majors, so was the Soviet Union now goading the British into undermining established practices of coordination in the governance of international finance. This was ultimately a triumph of the City, which had long been a fan of the Soviet Union's creditworthiness, and had maintained a cozy relationship with the communists even at the height of the Cold War.[44]

The short sketch of British financial history the London office sent back to Moscow noted that already in 1961 the British were flouting the Berne Union by granting export credit for fifteen years, and expanding the volume of credits as well. In April 1961, British Board of Trade President Reginald Maudling announced the government would be happy to include the socialist bloc in this new policy, although only Yugoslavia

---

[42] The timing of this opening also explains the sudden forcefulness with which the Soviets lobbied Japanese political and business circles for long-term loans in 1964, documented in Sanchez-Sibony, "Economic Growth in the Governance of the Cold War Divide."

[43] The report has the year of the Union's establishment as 1923 and seems unaware of its roots in the Great Depression.

[44] A short discussion of the Berne Union, German complaints to the United States about British indiscipline, and the British government's arguments that Soviet creditworthiness and purchases of factories in England would help British workers is in Angela Stent, *From Embargo to Ostpolitik. The Political Economy of West German–Soviet Relations 1955–1980* (Cambridge: Cambridge University Press, 1981): 147–151.

was ever offered long-term credits before 1964. Edward Heath, who had succeeded Maudling's successor at the board, reaffirmed British commitment, which immediately prompted the Soviets to send a delegation of Soviet financial experts to negotiate a credit line. By February 1964 the British government had guaranteed the Soviets a loan for 100 million pounds, about 250 million rubles (or US$280 million) for the purchase of complete equipment.[45] This is the line of credit the Soviets then drew from to purchase those polyester plants in September, after which they turned around and raised another twenty-four million pounds from their longtime partners at Midland Bank for more purchases, all endorsed by Great Britain's Export Credit Guarantee Department. The Soviets ended up using half of that 100-million-pound credit line before the line expired. But as they liked to emphasize, it had set a precedence the Soviets could use in London and throughout the capital-exporting countries of the industrialized world.[46]

The novelty of long-term finance ushered the Soviets into an uncertain domain of risk. Finance rendered large investment objects a greater degree of international comparability, but the still largely partitioned world of Bretton Woods meant that credit terms had to be weighed in terms of the differing interest rates in each country, the inflation rate of different national currencies, and possible devaluations unsuspected at the moment of a deal's signing. Or at least a degree of lip-service was paid to these new concerns over risk. But the fact is that the British had opened the door to a flood of socialist interest. Very quickly the socialist countries came to the London financial community cap in hand. Czechoslovakia quickly signed a twelve-year loan, and Bulgaria, Poland, Hungary, and Romania were actively seeking one at the beginning of 1965. China negotiated a medium-term loan for 4.5 million pounds. In the Soviets' estimation, "the English are still weary of giving China long-term credit, as they don't trust its creditworthiness."[47] Inadvertently, however, this created a certain degree of competition for credit and British industrial goods among socialist countries, raising the price of both. "All these interventions were conducted without any coordination among socialist

---

[45] RGAE, f. 413, op. 31, d. 641, ll. 74–75. The details were as follows: The British guaranteed credit for nine months from the signing of the financial agreement. If the Soviets concluded a deal within those nine months, they would have to pay the first installment within three to four years of the signing of the deal, but no later than within six months from the date of the last shipment of the equipment delivery. The last payment had to be made no later than thirteen to fifteen years from the signing of the contract. Accounting for an average delivery time of three years for most equipment, what this amounted to in practice was an effective loan of eight and a half years.

[46] Ibid., ll. 75–76.   [47] Ibid., ll. 77–78.

countries," the Soviet London office lamented.[48] Markets, even infant ones, cut both ways.

And still the import/export gap persisted for the British. The answer to the problem of the British balance of payments turned out to be even easier credit.[49] Dryly put: "In these conditions, with the availability of the necessary export resources, we could already now significantly expand the export of our goods to England. There are also conditions for the purchase in the English market of a number of goods necessary for our national economy, for cash, for medium-term company credit, and long-term bank loans."[50] And that is what they did.

****

The year 1965 created another gap, even if this one was not the focus of the disputes that continued to be aired in the drab government offices of London and Moscow. Great Britain, one of the Soviet Union's main traditional partners since the 1920s, had started the decade of the 1960s with a sizable lead over its allies in terms of trade with the Soviet Union. This gap had been closing throughout the first half of the 1960s, as West Germany and others began to normalize their economic relations with the Soviets. West Germany even recorded a higher trade turnover than Great Britain in 1962 and might well have entrenched its position as the Soviet Union's first trade partner had the United States not vetoed Germany's pipe exports already under contract. With the gates of British capital cracked open just enough in 1964, however, the trade turnover the British recorded for 1965 raced well ahead of its allies again. It stayed ahead until the 1970s, when another gate was opened to continental Europe allowing for the flow of red energy that would reshape the continent.

Perhaps this gap was the reason that, when future Board of Trade president Roy Mason arrived at the offices of the Soviet Foreign Trade Ministry in Moscow in May 1966, some of the fight had left the British representative. He acknowledged the other gap, the one of discord, as the ritual went. But he "did not want to repeat everything that had already been said so many times."[51] He wanted to talk ships and was there to represent the waning shipyard interests of a British interest group that

---

[48] Ibid., l. 78.
[49] Ibid., they cut the minimum to secure a medium-term credit of three to five years at 5.5 percent interest from 100,000-pound deal to 50,000 pounds. For long-term credit, they cut the interest rate to 5.5 percent for the first five years, followed by the earlier 6.5 percent for the rest of the loan period. The Bank of England would place these state-guaranteed export loans among sixteen designated banks from England and Scotland.
[50] Ibid., l. 80.   [51] RGAE, f. 413, op. 31, d. 1106, l. 21.

called itself the "Russian club of shipbuilders." This ended in the mono-
logue of market instruction documented earlier in the chapter.[52] There
were also limits to what finance could do to render British industry
competitive. When a British trade representative went back to England
to check on Soviet claims that their offer for equipment for the production of laminate plastic – used to surface kitchen counters and table tops
for the modern kitchens the Soviets were then building – was not competitive, he found that in fact British firm Formica had offered the more
competitive offer: a £3.25 million sterling loan for thirteen years at 5.75
percent interest rates compared to the £3.5 million for ten years at 5.9
percent offer that won the order for a French competitor. The Soviets
stressed that the reasons the French had won that order were technical
rather than commercial: The French firm had offered a more modern
process for the production of plastic laminate, with a greater degree of
automation.[53]

In fact the archival documents in Moscow, neatly ordered by country
and year, show that the Soviet–British commercial relationship was by far
the most acrimonious, despite being the largest, among Western
European partners. One obstacle to it that created tension involved the
extent to which British industry relied on American patents, making their
products subject to American sanctions. Another were the endemic
delays in British delivery schedules despite contracts, which extended
even to consumer goods, a scandalized Deputy Minister of Foreign
Trade Mikhail Kuz'min told Board of Trade Minister Edward
Redhead in 1965.[54] And in what archives show to be an almost exclusive
problem of Soviet relations with British industry, the Soviets regularly
complained that equipment that was sent on time was occasionally so
bad that it could not be mounted for years, leading to claims for recom-
pense that seems almost inexistent in trade with other countries. This
was the case, for example, with equipment the engineering conglomerate
Vickers-Armstrongs sent for the production of nylon salts used in textile
and plastic manufacturing, which had not been able to be put to use for
two years and had led to the idling of other factories down the chain of
production. Kuz'min demanded that Vickers-Armstrongs make good on
those losses, even threatening to go to the press and tarnish the

[52] Ibid., ll. 34–37. Repeated again for the benefit of Mason's boss, Douglas Jay, a few
weeks later.
[53] RGAE, f. 413, op. 31, d. 574, ll. 132–133.
[54] Ibid., l. 97. Of five million rubles contracted with V/O Tekhmashimport at the moment
of this meeting in September 1965, two million were being delayed, including gas
equipment from Humphreys and Glasgow (H&G), and equipment for plastic factories
from Simon Carves Engineering.

reputation of the firm.[55] Vickers-Armstrongs ended up agreeing to pay almost twenty million rubles later that month, consenting to reequip the factory within 6–8 months and supply the needed salts to the idle nylon factories.[56] But not before objecting to some quintessential problems in Soviet translations of Western values: "The calculation of lost profit is made in domestic prices, which are twice as high as the prices existing in the world market," the company noted. "Also very high is the calculation of the profit percentage."[57] Another such bruising with Humphreys and Glasgow saw a company representative refusing to pay a fine for reneging on their contract schedule, arguing that their own deliveries in England were late by as much as six to eight months, and asking the Soviets "not to remind him about delays in deliveries every day."[58] That day, the Soviets swore never to sign another contract with Humphreys and Glasgow; but that supposed, the British businessman retorted, that his firm was at all interested in another Soviet order.

Whether or not the Soviets actually countenanced going to the press about any of this, it seems likelier that they were above all trying to counter an earlier threat from the British government to go back on the case-by-case liberalizations of Soviet goods if Soviet purchases of British equipment did not reach £50 million in 1965 – a volume it surpassed by about 10 percent, perhaps partly in response to that threat.[59] Further liberalization within a state-managed framework was an interstate checkers game of arithmetic market growth. Within the prescript of these structures, diplomacy, with its oscillating rhythms of persuasion, pressures, and ultimatums, aimed not at any relentless project of market creation, but rather at the satisfaction of socioeconomic constituencies that were the bread and butter of national politics, particularly in Great Britain. In facing administrators and public officials the Soviets pointed to what their counterparts elsewhere were doing; they wanted the British to know that the French were liberalizing imports of Soviet consumer products, "while England, as we have learned, is going to take some measures in the near future that will worsen its trade regime with the socialist countries," a cautioning Aleksei N. Manzhulo told Board of Trade President Lord Jay in the summer of 1966.[60]

There was another side to the acrimony in industrial relations between the two countries, one that Soviet officials did not bring up in their

---

[55] Ibid., 96–99.
[56] The agreement is in ibid., ll. 85–86. This was well above their first offer of compensation: 1.61 million rubles and 3,700 tons of salt, in ibid., ll. 60–61.
[57] Ibid., ll. 72–77.   [58] Ibid., ll. 65–66, in a meeting in November 1965.
[59] Ibid., l. 100.   [60] RGAE, f. 413, op. 31, d. 1106, ll. 82.

business discussions with British political and corporate leaders. Although the drive to expand the presence of Soviet industrial products in Western markets has often been attributed to the Brezhnev leadership, a decree to expand industrial exports to Great Britain ten-fold had already been approved under Khrushchev, putting in motion bureaucratic gears and mechanisms that generated follow-up reports from the mid-1960s.[61] An expansion of anything in the Soviet Union meant, from a bureaucratic perspective, an expansion of problems and deficiencies. They must have made for anguished reading in Moscow, even if the literary genre of the report was familiar: the litany of shortcomings (*nedostatki*):[62]

systematic and large delays in the delivery of equipment against the deadlines accepted under contractual obligations; extremely long and totally uncompetitive delivery times offered by industry for exported equipment, machinery and instruments; the existence of many and serious defects in the products supplied for export and weak response from our industry to individual wishes arising from the conditions and requirements of the foreign market; lack of a sufficient production base to manufacture certain types of equipment that are already or could be in demand on foreign markets, as well as unacceptably long coordination of export opportunities and in many cases refusal by our industry to manufacture certain types of equipment and products; a limited range of products suitable for delivery to the English market, given the different technical requirements of this market from ours (voltage in electrical equipment, inch system, etc.).[63]

The real-world examples arising from this record of incompetence were, if anything, more alarming. For one, it turned out that delays were often as long as the ones that had prompted the Soviets to ask for restitution from British companies. "Constant delays in the delivery of almost the entire range of machines, equipment and devices cause acute dissatisfaction among customers, who in some cases raise the issue of canceling orders," the report warned.[64] And that was despite the fact that the Foreign Trade Ministry's departments were already having "difficulties in obtaining acceptable and competitive delivery times from industry, even for ordinary, uncomplicated standard equipment."[65] Some of these ran to fourteen months when competitors regularly delivered those products in six. And so it went, down the list.

---

[61] RGANI, f. 5, op. 58, d. 201, ll. 81–98. The decree was promulgated on September 17, 1964.
[62] See Oscar Sanchez-Sibony, "Soviet Industry in the World Spotlight: The Domestic Dilemmas of Soviet Foreign Economic Relations, 1955–1965," *Europe–Asia Studies* 62, no 9 (2010): 1555–1578.
[63] RGANI, f. 5, op. 58, d. 201, l. 84.   [64] Ibid., l. 85.   [65] Ibid.

Perhaps the most distressing problem was the refusal of many industrial managers to accede to the demands from Moscow.[66] Soviet industry had refused to take on orders from Mashinoeksport for frames and gutter guards, which England imported to the tune of 650,000–750,000 rubles, mostly from India. Aviaeksport informed that industry refused to offer helicopters, and small and agricultural aircraft for export to England. Stankoimport, which despite the name was also responsible for exporting machine tools, was forced to cancel several products already under contract despite the fact that they figured in the catalogs of machine tools available for export used by Gosplan. In other instances, industry refused to make available certain machine tools because of a lack of clarity over the patents they were built from.[67]

Despite Moscow's comprehensive efforts, the drive to expand industrial exports to British markets failed. The ten-fold increase never happened, certainly not in the 1960s. By the end of the decade, export volumes for industrial products remained where they had been at the beginning of the decade. Only later in the 1970s, as part of deals involving re-exports to Global South countries, did the Soviets finally make inroads, matching and exceeding the goals set by the Khrushchev administration. Through the 1960s, industrial exports to Great Britain accounted for one to 2 percent of all exports, while fully half of the imports from the island were industrial goods. Continued efforts throughout the 1970s raised the ratio of industrial exports to between 3 and 5 percent. All the while, British industrial imports remained the largest category in the bilateral relationship.

Whereas Soviet pressure on Great Britain for liberalization succeeded spectacularly, Soviet attempts to change the structure of its exports to Great Britain failed just as dramatically. The contrast is one of systems and allies. Despite the reputation of the Soviet system as a command economy, Moscow's edict was circumscribed by decentralized fields of power and structures of domestic political economy we have yet to investigate with any kind of archival empiricism.[68] But it was clear that when it came to exports, Moscow's command over industry barely matched the moniker. The bankers and industrialists allied to Soviet liberalizing purpose were a different kind of partner altogether. In that endeavor, the Soviets were adding weight to a power shift in global

---

[66] This too had been a problem from the moment Soviet engagement in foreign markets acquired some weight from the mid-1950s, as documented in Sanchez-Sibony, "Soviet Industry in the World Spotlight."

[67] RGANI, f. 5, op. 58, d. 201, l. 89.

[68] A good primer to start is Douglas Rogers, *The Depths of Russia. Oil, Power, and Culture after Socialism* (Ithaca: Cornell University Press, 2015): chapter 1.

capitalism that sought, in tandem with Moscow, to recentralize allocative economic power away from its seat in Washington and its state allies in Europe. Of course, the performative politics of the market with which the Soviets encouraged Western liberalizing efforts were only as effective as the material weight the Soviets could bring to bear; the pace was slow but it grew at the speed of globalization. Ultimately it depended, not on the arithmetic growth of state-managed trade policy, but on the geometric growth whose potential lay with finance.

****

It is perhaps again the juxtaposition of British financial competitiveness contrasted with its relative industrial decline that also best explains the timing and form of a new kind of cooperation that would, in time, become an important vector of global financialization.[69] As with so many other social developments, this one would make of the Global South a laboratory of new forms of debt creation that would redraw the flows of global capital only to redound negatively on British society itself a decade later. In the second half of the 1960s the Soviets had begun to advocate for a new form of cooperation in Global South countries. What this amounted to in England was a banking community raring to utilize the particular network of exchange the Soviets had built over time through aid and development policies. British financiers, looking for opportunities a compartmentalized domestic economy could not contain, sought out the Soviets in their offices in Moscow to finance projects that could utilize some of the more competitive British technology by matching it with the kinds of lower-order industrial technologies the Soviets had competitively marketed all over the Global South. A May 1968 proposal from the Bank of London and South America (BOLSA) can serve as example, even if at this early stage it did not come off. BOLSA bankers wanted to capitalize on the ongoing, Bretton Woods–delimited cooperation between the Soviet Union and Rolls Royce, and to relocate it to Latin America. In fact a first suggestion did not even involve Soviet production, with BOLSA financiers seemingly asking permission on behalf of Hungary: The bank could organize the marketing of diesel locomotives in Latin America with motors from Rolls Royce and chassis

---

[69] Everything in the Soviet archives agrees with David Edgerton's oft-repeated critique of the tenacious narrative of absolute British industrial decline. Edgerton emphasizes its absolute success, which certainly accounts for the eminent position of Great Britain in Soviet foreign trade, while making allowances for its relative decline. An early example is David Edgerton, "The Decline of Declinism," *Business History Review* 71:2 (1997): 201–206.

from the Budapest-based Ganz-MÁVAG Locomotive, Wagon, and Machine Works.[70]

What the Soviets wanted to export was equipment for power stations. The bankers from BOLSA were not acquainted with the new material relationship the Soviets were building with the right-wing military dictatorship that had established itself in Brazil in 1964 – a relationship that was causing an insistent stream of denunciations from the Soviet Union's allies in Cuba. But this was precisely the kind of intelligence BOLSA's bankers had gone to Moscow to gather. The British bankers discovered that Brazilian specialists had visited hydroelectric plants on the Volga and the Angara in Siberia, along with factories in Kharkov and Leningrad. The Brazilians had liked what they had seen, and the Soviet energy machinery export agency, Energomasheksport, had tried to enter into cooperation with English Electric for the construction of a power station in Brazil, the Soviets informed.[71] English Electric was at that very moment folding into the British General Electric Company (GEC).[72] The bankers in turn told the Soviets that cooperation prospects under merger conditions were not great, and worse still without the state financial guarantee that the participation of large industrial conglomerates could bring in their wake.[73] Brazilian law on loan guarantees still required the kind of state involvement primed under Bretton Woods. The other main difficulty, the bankers advised, was competition from the United States. To compete in Brazil and Latin America more generally, the Soviets had to offer competitive credit conditions, as many firms there paid more attention to credit conditions than to prices, they argued.[74] Here was a cooperation to dislodge an American hegemony in the region that had earlier itself displaced that of British finance over the course of the twentieth century: British financial experience and networks coupled with the experience the Soviets had accrued over decades in large-scale industrial construction.

Although these kinds of cooperation started to take on volume at the turn of the 1970s, they had in fact been broached discreetly since the mid-1960s. As David Engerman has shown, this dynamic existed in piecemeal form already from the 1950s.[75] Despite much Cold War

---

[70] RGAE, f. 413, op. 31, d. 2296, l. 18.

[71] The Soviets had broached the issue with English Electric as early as November 1967, in RGAE, f. 413, op. 31, d. 1677, ll. 3–4.

[72] One of the largest industrial conglomerates in the UK, and unrelated to the American GE.

[73] RGAE, f. 413, op. 31, d. 2296, ll. 19–21.   [74] Ibid.

[75] A point made convincingly in David C. Engerman, *The Price of Aid. The Economic Cold War in India* (Cambridge: Harvard University Press, 2018).

propaganda and its reflection in Cold War histories that see aid politics in strict binary terms, aid projects were often hybrid, incorporating elements from both sides of the Cold War divide.[76] Suggestions for a more cooperative approach across the East–West divide toward the Global South was a mere recognition of what was already happening on the ground. In fact when the Austrians suggested in 1964 that they wanted to help the Soviets in their construction of steel mills in India, they could point to the fact that they were already conducting similar forms of cooperation with Czechoslovakia and Hungary.[77] Half a year later, while the Soviets were urging the Austrians to show them concrete proposals, they thought of these kinds of cooperation as part of their overall aid strategy, to be handled by the Soviet aid agency (the *gosudarstvennyi komitet po vneshnim ekonomicheskim sviaziam*, GKES).[78] In December 1964 another deputy foreign trade minister pointed Groupe CIFAL's President Pierre Detoeuf in the same direction. The French international trade consultancy and import/export firm had already sounded out the intended recipients of this cooperation in India, and Detoeuf mentioned that the firm already had cooperative projects of the kind with Polish foreign trade organizations in Africa and Asia. In 1965 another French firm offered cooperation on a steel mill in Algeria and equipment for the Greek food industry. But off to GKES they had to go.[79] And again when Liberal Party leader Jo Grimond informed the Soviets in 1966 that there was interest in Great Britain in incorporating British technology licenses into Soviet production for export to Global South countries, the Soviets responded that they preferred to keep to themselves the production arising from expensive Western technology licenses.[80]

---

[76] The head of the Soviet aid agency, Semyon Skachkov, complained about this as early as 1961, in a report uncovered in Sanchez-Sibony, *Red Globalization. The Political Economy of the Soviet Cold War from Stalin to Krushchev* (Cambridge: Cambridge University Press, 2014): 240–244.

[77] RGAE, f. 413, op. 31, d. 57, ll. 48–49.

[78] RGAE, f. 413, op. 31, d. 572, ll. 42–43. Sara Lorenzini offers a useful summary of East–West cooperation in the Global South, interpreted in a Cold War narrative arc of early Soviet autarky followed by ideological exhaustion and disillusionment, in "Comecon and the South in the Years of Détente." The Cold War prism, as ever, misguides interpretations of Soviet intentions; Soviet eagerness to promote this kind of cooperation precedes détente by many years, and had ultimately little to do with disillusionment.

[79] RGAE, f. 413, op. 31, d. 116, ll. 96–98. CIFAL, created in 1946 as the *Compagnie d'Ingénierie France-Amérique Latine*, was an import/export group for French technology and its pitch, confirming Engerman's argument, was that they could help deliver parts that for one reason or another the Soviets did not want to deliver, or could not deliver swiftly. The 1965 example is in RGAE, f. 413, op. 31, d. 632, ll. 49–52. Later that year another French company approached the Soviets to cooperate on the construction of a steel mill in Aswan, Egypt. Ibid., ll. 65–66. And so it went.

[80] RGAE, f. 413, op. 31, d. 1106, l. 107.

Slowly, the Soviets began to take the initiative, arguing in the run-up to negotiations for a new long-term trade agreement in 1968 that one of the paths forward was through joint deals in the Global South, like the one that had placed 200 Perkins engines in Soviet cars for export to third countries.[81] They had cooperative arrangements of the sort with France, Japan, and Finland, and were looking forward to having them with Great Britain. The British state, however, seemed focused still on trade balance. Later that year, during the negotiations for a long-term trade that would yield an important victory for the Soviets in their drive to have the British liberalize their trade to the East, the British would insist, ultimately in vain, on a clause in the agreement that would trigger consultations in case of a trade imbalance.[82] They were slow to change gears but not so the Soviets. By 1970, the latter had developed their position on where competence lay for these kinds of cooperative endeavors within their bureaucracy; when a British official asked Gosplan whether the planning agency might veto the cooperation between British firms and Energomasheksport, the answer made the new dispensation clear: "The issue of the possibility of joint deliveries of power equipment to markets in third countries is entirely within the competence of Energomasheksport and the relevant British companies, and if such an agreement is reached between them, it will not meet with any objections from our side."[83] The Soviets had remained open to these offers of cooperation, so much so that they kept reminding the Austrians over the years about their 1964 proposition. Reticence from Western officialdom, coupled with the proliferation of prospects later in the decade, had encouraged the Soviets to take the initiative. Continuous Western prodding to establish partnerships in the Global South also beat a particular bureaucratic path; while Global South state officials tended to visit GKES offices, Western officials and businessmen knew only the halls of the Ministry of Foreign Trade and pitched their growing number of business proposals there. The consequence over time of this insistent drum of Western business was the Soviet bureaucratic relocation of this kind of exchange from its conceptual place as an object of aid to one of a more transactional, financialized sort, amenable to the Ministry of Foreign Trade and joint commissions with partner countries under the ministry's remit. The only inhibition was that these proposals were coming from state officials, and they were in effect an attempt to drum

---

[81] The meeting between Patolichev and Board of Trade President Anthony Crosland took place on June 6, 1968, in RGAE, f. 413, op. 31, d. 226, ll. 26–30.

[82] Ibid., ll. 40–44. Pressures for the long-term agreement now also came from British firms, British officials admitted in May, in ibid., ll. 15–17.

[83] RGAE, f. 4372, op. 66, d. 3715, l. 13.

up more business for domestic constituencies on the back of relationships the Soviets had painstakingly developed over the preceding decade.

The financiers also wanted to seize on the special relationships the Soviets had built with those areas of the world that capital had marginalized during the famous – and West-centered – *trente glorieuses*. But unlike the state officials, they brought something to the cooperation that was of value to the Soviets. Along with similar connections to Western domestic industries that state officials also had, the financiers brought with them knowledge of Global South markets and relationships to Global South actors. Already many of the proposals coming from Western private firms had sought Soviet participation in order to strengthen their credentials vis-à-vis haute finance. For example, when French steelmaker Schneider-Creusot (now Schneider Electric), sought Soviet cooperation in building a steel combine that the French company had won the right in 1965 to construct in Aswan, Egypt, they demanded a quick decision from the Soviets because their participation would impinge on the volume and quality of credit the project would get in France.[84] The French government had refused to finance the full US$100 million the steel mill cost, opting for half that amount instead, and the French firm wanted the partnership with the Soviets to lend the project credibility with financiers.[85] In fact, before cooperation among CMEA members in the Global South became common, Schneider-Creusot was suggesting that if the Soviets did not want to take the lead, they could both invite a third partner from the socialist bloc into the project. In a reversal of the usual dynamic, it was Schneider-Creusot's director who was the one saying that it would all depend on the terms of the credit the Soviets would offer. When he suggested they could form a consortium, the Soviets responded they had no experience with that sort of cooperation, and they would have to study it.[86] Corporations and states alike were grasping at the new possibilities the new developments in debt-making arrangements were producing during the second half of the 1960s.

The prize in this fluid context was a direct relationship to finance. By the second half of the 1960s finance too was throwing its hat into the

---

[84] RGAE, f. 413, op. 31, d. 632, ll. 65–66. What they received instead was a proposal from the Soviets offering their industry as sub-supplier, as their organizations had already studied the project five years earlier and decided that the region's iron ore was not amenable to the processes the Soviets had developed for their own. The Soviets did not want to be responsible for a project which outcome relied on technology they could not guarantee, but they would gladly cooperate with Schneider-Creusot if the French firm took on all responsibility. In ibid., ll. 67–70. Another interesting moment: Despite their insistent financial requests elsewhere, the Soviets here offered only a five-year loan on whatever Soviet equipment was drawn.

[85] Ibid., ll. 71–73.   [86] Ibid.

ring. Broad-ranging discussions of different kinds of possibilities opening
in the financial world often ended with offers to join the Soviets in deals
the Soviets had concluded. In March 1966 the French bank Paribas, for
example, seized on a Soviet deal with Iran for the construction of a steel
mill; they offered their financing services in case the Soviets might look
kindly on deliveries of parts and equipment from French steel conglomerates.[87] And that direct relationship was no doubt the reason behind the
restrained excitement palpable in the memo of a meeting at the Soviet
embassy in London with the vice president of Barclays Bank Dominion,
Colonial, Overseas in May 1970, who noted that his bank had been
remiss in not following its competitor, Midland Bank, into a long business relationship with the Soviets. They were now ready to visit around
the foreign economic relations bureaucracy of the Soviet Union to offer
their services in the forty-two countries where they did business, mainly
in Africa, the Middle East, and the Caribbean. "It gives the impression
that [the vice president], in his conversations with the heads of Soviet
economic organizations, will probably touch upon the question of forms
of participation of the bank (in lending, etc.) in Soviet trade and other
relations with countries in Africa and the Middle East."[88] And they
brought capital, even if at the end of the 1960s it was still more expensive
than the subsidized kind states could bring to bear. Increasingly, however, it was freer to flow across borders at their command. Unlike
Austrian officials in the mid-1960s, the bankers at BOLSA could take
Soviet officials directly to the basin of the Água Vermelha Dam on the
Grande River in the south of Brazil, where by 1971 the talk was no longer
prospective. In December that year, they were intermediating for the
Soviets on negotiations over how local labor expenses were to be paid.
They expected construction to start within the next four to five months,
but at any rate their man in Brazil stood ready to give the Soviets more
detailed information as it became available.[89] The Brazilians needed US
$35–40 million, and BOLSA wanted the Soviets to enter into a consor-
tium with them for US$5–7 million of that amount.

The Soviet Union had one more thing to offer finance that went to the
core of haute finance's quiet accretion of social power that decade:
credibility. At a meeting in Moscow, BOLSA representatives had
observed that "at the present time Brazil is quite popular in the capital
market."[90] The Soviet Union, the bankers argued, would lend these flows

[87] RGAE, f. 413, op. 31, d. 1158, l. 25.   [88] RGAE, f. 413, op. 31, d. 3643, ll. 35–37.
[89] RGAE, f. 7590, op. 17, d. 259, l. 74.
[90] Ibid., l. 75. Just two months earlier, the Banco Banespa, a regional bank tied to the state
     government of Sao Paolo, had guaranteed a US$50 million Eurodollar loan for six years

even more credibility through its participation in the bank consortiums that were being constructed to facilitate them. For despite so much academic output today seeing everywhere and everywhen socialism's rot and decline, the socialist world had in fact been deeply trusted by the financial community for decades. An eighteen-bank consortium had that very month arranged for a US$50 million loan to Hungary for five years at an interest rate 1 percent above the Eurodollar deposit rate, and it could easily arrange another one for the Soviet Union for US$200 million on even better terms, the bankers said.[91] In other words, what had formerly been the purview of aid agencies, the state-to-state financing of industrial construction around the world, was quickly coming under the auspices of the banking community. This was not the rise of the market, but the securitization of state prerogative around the world. Cold War binaries have never quite captured the logic of development aid, but the Cold War had certainly impinged on its geography. As capital broadened geographical horizons beyond geo-ideological alliances, that Cold War logic, such as it was, was interrupted beyond recognition. And the Soviet Union had been brought to the center of that interruption. The socialists had won a Cold War.

★★★★★★★★★★

Having grown close to the Soviets over cooperation in South America, BOLSA bankers, as many others would over time, became valuable informants on the financial community in London itself. By the turn of the decade, the importance of these exchanges of information grew in tandem with the profit to be gained from the new frontiers of capital the partners were plumbing. During lunch at BOLSA's offices in London, the Soviets learned that the Rothschild Bank had received support from the Bank of England to lend credit to the Soviets for the exploitation of the Udokan copper deposit in the Baikal region of Russia, a great project that would eventually give rise to one of the largest copper mines in the world. BOLSA was not speaking as an agent of the Bank of England, but rather on behalf of Rio Tinto and other corporations interested in internationalizing the loan.[92] "The directors at BOLSA," the November

at an interest rate 2 percent above the Eurodollar deposit rate for the Companhia Energetica de Sao Paolo (CESP), the region's state-owned electricity company.
[91] Ibid., ll. 75–76. All they would need was to arrange a smaller loan first, presumably to test the waters. They could then move on to a bigger loan for either domestic construction or for cooperative industrial projects in the socialist bloc.
[92] Rio Tinto needed the help. Representatives from the firm had been to Moscow in October that year to discuss what the Soviets found to be a woefully incomplete proposal for the mine's construction. They were sent home and asked to try again and

1970 memo recorded the bankers saying, "are ready to use their broad international contacts to take the initiative to create an international consortium that would include Japanese and Western European banks. In their opinion, such an approach to the problem of credit would make it easier to solve the problem of equipment supply, which will be manufactured not only in England, but also in other countries."[93] And it was not just the interests of the Bank of England and British workers they were betraying, they were also there to steer the Soviets in the direction of certain clients rather than others. The Soviets had chosen the British Steel Corporation as their partners for the exploitation of an iron ore deposit in the Kola Peninsula. BOLSA wanted to let them know that British Steel was an "unreliable partner."[94] The newly formed state company had no means for producing its own mining equipment and was itself a consumer of iron ore. It had nothing to offer the Soviets, the bankers maintained. Guest, Keen, and Nettlefolds (GKN), on the other hand, would do nicely. The Soviets were also informed they had chosen badly in their partnerships to bring about the containerization of their shipping, and that they should involve the much more capable and experienced British Rail.[95] In the neoclassical version of economics, finance merely intermediates. Perhaps there had been some truth in that during finance's quarter century–long repression under Bretton Woods. But the wheel was turning again.

The BOLSA bankers were perhaps taking the Soviets out to lunch precisely because a director from the Bank of England was about to visit Moscow to check in on a sizable list of large Soviet projects that needed foreign funding. The import/export gap was now two decades old, and slowly losing urgency as finance sought profit in the socialist world. The bank director professed having a "broad view" of the subject, and his Soviet interlocutor declared that there was "no longer a need to talk about the imbalance," but rather a need to "pay attention to the development and expansion of exports and imports above all."[96] This was the party line on the matter, expressed by Patolichev in the spring of 1970 with something of an edge. The problem needed to be resolved through the expansion of trade turnover, he said. In 1969 the gap grew from the increased delivery of diamonds that Great Britain then reexported, which if excluded from accounts calculations would result in

---

do better, and present a more detailed proposal. In RGAE, f. 413, op. 31, d. 3643, ll. 21–24.

[93] Ibid., l. 3.

[94] Ibid., l. 4. The words seem to be verbatim and surrounded by quotes also in the memo.

[95] Ibid.   [96] Ibid., l. 12.

a rough balance of payments. In fact the Soviets had good relations with diamond syndicates, he noted, worryingly for the British, and could easily establish direct sales with them. But this would not result in increased trade between the two countries, he concluded.[97] Half a decade earlier, this veiled threat might have been met with even greater rancor, but that spring the British wanted simply to know "in which areas the English side can compete with Japan."[98] This was precisely the kind of market logic in bilateral talks that the Soviets had worked to establish over the last decade and would continue to develop. The softened tone was a small Soviet victory representing the softening of the mechanisms of discipline that came with the twilight of Bretton Woods. The discursive and practical vectors through which the British now apprehended their place within an international arena of competition could not only have been of a Soviet provenance, but the internalization of this logic was real, and expressed with increasing frequency by the British in echo of long-standing Soviet discourse. "England, like Japan, barely has natural resources of its own," the British now reasoned in their appeal for Soviet business. "Therefore the forms of economic cooperation that have developed between the USSR and Japan are applicable to England."[99]

The soft tone was no doubt also a function of the fact that Patolichev's interlocutors that day were not state officials, but of a different kind of British industry-promoting entity: the Confederation of British Industry (CBI), a business lobbying group formed five years earlier.[100] The fact that non-state networked business was now making the rounds around the industrial bureaucracy in Moscow was not coincidental. Networked productive and marketing capacity, after all, was also what financiers were organizing for the Soviets, and another reason why Soviets and financiers had found mutual cooperation so congenial. Finance, we will see, had been both the medium and the purpose of the compensation trade in gas that the Soviets had succeeded in organizing by the turn of the decade, which in turn became the template for the socialists' insistence on compensation trade. This insistence irrupted in 1970 with little care for ongoing negotiations, a British official observed a year later to one of the Soviet deputy ministers of foreign trade.[101] Negotiations for a new process for the production of plastics, for example, were suddenly upended after two years when the Soviets suddenly introduced the

---

[97] Ibid., ll. 39–40.   [98] Ibid., l. 40.   [99] Ibid.
[100] Director-General Campbell Adamson and CBI's director Arthur Norman. The meeting dates from March 23, 1970. RGAE, f. 4372, op. 66, d. 3713, ll. 19–21.
[101] RGAE, f. 413, op. 31, d. 4396, ll. 23–26.

condition that the deal be paid with plastic from the new production process. Since then, negotiations essentially stalled.

Unsurprisingly, when the CBI directors moved on from the offices of the Ministry of Foreign Trade to those of Gosplan, they encountered there as well the Soviet pitch for compensation trade – along, of course, with the party line on the British trade they encountered everywhere in Moscow. And the discussion over it also made clear why partners in finance were preferable. The multi-layered organization of exchange that the Soviets demanded through compensation trade was a problem for industrialists. States and its officials had earlier been able to provide a crude approximation of a many-sided exchange practice through trade lists. Financiers, with their long rolodex of partners in industry, and their increasing international reach, supercharged it. For the industrialists represented by CBI this Soviet request for compensation trade was trickier: "The proposal offered by the Soviet side to repay loans with the production from the enterprises to be constructed creates difficulties for British suppliers, since these firms are not, as a rule, importers of raw materials or other products manufactured with the help of imported equipment," the directors confessed.

The Soviet response was enthused with the new possibilities opening up. Gosplan officials suggested that British industry could organize consortia of British firms and banks in order to execute specific projects. This would entail a different practice than CBI was used to, the industrialists replied, but they could try to take on this task of coordination.[102] This was, of course, the organizational form finance had begun to routinely model. Trickier still, the industrialists agreed with the Soviets that for larger projects like the Udokan mine, larger outlays of capital would be needed than could be provided by one country.[103] As with joint projects in the Global South, the industrialists were dependent on Soviet networks and Soviet forbearance for participation. Finance, on the other hand, actively offered options and solutions.

So it was a sign of the times, then, that industrialists encountered a more negative reception to their proposals for the configuration and internationalization of foreign involvement in Soviet projects than bankers, a reversal from the 1960s. When Rio Tinto suggested that the company might be able to attract the cooperation of a Canadian firm for the exploitation of nickel reserves in the Orenburg region south of the

---

[102] RGAE, f. 4372, op. 66, d. 3713, l. 20.
[103] Ibid. In the case of the Udokan mine, internationalization meant Japan, or rather the other way around: It was Japan's project that was being internationalized through British capital.

Urals, they were told that the Soviets already had firm interest from Japan and that they did not need Rio Tinto's help on that score.[104] Gosplan officials wentfurther, answering Rio Tinto's suggestion that the company be the main hub for relationship building by telling the British representatives that the Soviet Union might well simply establish direct relationships with those other companies instead.[105] And neither did the Soviets find the company particularly helpful in the financing of the project. As in the past, Rio Tinto's main reference for finance was the British state's Export Credit Guarantee Department, which was raising interest rates in 1970. The retort was cutting: "If credit conditions are going to change, then our conditions for cooperation can also change."[106]

By 1970, the logics and preferences of Soviet political economy had come to be well understood by British state officials, who now led with the kinds of tenders the Soviets had for so long emphasized. Answering his own question in a meeting with Gosplan's head of the foreign trade section Viktor B. Spandar'ian, the chairman of the East European Trade Council John Stevens noted that the way to increase trade turnover was through granting new bank and commercial credit to the Soviets, particularly in investment deals within Soviet borders. Spandar'ian referred to this as a "new, higher form of economic cooperation," to be developed along with the more traditional forms of trade.[107] The Soviets could point out that the Japanese had already entered into such credit-based forms of cooperative foreign direct investment involving timber – in a practice that resembled Japanese concessions of the 1920s and 1930s, minus the Japanese workers that labored in them. There were ongoing discussions with Japan on gas and the construction of a port in the Far East. The British were invited to do likewise, and animate investment objects of interest to British interests. Stevens, voicing the limits of British state officials more generally, was eager to look into the possibilities, it was just putting together the financing for it that confounded him – marking the difference with the Japanese state, which was much more active and experienced in organizing both industry and finance.[108] Competence and practice breeds imagination and command. In the 1960s, Japan had it; among British state officials, this great and terrible virtue was atrophying.

---

[104] RGAE, f. 413, op. 31, d. 3643, l. 24.   [105] RGAE, f. 4372, op. 66, d. 3713, ll. 40–41.
[106] In a meeting two days earlier, on October 20, 1970, RGAE, f. 413, op. 31, d. 3643, ll. 25–26. Gosplan was similarly unimpressed, in RGAE, f. 4372, op. 66, d. 3713, l. 41.
[107] The May 21, 1970 meeting is in RGAE, f. 4372, op. 66, d. 3715, ll. 11–14.
[108] Ibid., l. 13.

****

The turn of the decade, promising as it was for British–Soviet trade, became in fact an inflection point that reflected the larger transformation of the world economy, and the impending fate of the Bretton Woods system. The year 1970 proved to be the last time Great Britain clocked in as the Soviet Union's first trade partner among Western countries. And in fact that year Japan, with its dynamic, state-directed organization of economic life, had managed to just surpass Great Britain in trade turnover with the Soviet Union. Over the first half of the 1970s Great Britain was surpassed by France and Italy; West Germany, which had taken the number one spot in 1971, almost doubled the British turnover in 1973 as Soviet trade partner. The change was felt in real time. So much so, that the Foreign Office sent an official to the Soviet Ministry of Foreign Trade in June 1971 seeking answers: Why had trade with other Western partners over the last five years grown from 77 to 206 percent while trade with England had only grown 64 percent? Why were exports to England increasing while imports from England fell? Why was the number of trade staff in the Soviet Union's trade office in London growing while trade turnover diminished?[109] Great Britain started the 1970s as the first trading partner in the capitalist world; it ended the decade as its ninth partner.

The talk was no longer about the gap. That too was receding as a technique for moral suasion together with the system of strict trade balancing that lent it force – by the early 1970s, appeals in an ethical language of bilateral equilibrium were being replaced by a more transactional language of comparative probity in an international industrial market. In that 1971 meeting, attempting to blunt British grievances, the Soviets threw economic numbers at the British, recalled past glories of commercial collaboration, and disingenuously reproved contemporaneous rises in British interest rates that were in fact global.[110] But the relative stagnation of British–Soviet trade was real, and the truth was that it was not a problem the Soviets could resolve for the British. It was, however, a problem the Soviets had wanted and had helped put in motion. And it was as terminal for sectors of British society as it would be for the Soviet system as a whole.

It started from the fact that, as the Soviets promoted the transition to credit-intensive compensation trade, certain technopolitical assemblages found it easier to cooperate with the Soviets than others. Foremost among them were those involving the energy transition that had been ongoing on the European continent since World War II. Great Britain

---

[109] RGAE, f. 413, op. 31, d. 4396, l. 34.   [110] All of which they did, in ibid., l. 35.

transitioned to oil on the back of its former empire, and then became a net energy exporter through the eventual exploitation of energy resources then being discovered in the North Sea – necessitating a transformation in domestic political economy that centralized economic decision-making in London and, at large, helped Prime Minister Margaret Thatcher face down British coal miners and organized labor more generally in the mid-1980s. Meanwhile, much of continental Europe cooperated with the Soviets in order to deepen its own transition, spurring trade with the East and prolonging the economic life of its industrial regions in exchange for Soviet energy resources. Although the compensation trade the Soviets promoted came to involve many branches of its economy in complex and often wasteful deals, compensation trade in energy flourished. And it remained a continental trade.

The financialization occasioned by this loan-intensive and credit-prolonging continental exchange encouraged another kind of transformation: the decoupling of finance from national territory. Even as London's financial center known as the City became ever more involved in trade with the Soviets, the industry it used to serve did not benefit. In fact through cooperative deals with the Soviets like those in Latin America, British finance would help facilitate the deracination of industry from its birthplace in North England. If finance in the 1960s had helped British industry become one of the most important partners of Soviet industry, it now undermined the industrial relationship in favor of the Soviet Union's ambition to create markets for Soviet industry globally, and, perhaps more importantly, to create competition for Soviet industrial purchases in the rich world. There were winners and losers to the liberal transformation bankers and socialists had sought, and these were reflected in the Soviet statistical compendiums that cataloged the incontrovertible fall of Great Britain as a trade partner.

Meanwhile, in the fall of 1971 the annals of the Cold War record quite the diplomatic kerfuffle. On September 24, London expelled ninety Soviet representatives from the country on charges of espionage, and barred another fifteen who were abroad from reentering the country.[111]

---

[111] "British Expel 90 Russians for Espionage; Deny Re-entry to 15 more," *New York Times*, September 25, 1971. The *New York Times* reports were more alive with disinformation than actual information, reporting that this was the outcome of a defection earlier in the month of a "high official of the KGB" from outside the country. Interestingly, *The Guardian* reported correctly that the defector was from the Soviet mission in London, in "Britain Expels 90 Russian Diplomat Spies," *The Guardian*, September 25, 1971. Other deceitful forms of false representations seemed less geared at disinformation and more at inflaming and giving substance to the Cold War narrative, as when the Foreign Office hinted in its formal statement that plans for sabotage were for peacetime use, rather than in the case of war.

This was about a fifth of the 550 Soviet officials then in Great Britain. The whole episode had been well prepared, with the British ready to regale the press with thrilling tales of nefarious Soviet espionage and sabotage planning.[112] It had been prompted by the accidentally timed defection on September 3 of KGB agent Oleg Adolfovich Lialin, whose job had been to reconnoiter and identify sites for sabotage and infiltration in case of war. His cover was the trade delegation. In April a nervous Lialin had walked to a police station to give himself over as a double agent giving information to the British from inside the KGB. This lasted until a drunk-driving arrest in the morning hours of August 30 forced him to defect, lest he be taken back to Moscow and be fired for incompetence, which would have meant a significant loss to British intelligence; or it may be that the incident catalyzed fears that his estranged wife had revealed to his fellow Soviet spies in London his disaffection with the KGB, and that it was this that might get him recalled.[113] Whatever the case, the timing was propitious; British counterintelligence had been tracking the ballooning number of intelligence officers in England, not least through Lialin's own information, and had wanted to deal a blow to Moscow's ability to gather intelligence in the kingdom. The MI5 called this Operation FOOT, and it was scheduled for October, but was pushed up to September 24 after Lialin's drunken blunder. All told, some 180 Soviet citizens left Great Britain a week later, boarding a ship back home to the tune of Fiddler on the Roof's "If I Were a Rich Man."[114]

Operation FOOT had caught the Soviets by surprise, and proved, by all accounts, devastating to Soviet intelligence efforts in Great Britain. The Soviets might have been better prepared had they shared observations from all their interactions with the British, because the fact is that the latter had expressed their exasperation over the expanding size of the Soviet mission for months, for example bluntly stating in June in Moscow that they did not understand why the number of Soviet trade officials grew in Great Britain while trade volume fell, and that they would rather it were the other way around.[115] According to the reports given to the press as part of Operation FOOT, the bulk of Soviet

---

[112] John M. Lee, "Britain Tells How Soviet Spread Its Spy Network," *New York Times*, September 25, 1971.

[113] The whole affair is covered in Christopher Andrew, *Defend the Realm. The Authorized History of MI5* (New York: Alfred A. Knopf, 2009): 567–575.

[114] As reported in "Expelled Soviet Aides Leave Britain by Ship," *New York Times*, October 4, 1971.

[115] RGAE, f. 413, op. 31, d. 4396, l. 34.

espionage had centered precisely on industry and technology, even if rather than highly sophisticated and daring acts of espionage, Soviet efforts seemed to have involved trying to convince British computer engineers to consult with the Soviets on technology whose export was prohibited in the often arbitrary and increasingly pointless CoCom lists.[116]

The Soviets predictably reacted to this Cold War indiscretion with performative anger: "As for rectifying the situation created solely as a result of the actions of the English government, the English side will have to work hard to normalize relations between our countries," went one such performance that fall at the European department of the Ministry of Foreign Affairs.[117] The Soviets would continue to huff and puff for months, complaining rather disingenuously that they could not properly discharge their work on trade with a reduced trade mission – never mind that it remained larger than most other Soviet missions around the world.[118] This well practiced passive aggressive posture notwithstanding, the intrusion from bumbling intelligence services did exactly nothing to alter the material course of the Anglo-Soviet relationship. In fact, passive aggression was not even the prevailing Soviet posture. The abiding attitude remained what it had been for the last decade: It could be described as market optimism. Where at the end of the Bretton Woods international political economy the British expressed pessimism over being left behind in the sustained rapid growth of Soviet commerce, Soviet officials played the unlikely role of the optimistic, encouraging partner. So much so, that in the 1971 end-of-the-year assessment exercise of Soviet–British commercial relations and its prospects for the future, the Soviets felt compelled to console the British with affirmations that English firms "were and remain our important commercial partners," and, contradicting their outrage at the expulsions, that their foreign commercial organs "carry out a lot of work on exports and imports in the English market."[119]

More than anything, these talks illuminated the extent to which the Soviets had imposed the terms and parameters of commercial practice while maintaining their performative liberalism, and how far the British had gone in both accommodating these while adapting their discourse to changes of political economy then taking place. The British now stressed that the way forward was the inclusion of their firms on compensation

---

[116] Lee, "Britain Tells How Soviet Spread Its Spy Network."
[117] RGAE, f. 413, op. 31, d. 4396, l. 14.   [118] Ibid., l. 3, for example.
[119] In a meeting on December 30, 1971, RGAE, f. 413, op. 31, d. 4396, ll. 1–4.

terms in the large infrastructural and mining projects then being considered in the Kremlin; they even made a pitch to render services and machinery on credit for a large irrigation project the Soviets had intended for the Smolensk region, to be repaid in agricultural products.[120] This, of course, was the very thing they had resisted for years while complaining about the gap and using the quota system to encourage their exports to the Soviet bloc. None of the disadvantages of the financialized, long-term compensation trade deals had fundamentally changed for British business. But in the context of the rising interest rates that the Soviets had started to complain about at the turn of the decade, there was a competitive edge in attracting Soviet business through the stabilization inherent to long-term credit and compensation deals.[121]

The rise of international competition the British were beginning to feel and that the Soviets had promoted also generated the end of the Soviet Union's liberal moral high ground. In the wake of the political victory over British liberalization of trade toward the East, arguments for further liberalization rang false.[122] And yet the Soviets were still at it. One of the reasons for the downturn in trade, they tried to explain, was that transistor radiograms and television exports were only fulfilled by 50 percent because the British took too long to remove quotas on them. As if those items would have moved the needle on trade turnover. The British were no longer having any of it. The 1969 long-term trade agreement had reduced quotas and limits to a minimum; only 1 percent of Soviet products were now impacted by them. And all the while, the Soviets were limiting competition in their own markets by insisting on uncompetitive imports from socialist bloc countries.[123] Under the economic compartmentalizations of Bretton Woods the Soviets had not had to answer to the contradictions of their liberal posture; their victory brought with it a reversal of the ethical discourse they had used for so long. In the twilight of this discursive exhaustion, we will see, only energy remained.

---

[120] Ibid., ll. 1–2.

[121] As one complaint went in June 1971, "one of the factors preventing the purchase of English engineering products is the increase on the English side from October 1, 1970 of bank credit interest from 5.5 percent to 7 percent for the sale of machinery and equipment on conditions of long-term credit." In ibid., l. 35.

[122] In fact, in talks elsewhere in Europe, Great Britain was described as exemplary in relation to the strides it made toward liberalization, for example in France in RGAE, f. 413, op. 31, d. 3680, l. 11.

[123] RGAE, f. 413, op. 31, d. 4396, ll. 36–37.

3   Austria
Bretton Woods and the Soviet Politics of Liberalization

Minister of Foreign Trade Nikolai Patolichev was apologizing to the Austrian ambassador. It was only May, and 1964 was already looking like a bad year. He blamed the temporary decrease in Soviet–Austrian trade on the bad harvest, which had forced the Soviets to shift their trade to grain-growing partners. But this was only a bad year in a stellar stretch of years. If one counted freshly signed contracts for delivery in subsequent years, Patolichev argued, then trade levels were in fact much higher than those that had been stipulated for the year in their long-term trade agreement signed almost four years earlier in December 1960.[1] That five-year trade plan was coming to an end in 1965, and Patolichev was hopeful a new one could be signed soon. Balances were clear, trade volume had grown beyond expectations, and new deals were in the pipeline. The Bretton Woods system of capital controls and strict accounts balancing had worked to everyone's benefit, small and large countries alike. Its steady, predictable quality had even created certain dependencies, for example, in sales of fittings, for which an Austrian firm had rearranged its production to Soviet specifications only to see sales volumes decrease in 1964.[2] The necessity for balance under Bretton Woods conditions meant that countries throughout Europe had welcomed the Soviet Union's long-term, list-based approach to foreign trade.[3] Trade growth had been continual across the board, with no serious disruptions from the Soviet side until then. Over time, Western countries even learned to time negotiations over annual and five-year trade agreements to the rhythms of the Soviet plan itself, the better to lobby for the interests of their national enterprises.

---

[1] RGAE, f. 413, op. 31, d. 57, ll. 1–3.   [2] Ibid., ll. 15–17.
[3] It is important to note that the "embedded liberalism" constructed in Bretton Woods in 1944 was seen by its British and American architects as compatible with the centrally managed economy of the Soviet Union, which weighed participating in its institutions. See Eric Helleiner, "The Life and Times of Embedded Liberalism: Legacies and Innovations since Bretton Woods," *Review of International Political Economy* 26:6 (2019): 1112–1135.

The Bretton Woods system had failed to establish itself in the first instance. Launching the institutions themselves and getting everyone to agree to their legal frameworks in that New Hampshire town in 1944 had proved of no immediate use in establishing the pegged exchange rate system of convertible currencies that was its ultimate aim. Trust cannot be decreed. It took care, coordination, strict capital controls, technological transfer, miracle growth, social stability, and sheer discipline from a hegemonic authority to nurture and grow the reserves of international American dollars in Europe for the system to work. To this end, schemes like the Marshall Plan and the European Payments Union were devised to create a modicum of international goods circulation as the United States and its junior allies in Europe nurtured the world out of a quarter century of autarky. The training wheels came off the Bretton Woods project at the end of 1958 with the belated introduction of currency convertibility between the US dollar and the leading European currencies. This is the tentative, coordinated international context that came to welcome – tentatively, coordinately – the reassuring predictability of negotiated Soviet trade plans. Despite American hostility, Western European governments came to appreciate the advantages of a system of East–West trade that promoted bilateralism and state-to-state negotiation over competition and market discipline. This was particularly true of small countries and non-conglomerate business. There, geographical and historical advantages could be leveraged to great effect in a trading context in which bilateral trade accounts needed to clear. The dollar constraint was a common denominator all parties, capitalist or communist, accepted. During the first two decades of the Cold War, the world learned to trade again on the strength, not of the dollar, but of dollar-denominated barter. This commerce was, at best, lightly financed with short-term loans that enabled quick turnover. The finance itself was mostly arranged by those Western companies whose products were being bought, usually in cooperation with national governments that managed trade licenses and often subsidized interest rates for borrowers in order to stimulate domestic industry sales abroad.

But what would happen when the US dollar stopped being scarce and acquired real allocative power internationally? This is the dilemma Austria was facing in the mid-1960s. And the face of that dilemma was the Soviet Union. The excess of the US dollar beyond US borders – the dollar glut – could potentially mean a drastic reorganization of international trade to the advantage of actors with real market power. Accounts clearing had allowed the logic of political borders and their instruments in state agencies an important relevance in negotiations over exchange of goods, services, and capital. This was sustained in what neoclassical economic theory sees as the inefficiencies of barter but might be better understood as diplomatic trust-building exercise in international political economy. In practice, clearing was also the hammer used to force the capital-scarce Soviets to buy or sell more than they wanted. The lists of goods to be exchanged were first drawn up on the basis of Soviet negotiations with individual firms inside the capitalist partner; resulting imbalances then were usually negotiated on moral grounds of mutual friendship and the ideologically unassailable argument of trade expansion. It is at that stage that the Soviets found themselves on a weaker footing; Western government bureaucrats, all sides understood, could not force sales and purchases on private companies.[4] This made deflection easier; when the Soviets complained about the lack of progress their industrial products were making in Austrian markets, as they did for instance in December 1966 in a meeting with Austrian Vice-Chancellor Fritz Bock, the Austrians had an easy time blaming the Soviets for it.[5] Their products were of low quality; product advertisement was poor; product service was non-existent; and "competition in the world market" had intensified. Bock, meanwhile, could remain plaintive, lamenting that despite all his efforts "he cannot force Austrian firms to buy goods that do not suit them."[6]

The Soviets asked in turn that state agents not underestimate their power to push Soviet goods in domestic markets, and to make renewed efforts, while in the same breath they complained helplessly that Soviet industrial goods had sold at an annual rate of 10 percent of the amount stipulated in the lists.[7] Accounts ultimately had to balance, and while Austrian trade officials could hide behind notions of domestic demand and supply, the Soviets had no such recourse. The burden of balancing thus often fell on the Soviets. The perennial weakness of the Soviet negotiating position goes some length in explaining the differing attitude toward the bilateral trade lists negotiated on an annual and quinquennial basis. Western negotiators under strict capital constraints saw the lists in light of the kind of indicative planning their own countries practiced. In 1964, for example, the Austrian delegation worried only about the optics of the trade agreement, trying to make sure the lists of goods to be exchanged over the next five years showed annual increases in trade

---

[4] See, for example, the desultory response of the Austrian ambassador in the face of Soviet complaints that an Austrian firm was systematically failing to buy Soviet machines and equipment provided in the lists. The ambassador's response was to bring this to the attention of the firm when he got back to Vienna. In RGAE, f. 413, op. 31, d. 572, ll. 1–2, in a meeting dated November 30, 1965.

[5] The Soviets thought this "an excuse," in RGAE, f. 413, op. 31, d. 1930, l. 3.

[6] RGAE, f. 413, op. 31, d. 1104, ll. 67–68.   [7] Ibid., ll. 68–69.

turnover, whether or not these were achieved later in practice.[8] The Soviets, however, saw the lists less as an exercise in aspiration and more as a document that could be used in future annual reviews to make concrete demands and formulate claims and complaints. Where the lists are concerned, the Soviet delegate explained, "we are used to approaching them from the basis of real possibilities."[9] This should stand in contrast to the widespread assumption that Soviet trade was largely a means of plugging the leaks and amending the deficiencies of planning.

In 1964, however, the brute limits of dollar scarcity had forced the Soviets to cut down on Austrian imports, prompting Patolichev's apologies. The Austrian response was to acknowledge the Soviet Union's difficulties "arising sometimes in relation to the clearing of accounts." In this spirit of compromise, they would "not insist on strict balancing of deliveries" and would be "ready to discuss later the question of balances."[10] What this augured for the Soviet–Austrian relationship was a struggle over the organization of their bilateral trade. The Soviets wanted to bring that relationship within the purview of a wider market denominated in hard currency. In other words, they embraced the potentialities of convertibility, which opened products up to the full force of competition across political boundaries. Competition, of course, had always existed, and it had always been a primary vector of Soviet bargaining strategy – recited incessantly as the mantra of Soviet political economy. But convertibility intensified competition, opening the field of play beyond national boundaries, weakening all arguments based on clearing, and equipping purchasers with the bottom-line rhetoric of market discipline.

The reordering of trade away from clearing would be a sticking point over the next few years. Already as soon as the Soviets introduced the idea, the Austrians were quite straightforward with their anxieties, fearing that "in case of a withdrawal from clearing, Soviet exports to Austria will be much faster than imports, and the currency earned in Austria will be directed to purchases in other countries."[11] This was precisely the kind of flexibility the Soviets were looking for.[12] By 1966, trade officials could boast that "a majority of countries conduct their accounts with the USSR in convertible currency." Confirming what was attractive to the Soviets

---

[8] The Austrians, in fact, considered "the position of the Soviet delegation to be too firm and assured that the Austrian side will in no way reproach the Soviet side for not fulfilling this or that list contingent." But, during the negotiations of the lists in November 1964, they asked "to be kept in mind that their delegation could not return home with lists showing a decrease in trade compared to 1964." RGAE, f. 413, op. 31, d. 57, l. 22.

[9] Ibid., l. 31.   [10] Ibid.

[11] Ibid., l. 47. The Austrians had already experienced this with their Yugoslav partners.

[12] Ibid., l. 48.

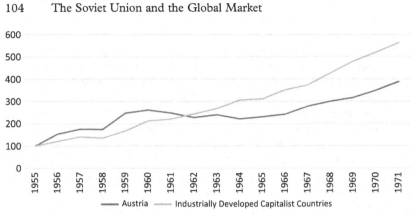

Figure 3.1 Trade growth (1955 = 100)[15]

about the arrangement, the official continued: "This form of accounting is profitable for both sides, but of course it requires a high degree of competitiveness from the goods on offer."[13] The Soviets noted approvingly that the IMF very much agreed with them and was conducting its own pressure to move Austria into convertibility.[14] As the figure below shows, trade with Austria peaked in 1960; it would take seven years to reach that height again, even as trade with the West continued its growth unabated (see Figure 3.1). Without a resolution to reorganize trade around hard currency, the relationship stagnated to the benefit of other partners.

The negotiation of a new five-year trade agreement in the summer of 1965 finally moved the commercial relationship beyond the 1960 peak, but the gap with the rest of Europe grew wider – a strange dynamic given Austria's geographical proximity and historical ties to Eastern Europe.[16] In this second half of the 1960s, the Soviets poured on the pressure to get the Austrians to liberalize their trade, which "would undoubtedly promote the expansion of trade between our countries, since Soviet foreign trade organizations and Austrian firms would have a great opportunity to

---

[13] RGAE, f. 413, op. 31, d. 1104, ll. 1–2.   [14] Ibid., ll. 10–11.
[15] Constructed from the *Vneshniaia torgovlia SSSR za … Statisticheskii obzor* series for each year published in Moscow by *Vneshtorgizdat*. "Industrially developed capitalist countries" is the category the Soviets used in the series to refer to Western Europe, the US, Canada, and Japan.
[16] The gap is comparatively relevant because it is measured, as the chart shows, in terms of the pace of growth, rather than absolute volume, since small countries like Austria would naturally trade less volume. The negotiations can be found in RGAE, f. 413, op. 31, d. 572. The agreement for 1966–1970, with the lists of exchange goods, is in RGAE, f. 413, op. 31, d. 656.

maneuver when selling and buying goods."[17] The Soviets added to this an old saw: Large orders were going to England, France, and Italy because they give credit for ten to fifteen years, while the Austrians could not even muster eight years.[18]

In Austria, business circles were split on the issue, but the fear of leaving the protection of Keynesian capital controls and trade clearing in order to enter an integrating world market kept the government immobile. This, at least, was the Soviet view, stated in a report that concluded that "in the context of intensified competition in the world market that led to a decrease in the expansion of Austrian exports, which are vitally important for its economy, a certain part of the ruling circles and industrialists of the country are compelled to objectively consider the need to preserve for Austria the traditional markets of the European socialist countries, among which the Soviet Union is Austria's largest partner."[19] All the while the Soviets, agents of that global market integration the Austrians feared, continued to advocate for an end to the commercial and financial practices of a Keynesian past and for a future in which international capital may be allocated according to the laws of competition rather than national interest.

The Soviets, needless to say, maintained for themselves the privilege of an institutional monopoly to organize their foreign trade and decide centrally what came in and went out of their country. This could lead to complaints. Soviet organizations, for example, could easily visit potential suppliers and find out what the conditions are for whatever they needed; Austrian companies, however, needed an invitation to Moscow, inevitably depriving others perhaps more competitive of the opportunity. In their dealings with Moscow, Western firms had just as often to act as agents for other firms as direct suppliers.[20] More consequentially, however, the Soviets directed this monopoly in two main directions. First they used it to plan enormous growth in their foreign trade, well beyond that of their overall economy, and well above that of the global international trade. In fact, the foreign trade they planned invariably fell short, as we have seen, of the exchanges that actually occurred. And second, they used the concentrated force of that monopoly – the door to a measure of industrial aptitude and inestimable riches

---

[17] RGAE, f. 413, op. 31, d. 1675, l. 81. A meeting on that same day with a different Soviet apparatchik yielded much the same line: Clearing was simply less "flexible." That particular talk added the ostensibly assuaging information that France, Italy, and Norway had successfully transitioned to liberalized, hard currency trade, in ibid., ll. 83–86.

[18] In ibid., ll. 79–82, for example, in talks on March 15, 1967.

[19] RGAE, f. 413, op. 31, d. 1930, l. 4.   [20] RGAE, f. 413, op. 31, d. 2293, l. 43.

in natural resources – to liberalize, commoditize and otherwise integrate European (and international) offerings into competitive markets. This was stubborn work. And it looked something like the lecturing Manzhulo performed on an Austrian foreign ministry envoy in March 1968, to whom he lobbied for an "improvement in the political conditions of trade" between the two countries:[21]

Here, first of all, it is necessary to solve the issue of improving the regime for the import of Soviet goods into Austria, which is much worse than what Austria provides to its Western partners. It is well known that the import of Soviet goods is fully covered by the licensing system, i.e., Austrian companies must obtain a permit for each individual import of Soviet goods. This situation makes it operationally difficult for Austrian firms when purchasing goods from Soviet foreign trade organizations. It introduces an element of uncertainty and is completely inappropriate in relation to the state with which the most favored nation treaty exists. [Manzhulo] stressed that extending the liberalization regime to the import of Soviet goods into Austria would also facilitate trade between the two countries.

Then Comrade Manzhulo said that the clearing of accounts system currently in place between the USSR and Austria does not encourage the expansion of our trade, and sometimes even limits the possibility of individual transactions. In our opinion, there is a need to move to freely convertible currency exchange. Transition to accounts in a freely convertible currency will help to increase the volume of trade transactions and expand the range of traded goods.[22]

The proof of his words was in the statistical data of trade with Norway and Sweden, where there was a substantial increase in trade after the transition to convertible currency, Manzhulo closed triumphantly.

The next month the Austrians finally conceded to discussing a new governing arrangement that could come into effect after the end of the trade plan in 1970.[23] Their proposal, however, was for a hybrid approach in which the bulk of the trade would be set down on lists, while individual deals not sanctioned by the lists could be accounted for in hard currency with the cooperation of Austrian banks.[24] This could be a temporary arrangement until the inevitable transition to a fully liberalized govern-ance, and it would at least have the virtue of legalizing transactions in hard currency that were already taking place, the Austrians offered.[25] For

---

[21] The talk, which took place on March 19, 1968, is in RGAE, f. 413, op. 31, d. 2293, ll. 8–12.

[22] Ibid., ll. 9–10.

[23] In a series of talks from April 2–4, 1968, in RGAE, f. 413, op. 31, d. 2293, ll. 15–23.

[24] Ibid., l. 21. The Austrians had in mind purchases of Soviet resources—nickel, apatite for fertilizers – that the Soviets had refused to include in the plans and which the Austrians had to buy elsewhere anyway.

[25] Ibid., ll. 21–22.

the Soviets, the transition was "well overdue."[26] The Austrian proposal changed nothing in practice, given the Soviets had always responded positively to Austrian firms who bought or purchased non-listed goods in hard currency. The Soviets were willing to wait until the Austrians took the plunge to full liberalization; they had no choice.[27] And anyway, with the world liberalizing out of Keynes' Bretton Woods shackles, the Soviets knew that the future was on their side.

✶✶✶✶✶✶✶✶✶✶

Natural gas, itself a liberalized product not subject to lists or licensing, powered the exit out of the doldrums in which the Soviet–Austrian economic relationship had languished.[28] Despite appearances, it is not preciously symbolic to note that this small country, lacking any energy needs of a continental scale, ended up playing such a pivotal role in the continent's transformation. Austria, central to Nazism's abortive European project, had emerged from the war as a rare space of East–West neutrality. Its state oil and gas company, ÖMV (Österreichische Mineralölverwaltung, or the Austrian Mineral Oil Administration) was the genealogical product of the control of that space by Nazis and then Soviets.[29] Ostensibly formed from a Nazi-era enterprise, but in practical terms the successor to the Soviet Mineral Oil Administration (Sowjetische Mineralölverwaltung, or SMV), ÖMV governed the energy regime change that was socially general and chronologically parallel to that in all of Western Europe, all the while retaining a practical experience of Eastern Bloc commerce – including a particularly intense

---

[26] Ibid., l. 22.

[27] Ibid., l. 23. This Austrian reticence and practice of half-measures in the liberalization of its commerce and finance contrasts with something Patolichev told a German political leader in December 1971: "Austria, for example, immediately made the decision for full liberalization of its imports from the USSR." This is disingenuous, but well established in Soviet performative efforts to create a sense of market-like competitive pressures when speaking with partners; the accuracy of these descriptions was secondary to the political task market language was meant to perform for the Soviets. In RGAE, f. 413, op. 31, d. 4407, l. 4.

[28] The Soviets themselves noted this in RGAE, f. 413, op. 31, d. 1331a, l. 2. The story of the deal's negotiations, mostly from a Western perspective, is documented in the excellent Per Högselius, *Red Gas. Russia and the Origins of European Energy Dependence* (Basingstoke: Palgrave Macmillan, 2013). This gas-powered exit was the hope Vice-Chancellor Bock expressed explicitly at the end of 1966, once the Austrian government realized it had to push for a more integrative approach to the gas deal involving several different Austrian companies, as he expressed to Patolichev in RGAE, f. 413, op. 31, d. 1104, l. 71.

[29] Högselius, *Red Gas*, pp. 45–46. Högselius further points to the company's practical experience with systems building in oil and gas production and transmission, which briefly made the small country Western Europe's largest oil producer in 1955.

experience of Soviet actors during the country's first postwar decade. Having successfully promoted domestically produced natural gas as a clean alternative to coal, ÖMV and Austria more generally anticipated that there would soon be a relative, demand-driven shortage of gas. As small private energy companies in Austria began to combine efforts to undo ÖMV's gas monopoly by bringing gas from abroad, ÖMV leaned into its peculiar lineage. At the beginning of 1964 the Soviet Union announced the construction of a gas pipeline bringing Ukrainian gas to Czechoslovakia. By November that year, an Austrian delegation was conveying the country's enduring interest in Soviet gas and its readiness "to participate in the manufacture of gas pipeline equipment."[30] Neither the Soviets nor the Austrians were ready to exchange material opinions on the matter, they both acknowledged, and the Austrian expression of interest was ultimately not the comprehensive, long-term, heavily capitalized proposal the Italians would extend a half year later. The Austrians merely looked to fold exports of pipes and imports of gas – not explicitly linked – into the upcoming long-term trade agreement negotiations.[31] If further proof is needed to show that abundant gas supply on one side and eager demand for gas on the other would not, of its own, prod the continent into a socioeconomic reconfiguration, consider this: A mere few weeks before an Italian coalition of national industrial, financial, and political power produced exactly that outcome, insistent Austrian interest in gas imports produced only a vague request for more time to consider the issue.[32]

Once Italy had clarified the possibilities of the kinds of financial and material infrastructures such a project might put in place, the Soviets began fanning competitive flames throughout the continent.[33] These were complemented by all sorts of rumors. Were the Soviets carrying out secret negotiations with the West Germans? Were they offering the Germans better prices?[34] Domestically Ferngas, a coalition of three different private-sector companies that had been actively talking with Algerian

---

[30] RGAE, f. 413, op. 31, d. 57, l. 49. Although I have not found an earlier expression of this interest in gas, it is obvious the Austrians had already broached the issue before this November 20, 1964 encounter.

[31] As per the December 4 protocol auguring the negotiations, which merely expressed Austrian desire for Soviet gas and Soviet desire to expand deliveries of Soviet machines and equipment to Austria. Ibid., ll. 66–67.

[32] In a May 26, 1965 meeting at the Soviet Ministry of Foreign Trade in RGAE, f. 413, op. 31, d. 572, ll. 42–43.

[33] The Soviets did not fail to note this, as per the four-page 1967 report from the Ministry of Foreign Affairs, RGAE, f. 413, op. 31, d. 1331a, ll. 1–4.

[34] RGAE, f. 413, op. 31, d. 1104, ll. 13–16, in a meeting in Vienna on June 9, 1966.

and Dutch gas companies, started actively courting the Soviets as well.[35] They offered hard currency and a measure of coordination for the export of pipes, even as they took up the responsibility to finance their purchases with their own national banks.[36] But in the nationally segmented economic life of Bretton Woods, state industrial management meant state-centered networks of economic coordination. Which is to say, like ENI in Italy, ÖMV had a useful partner in VÖEST (now Voestalpine AG), a state-owned steel company with a peculiar genealogy similar to that of ÖMV. The Austrian state had paid attention. Both the Italian deal and Soviet unresponsiveness effectively communicated to the Austrians to scale up their offers, and by 1966 VÖEST too was making trips to Moscow to negotiate directly the pipeline side of a gas-for-pipe deal – and discrediting the offers by private-sector actors as unserious "noise."[37] By the end of the year, the Austrian ambassador finally made a formal offer, a year and a half late and, one might add, a dollar short.[38] This too the Soviets conveyed clearly. Although the Austrians had offered competitive prices on the individual commodities involved, both the financing and longer repayment horizons the Italians were being forced to propose were missing. The Soviets "were negotiating with Italy on gas with the Italians supplying pipes and necessary equipment on credit with later payment of their cost with Soviet gas supplies. On those same conditions we would agree to hold negotiations with the Austrians."[39] In other words, the Soviets were not looking merely for hard currency, or better pipe technology. They were looking for a new, durable, financialized relationship.

What is more, when VÖEST came fully onboard that December, the Soviets brought them up to speed on the preconditions of their negotiations

---

[35] Ibid., ll. 46–47, offering a price of $16 per 1,000 cubic meters, which was above the prices the Soviets finally settled on with ÖMV.

[36] RGAE, f. 413, op. 31, d. 1675, ll. 102–105. The Soviets never quite closed the door to Ferngas, which continued meeting with them, providing the Soviets with a competitive counterpoint to ÖMV and a useful source of information. See RGAE, f. 413, op. 31, d. 2294, ll. 65–68. This would pay dividends later in the talks with ÖMV.

[37] RGAE, f. 413, op. 31, d. 1675, l. 91.

[38] RGAE, f. 413, op. 31, d. 1104, ll. 61–62. In a meeting with Kuz'min on December 4. The Soviets wanted a competitive offer. When the Austrians proposed a three-way meeting with the Italians, Kuz'min demurred: "The negotiations will be more productive on a bilateral basis, taking into account the interests of each of the negotiating parties." This came in the wake of Pesidium chairman Nikolai Podgornyi's visit to Vienna in November, in which he encouraged the Austrians to participate in the gas pipe construction with Italy.

[39] Ibid. Kuz'min repeated this exact formulation a few days later in a meeting with Austrian Vice-Chancellor Fritz Bock, stressing again the financial character of the deal by way of clarifying Patolichev's earlier, broader invitation to the Austrians to participate in the project. This meeting took place on December 8, in ibid., l. 67.

with the company.[40] These consisted of five points.[41] The first made sure they understood that the pipe construction on Austrian territory was their affair and did not concern the Soviets, and the fourth point established simply that commercial relations would be negotiated. The remaining three points, however, were related to the main Soviet concern: the financial relationship. VÖEST was to know that the Austrians would be responsible for financing their participation in the overall deal the Soviets were working out with Italy, and that repayment would start much later, only after the gas started flowing. The fifth point pertained directly to VÖEST in a way the others did not. The steel maker was set to buy much more fuel and iron ore from the Soviets than Austria could muster, given all the pipe it had to produce. The Soviets wanted to establish, before any proposals were exchanged, that payment for these would run exclusively through their annual trade exchanges, and "without any link to the payment of the pipe or loan repayment." Even as the new relationship would require an intensified exchange in all manner of ancillary products, the Soviets quickly moved to effectively safeguard the new financial relationship and make sure these auxiliary issues did not degrade the relationship's time dimension – that is, by making sure those other products would not help pay down the pipe loan more quickly. The VÖEST delegation received the message loud and clear, countering that they were interested in the fastest possible repayment and requesting that both sides discuss increasing gas deliveries on account of exports to Bavaria.[42]

The reasons for the temporary demise of the Algerian deal at this moment are equally instructive.[43] Interest in Algerian gas had been as pan-European as that which the Soviets were experiencing. The technical challenge of building a system of pipelines to take it across the Mediterranean Sea was difficult but feasible, and the ultimate price of the gas was deemed very competitive in Europe, especially given the high calorific value of the gas. The financing, however, was haphazard, conditional, and uncoordinated. And Algeria was ultimately a poor partner with which to achieve this technopolitical challenge easily. According to

---

[40] RGAE, f. 413, op. 31, d. 1675, l. 106.

[41] RGAE, f. 413, op. 31, d. 1104, ll. 74–76, in a meeting on December 9.

[42] Ibid., l. 75. This was the first such inclusion of German interest, and a sign that the Austrians had been busy assembling the necessary technopolitical coalition.

[43] Gas from Algeria would flow in small quantities as liquefied natural gas (LNG). In 1976, ENI would once again break new ground by leading the construction of a major pipeline to Sicily, whose gas began to flow in 1983. Per Högselius, Anna Åberg, and Arne Kaijser, "Natural Gas in Cold War Europe: The Making of a Critical Infrastructure," in Per Högselius, Anique Hommels, Arne Kaijser, and Erik van der Vleuten, eds., *The Making of Europe's Critical Infrastructure. Common Connections and Shared Vulnerabilities* (Basingstoke: Palgrave Macmillan, 2013): 32.

VÖEST's report to the Soviets, the Algerians had been offered money from the United States, but on the condition that the Algerians invest 40 percent of their own funds in the project. The Algerian government approached Spain and England for credit, as well as Austria, but as far as Austria was concerned, this was not particularly attractive, since Algeria "had nothing to pay" for this.[44] Here is an interesting contrast illuminating the factors that made the Soviet Union especially adept at pushing for the financialization of its foreign relations. The socialist power had the natural endowments, yes, but it had more than that. Its markets were deep enough, its production diversified enough, and it had rooted its economic relationships deeply enough to make its partnership as attractive as its escalating financial demands were enthralling. And when these qualities did not suffice, the Soviets motivated domestic corporate constituencies in their partners to work on their behalf. To sell steel, for example, VÖEST was ready to activate the European subsidiaries of American powerhouses Westinghouse and General Electric to offer top of the line compressor stations necessary to move the gas. General Electric had already agreed before VÖEST had even met with the Soviets.[45]

By 1967 Austria became the first Western country to draw gas from the Eastern Bloc, but this entailed the draining of a gas field straddling the border with Czechoslovakia, rather than the large-scale, continuous flow of either Ukrainian or Siberian gas.[46] Progress on the much larger deal stalled in Austria as it did in Italy. With Germany and France also clamoring to join, the Soviets seemed unprepared for the large array of options opening up before them – unthinkable only two years earlier. But they also needed their Western partners to take time to reconsider the limits of how they would construct this new relationship. In February 1967, the Austrians had already noticed a certain Soviet reserve on the deal.[47] Though usually aggressive in their deal-making, the Soviets had not called for a follow-up round of talks since December. With demand for gas in Austria surging, the Austrians decided in May to take the initiative and make a proposal. This involved a "small plan," which would see gas flow from the endpoint of the Bratstvo pipeline immediately, and a "big plan," which would require a new dedicated pipeline from the large fields to the east to bring the gas by 1971. The latter plan depended on negotiations with Italy, so the Austrians would not hold their breath.[48]

---

[44] RGAE, f. 413, op. 31, d. 1675, l. 92.   [45] Ibid.
[46] Although the idea was for Czechoslovakia to be compensated through increases in gas imports from the Soviet Union, making Soviet gas the ultimate currency of exchange. RGAE, f. 413, op. 31, d. 2294, l. 2.
[47] RGAE, f. 413, op. 31, d. 1675, ll. 88–89.   [48] Ibid., ll. 58–61.

It seemed a kind of deflection, this Soviet insistence that the techno-political project was complex and necessitated time, and the Austrians despaired in the first half of 1967 that the deal would ever move forward.[49] It was not deflection; Soviet diligence was earnest. Key to the project's execution was Czechoslovakia. As early as November 1966, the Soviets announced their intention to build a dedicated gas export pipeline to Czechoslovakia's western border.[50] They were not asking for permission, nor did they receive it. But in time, Czechoslovakia's Gosplan would enmesh the Soviets in an intense bout of negotiation over the transit price the small country would exact for using its soil. While Austria fretted in the spring and summer of 1967, while coming up with plans big and small, the Soviets were busy failing to protect their future profits against their westernmost socialist allies.[51] What these heated negotiations revealed was the early desirability of Austrian participation in the project. Austria, small and financially constrained, was the gateway to German pipe technology, a prize the Soviets had pursued ever since the United States had forced Germany to renege on its gas-for-pipe contracts in 1962. Where the two other potential partners, Italy and France, offered 1020 mm diameter pipe, Austria offered 1220 mm. Although Austria would only take in 15 percent of the 10 bcm of annual gas deliveries the Soviets were contemplating to export – with Italy taking 60 percent and France 25 percent, – the small country would deliver the same volume of pipe as its partners.[52] VÖEST's close ties to Germany meant that two of Germany's largest industrial conglomerates, Mannesmann and Thyssen, would act as subsidiary manufacturers of the pipe, which would use high-quality VÖEST steel.[53]

Although final gas delivery volumes were important for making sure the infrastructure building the Soviets envisaged was economical, the Soviets seemed nonplussed that enough demand would surface for the project to move forward. In fact they were justifiably confident that demand would be as inexhaustible as their Siberian supply. What continued to worry them to the point of uncertainty about the project's viability, was not gas demand but rather credit supply. The Austrians, for their part, worried about the apparently willful hiatus. Moreover, during the first half of 1967 Germany experienced its first recession in a decade, mild though it turned

---

[49] Högselius, *Red Gas*, p. 58.   [50] RGAE, f. 413, op. 31, d. 2294, ll. 1–4.

[51] Part of these negotiations, which extended from May to June, can be found in RGAE, f. 413, op. 31, d. 2294, ll. 15–34. The now classic explanation for this familiar Soviet failure to protect its economic interests against East European recalcitrance is Randall W. Stone, *Satellites and Commissars. Strategy and Conflict in the Politics of Soviet-Bloc Trade* (Princeton: Princeton University Press, 1996).

[52] RGAE, f. 413, op. 31, d. 2294, l. 16.   [53] RGAE, f. 413, op. 31, d. 1675, l. 55.

out to be, taking Austria with it and pressing VÖEST to entreat the Soviets
to release it from coal and iron ore imports they had contracted earlier and
which threatened to "go directly to the warehouse and greatly complicate
the maneuverability of the company."[54] Or the Soviets themselves could
make up for the absent demand with the enormous gas-for-pipe
undertaking. A push in July of that year to restart talks found the Soviets,
now assured of Czechoslovakia's cooperation, eager to see where the
Austrians had fallen on the financial question. Curiously, the Soviet trade
representative in Vienna had the distinct impression that VÖEST, which
ÖMV had agreed would take care of finance, "did not want to discuss
finance issues in the presence of ÖMV."[55]

By the time talks were restarted in September 1967, the ever-
expanding gas deal had insinuated itself into the larger Austrian dilemma
of the switch from list-based, balanced payment trade to hard currency
trade. While the Austrians held on to their ambiguous position, the
Soviets were using the gas deal to create a time frame for the corrosion
of nationally segmented trade. On the one hand, the Austrians insisted
that the pipe deal and the gas deal were legally independent of one
another, which would potentially mean that delays or nonfulfillment in
one would not affect the other. This would force the Soviets to settle
accounts through traditional current account balancing arrangements of
the type that had governed exchanges since the 1950s.[56] On the other
hand, the contract that the Soviets presented in September, would oblige
the Austrians to pay for gas with US dollars after repayment for the pipe
ran its course. A decade in the future though that was, the Austrians
could still not bring themselves to commit to substantial purchases
outside of the trade agreement, where balance could be more easily
planned and negotiated. The Soviets obviously objected, arguing that
"gas in Europe will be a deficit commodity for a long time yet, and the
Soviet side intends to get hard currency for it."[57] Moreover, a year earlier
Vice-Chancellor Bock had already agreed that the gas deal should run
parallel and unconnected to the trade agreements.

But it was predictably the technology of debt making that sunk the
September negotiations. September 4 was a Monday, and it marked the

---

[54] Ibid., l. 56.   [55] Ibid., l. 60.

[56] RGAE, f. 413, op. 31, d. 2294, l. 43. The Austrians also wanted the option to unilaterally
demand more gas – by a particular amount – after the end of the contract. The Soviets
obviously rejected the proposition, aware as they were already of the problems of supply
with which they would be plagued over the next two decades, as eminently argued in
Thane Gustafson, *Crisis Amid Plenty. The Politics of Soviet Energy under Brezhnev and
Gorbachev* (Princeton: Princeton University Press, 1989).

[57] RGAE, f. 413, op. 31, d. 2294, l. 44.

first day of negotiations beyond protocol proclamations. The Soviet delegation had arrived in Vienna the Friday before, and had quickly established some differences of opinion, but it was only after the weekend that the financial fault lines made themselves felt. The gap was the measure of the world the Soviets wanted against the world as it functioned under Bretton Woods. The Soviets wanted something in the area of a $100 million credit, for exactly as long as it would take to pay it back in gas. The Austrians, working with German banks, could only offer five years of debt relations.[58] The Soviets wanted the dollar to mediate the relationship, which would ultimately reflect the fact that gas was a dollar commodity. The Austrians offered a basket of one-third Austrian schillings and two-thirds deutsche marks, which they revealed reflected the national contribution each country made in pipe deliveries. The Soviets wanted interest rates competitive with those they had already received for other deals from England and Italy. Austrian credit, without the same kind of state subsidies businesses in other states enjoyed, was half a percentage point more expensive.[59] Neither side knew that in little more than a decade, the competitive, market-integrated, US dollar-denominated world the Soviets were pushing for would be standard. For now, this was still a Keynesian world, even if it was coming apart at the seams. The Austrians would hold it together, if they could, a while longer.[60]

This is not a story about how the tail wagged the dog, about how small countries forced systemic reckonings, not exactly. The reason is simple; capital resources, however obscured by the Cold War paradigm, are power. Capital deployed can maintain established practices, but also open new pathways for doing, which eventually comes to mean thinking. Austria, simply put, lacked the means to do, which is to say, it lacked the capital to follow through on the vision the Soviet Union proposed for the reinvention and deployment of global finance. The Austrians asked explicitly for a deal modeled after the oil deals of the past, which is to say, on the basis of relatively large but temporally delimited loans that

---

[58] "Changing the length of the loan upwards is completely unrealistic and it would be a waste of time to discuss the issue further." RGAE, f. 413, op. 31, d. 1675, ll. 44–46.

[59] Ibid. Later, the Austrians would try to link finance to the start of gas deliveries in 1968 rather than 1971. This would of course also have the effect of speeding repayments, which pushed against the Soviet project. See for example ibid., l. 42.

[60] Ibid., l. 43. Their anxiety over the future showed in their attempt to negotiate terms for after the loan repayment in order to assure themselves that Soviet gas revenues from Austria would be spent in Austria.

had not traditionally required bank guarantees.[61] While the volume and duration of the deal formed the core of the Soviet plan, these were the very characteristics of the deal that made it prohibitive for ÖMV to seek bank guarantees within Austria, where banks "lacked such resources." And what was more, "existing legislation in Austria prohibiting banks from taking risks in their operations will force Austrian banks to share the guarantee obligation with other banks, which will increase its value." The Austrians did not want these costs to migrate over to the cost of the gas, which as with their Italian parallel, was their main concern. As with the negotiations with Italy, the main Soviet concern was elsewhere. The kind of new relationship the Soviets wanted to establish was "not practiced in world trade."[62]

At the end of the first week of negotiations, the heads of both delegations visited the office of the conservative Austrian Chancellor Josef Klaus. In their report to the chancellor on the negotiations, both heads showed a complete agreement and understanding of the issues that separated them. The political atmosphere could not be more agreeable to business dealings. Chancellor Klaus himself offered an eloquent expression of how the European project was beginning to stretch beyond its self-imposed limits at the Eastern border and follow Brezhnev's invitation to develop "inter-European cooperation in economics, science, technology, and culture. Austria," he continued, "seeks to use all its capabilities to participate in the practical implementation of these proposals: from the construction of the USSR-Austria-Italy-France gas pipeline, to the introduction of a common color television system for all of Europe. And we are ready to participate in the water purification of European rivers and seas, and to participate in general measures to combat such diseases as cancer, cardiovascular ailments and others."[63] Détente, the chancellor wanted to convey, was not even détente for Austria, but an almost genetic compulsion for the country's postwar politics – even if Klaus was at the same time seeking an arrangement with the European Common Market that greatly worried the Soviets. The goodwill was expressed sincerely and continuously. Détente had not been and would not be the obstacle for the realization of this prospectively durable relationship; the multigenerational technopolitical association the Soviets wanted for their gas required a new deployment of money, which is to say a refurbished technology of international debt

---

[61] RGAE, f. 413, op. 31, d. 2294, l. 48. The Austrians "offered to establish a payment method similar to the oil contract," but the Soviets "rejected this proposal, citing the long duration of the gas supply contract and its high volume."
[62] Ibid., l. 47.   [63] RGAE, f. 413, op. 31, d. 1675, l. 39.

making, and Austria made painfully palpable that political goodwill alone could not oblige this.

The weekend had not moved positions very much.[64] The Soviets had raised the interest rate they were willing to accept to 5.85 percent, and the Austrians could agree to a loan repayment schedule of six years.[65] A plaintive, pessimistic mood set in. So much so, in fact, that the Austrians never even offered a price for the gas in the two weeks of negotiations.[66] The September talks came and went with all the major coordinates of a deal still to be negotiated.[67] Détente was not at stake, but each side had important goals to meet. As one after another source of gas fell from contention – Algeria, Holland – every month that passed made securing Soviet gas for Austria more urgent. The Soviets, on their end, needed an exemplary precedent out of Austria in order to move Italy out of its positions, and as a guide for prospective negotiations all over Western Europe. Both sides had clearly decided they would grind out these talks despite the gap separating their respective positions, meeting every month to advance the project, even if glacially so. The Soviets met the Austrians first on their urgency, agreeing to deliver gas as early as 1968, while the Austrians finally proposed a price more than a month after the failed September talks.[68]

It is a matter of empirical fact that the glue that held the talks together within a field of pecuniary struggle but broad goodwill and meaningful – rather than diplomatic or superficial – understanding was a performative insistence coinciding on the category of the market that each side used to cast their claims upon one another. In the absence of anything resembling a market, Soviets and Austrians bandied market discourse, and sought refuge in an ethics whose common denominator was the repeated recovery and deployment of market verities. Disagreements, it followed, were fertile grounds for performing the market. Consider these over the initial $12.80 per one thousand cubic meters the Austrians offered at length, anything above which "would make Austrian production uncompetitive in foreign markets."[69] Surprisingly, and circularly, ÖMV argued that importing large amounts of Soviet gas required the company to

---

[64] Ibid., ll. 35–36.   [65] Ibid., ll. 33–34.

[66] Although they had agreed that they would. RGAE, f. 413, op. 31, d. 2294, ll. 73–76.

[67] A final reckoning between the two sides on the last day, September 15, 1967, is in RGAE, f. 413, op. 31, d. 1675, ll. 30–32. The financing, the price of the pipe and the price of the gas were all left on the table to be taken up again at a later date. Only a month later did the Austrians finally offer a price: $12.8 per one thousand cubic meters.

[68] Over three days of meetings from October 25 to 27, 1967, in RGAE, f. 413, op. 31, d. 2294, ll. 82–92. The Soviets ultimately linked a better price offer to the offer to deliver gas in 1968.

[69] Ibid., l. 83.

attract new consumers among industrial firms, causing the very effect that justified the low price in the first place – since in the expansion of gas consumption to encompass Austrian firms, gas would become an industrial input whose price would have the potential of making Austrian production uncompetitive. What is more, the price of fuel oil, the direct competitor of natural gas, was decreasing all over Europe. The lack of any infrastructure that could produce something resembling market behavior meant that fuel oil, especially heating oil and the fuel oil used to produce electricity in the evening, was the first port of call for constructing a "market price."

The Soviets were well versed in market-making discourse.[70] They answered with a tighter kind of market logic. "The level of natural gas prices should be determined on the basis of market conditions for this product, taking into account various factors, including the competitiveness of products for export, but the latter cannot be taken as a base. Moreover, ÖMV should take into account that there was a firm request for gas by another Austrian gas company at a higher price."[71] Energy prices were unifying throughout Europe, ÖMV countered, and Austria was planning the organization of one company that would balance prices. This was a plausible argument, alluding as it did to the balancing role the great oil multinationals, with the help of the Texas Railroad Commission, had played for three decades, which had allowed the very constitution of the Bretton Woods regime.[72] The institutional rearrangements of energy the Soviets were advocating, which aimed to disorganize consumer prerogatives, was inimical with the regulated global energy regime of the West's golden years. Austria "is departing from the basic principles that determine the price level, which depends on the specific conditions prevailing in the market of a given country," the Soviets warned.[73] When ÖMV's director laid out the complex way in which domestic gas prices were decided – involving the Chamber of Commerce, the association of industrialists and a number of institutions responsible for the Austrian economy, – Soviet delegation head Osipov insisted on simplifying the

---

[70] The Soviets were well aware of the process for how gas prices were set domestically. With reference to Germany, see RGAE, f. 413, op. 31, d. 2985, ll. 82–83.

[71] RGAE, f. 413, op. 31, d. 2294, ll. 83–84. Here the Soviets were clearly instrumentalizing their earlier talks with Ferngas.

[72] Matthew T. Huber, "Enforcing Scarcity: Oil, Violence, and the Making of the Market," *Annals of the Association of American Geographers*, 101:4 (2011): 816–826; and "Fueling Capitalism: Oil, the Regulation Approach, and the Ecology of Capital," *Economic Geography* 89:2 (2013): 171–194. See also Roberto J. Ortiz, "Oil-Fueled Accumulation in Late Capitalism: Energy, Uneven Development, and Climate Crisis," *Critical Historical Studies* 7:2 (2020): 205–240.

[73] RGAE, f. 413, op. 31, d. 2294, l. 84.

equation to the idea that "the price is determined by the market and should be mutually beneficial," and that it was necessary "to take into account the actual situation on the European natural gas market."[74]

The argument here is not that the Soviets were somehow better at performing the market, or more loyal to market principles, but that this insistent performative practice characterized the field within which technopolitical objects were assembled that were as crucial to the social construction of Europe as they were to the development of finance. What is more, the Soviet Union was a central agent in both the construction and the sedimentation of market discourse through its performative politics. Market discourse did not produce the market, but then, neither is the transhistorical market category useful in assessing the way these sets of material exchanges were organized. There was no international gas market, and in the late 1960s it integrated Soviet gas.

From the fall of 1967 there would be nothing like the long break that had made the Austrians fear for the deal. Meetings continued closing the gap on price between the two parties all the way to February 1968. At that point, the Soviets made a firm proposal for $14.10 per one thousand cubic meters. ÖMV's board accepted. Time belonged to the Soviets; the only way to guarantee gas deliveries to Austria in 1968 was with a deal in hand. The Austrians were hoping Italy's ENI could use its much deeper financial resources to negotiate a lower price that ÖMV could then claim for itself. The Soviets, of course, preferred Austria to set price trends. And in fact, as Soviet offers to Italy show, there was a window of opportunity for the price of Soviet gas to have been lower still, but Italian intransigence and Austrian urgency for gas produced for the Soviets a price consonant with those of other natural gas providers.[75]

Meetings continued at a stubborn pace and the rest of the deal fell into place through the spring of 1968. The next task was to arrange for a price on the pipe, for which Osipov requested preemptively that VÖEST make a rational argument (*gramotno argumentirovat'*), meaning, one following basic market claim-making.[76] At once dangerous and irresistible, the Austrians found themselves trying to amend the deal before it was even realized. Soviet gas seemed to kickstart a doomsday clock, ticking away to the end of in-kind payments and trade balancing. The Soviets had been flexible in the past, and they were ready to hear out all Austrian proposals even then, but their first reaction to any talk about payment for gas imports after all loans had been repaid was to put the exchange on a dollar basis. Gas imports, in other words, would overwhelm clearing

[74] Ibid., l. 87.   [75] Högselius, *Red Gas*, pp. 62–66.
[76] RGAE, f. 413, op. 31, d. 2293, l. 7.

accounts by the mid-1970s, and the Austrian government was desperately trying to put ad hoc arrangements in place to postpone this presumed calamity. Their main play was to either sell more pipe or auxiliary
equipment around the immense pipe-laying project the Soviets would be
engaged with for years – and to keep the Soviets paying for all this in gas
beyond the initial loan.[77] But their negotiating position was weak. The
finance VÖEST had arranged was quintessentially of the Bretton Woods
regime, which is to say, arranged through private bank lending to
national firms and tied to the purchase of pipe, with the only distinction
that it ran for longer than the Austrians would have liked. The Soviets
should have been satisfied with their achievements in establishing the fact
of the gas-for-pipe deal, but must have been disappointed with the
financing terms; they ruminated out loud in Austrian presence that they
hoped to entice even better financing terms from Italy by offering the
Italians the chance to deliver equipment, especially if "Italian credit is
offered by banks through the government and we have the chance to use
it at our discretion."[78] The task of stretching and refashioning the institutional arrangements of Bretton Woods would have to wait for the
Italians. The best they could offer the Austrians was to consider using
any credit left on the account after the purchase of all the pipe on other
Austrian goods, always as long as the price on that pipe was low enough
for money to be left on the account. They could offer less than nothing,
in other words; for now, and as that price and finally the financing fell
into place before the summer, the Soviets were already thinking beyond
Austria. They were now thinking about liberated capital, and how it
could be internationally allocated in all the ways the Austrians dreaded.

****

The end of this long, breakthrough negotiation for Soviet gas was not
an end at all; it was the beginning of an imbricated laying of a continental
energy infrastructure that accumulated ever larger political assemblages
and allowed for the intensified social transformation of Western Europe,
along with the normalization of ever-increasing flows of international
finance. This is to say that in setting finance into motion and while
continuing to do so over the next couple of decades, it was a vector of
political power. And power's agents were drawn to it like a light in the

---

[77] And to involve more Austrian firms in the feeding frenzy. Ibid., l. 3. The Austrians
would continue trying after the deal was signed on June 1, 1968, for example in an
October 1968 meeting in which VÖEST offered 360,000 tons of pipe a year after the end
of the loan, in ibid., ll. 44–45.

[78] Ibid., ll. 3–4.

night. Austrian State Secretary for Nationalized Industry Josef Taus barely waited a few months from the signing of the deal on June 1 before making a wide-ranging, state-level – rather than firm to ministry level – tour of the Moscow bureaucracy to see about expanding the deal's prerogatives, in volume, time, and technological assortment. In what was to be one of the first bilateral joint commissions on economic and scientific-technical cooperation that would soon proliferate and play an important role in mediating the economic relations of the Soviet Union and its traditional partners, Taus wanted for the Soviet–Austrian commission a subcommittee to focus exclusively on gas supply arrangements.[79] The Austrian State Secretary wanted more, an easy but now necessary political action on behalf of his industrial constituents.

The gas-for-pipe deal stipulated that the Soviet Union would deliver gas over a twenty-three-year period. The Austrians would receive a small amount of gas already in 1968, an amount that would slowly increase until 1971, when the new dedicated pipeline would come into operation and deliver gas straight from Siberia at 1.40 bcm annually, for a total of 30 bcm. The Soviets would borrow just over $100 million to pay for half a million tons of pipe for the construction of that dedicated pipe; all of the pipe would come from Germany, half of which would use Austrian steel, which itself would use Soviet inputs of iron and coking coal.[80] This amount would actually be paid within the first seven years of the agreement. From 1975 to 1990 the Soviets demanded US dollars in the first instance, although they were willing to consider other proposals, as we have seen. Importantly, this deal of itself did not at all guarantee that the gas pipe to Western Europe would in fact be built. Without Italy, France or, it would later transpire, Germany, the contract signed on June 1 remained uncertain, despite its legally binding nature. After all, the pipe the Soviets had just secured was about one-third to one-quarter of the amount they calculated they would need to build the pipeline.[81] And yet Taus was right there in Moscow, asking the Soviets whether Austria could simply continue paying the Soviets in pipe after the loan was repaid by 1975 – which is also to say years after the operative pipe itself was supposed to have been built. The time delay would be useful for Austria; Taus was suggesting that his country, which lacked pipe-making

---

[79] In ibid., ll. 39–43, in a meeting on October 11, 1968, with Deputy Chairman of the Council of Ministers Nikolai Tikhonov. Tikhonov relegated the work to Osipov, who also met with Taus that very same day and promised to study the proposal; he also used the occasion to push once again for a transition of their bilateral trade to hard currency. Ibid., ll. 36–37.

[80] RGANI, f. 5, op. 61, d. 265, ll. 43–44.   [81] RGAE, f. 413, op. 31, d. 2293, l. 41.

capability at the time, could build a factory dedicated to the manufacture of wide-diameter pipe, but only if the Soviets could guarantee demand.[82]

We do not yet have the evidence to know whether the Soviet focus on Austria was a strategic decision to move the price higher, or whether the Soviets shifted their attention from Italy because they genuinely balked at proceeding from the extraordinarily low price the Italians proposed. It could have been chance or judiciousness, or inasmuch as both motivations are not exclusive, serendipitous. But the firm, even bold contract with a country that could not ultimately underwrite the project and bring it to fruition lays bare what the project was at its core: It was speculative. In every sense of the word, it was speculative. It sought to materialize in energy, steel, and machinery the kind of financial relationship they had long sought to have with the West. The pipe would produce and reproduce an endless relationship to time that would have the potential to put an end, at any moment of Soviet choosing, to the barter-like trade account balances of the Bretton Woods era. The creation of debt, etched into the durability of an immutable infrastructure and a nigh-irrevocable energy dependence, would finally allow the relationship to acquire a temporal quality it had so far lacked. Barter had been – always is – a relationship delimited by the time required to produce it, and discontinuous by nature, with no reproductive mechanism other than an always precarious sociopolitical will to continue it – this makes barter a favored practice of, for example, strangers or distant relations who prefer to keep the relationship that way and maintain autonomy.[83] Barter, in other words, was often a way to avoid relations of mutuality, trust, and responsibility. In this adverse context, the Soviets had developed list-based political commitments to temper barter's ever-existing possibility of disconnection, and that had made the Soviet Union's relative ostracism from global exchange easier, particularly in the first decade of Bretton Woods before list-based commerce became routine. What would cement that ongoing debt-based relationship was not diplomatic goodwill or geopolitical calculation, but capitalization, the language, logic, and practice of which was as commonplace in the West as it was in the East.

---

[82] Ibid., l. 40. They did not relent through 1969, when they kept pushing the same, for example RGAE, f. 413, op. 31, d. 2974, ll. 10–12. They were perhaps right to rush the Soviets into more contracts before the Soviets liaised directly with Germany. By June 1969, the Soviets were putting the Austrians off until the promising situation with Germany had clarified. See RGAE, f. 413, op. 31, d. 2974, ll. 13–14. By August Austria's fears had come true, in ibid., ll. 27–28, and by October these had been transmuted into fears that the Germans were getting a price 20 percent below the one the Austrians negotiated, in ibid., ll. 33–34.

[83] Caroline Humphrey, "Barter and Economic Disintegration," *Man* 20:1 (1985).

That common tongue, as well as the concord and agreements it sanctioned, brought forth the transformation of speculative endeavors, of unpredictable futures, into value in motion in the present. It brought 1971 down to 1968; it made of 1975 a potential construction site for a pipe factory Austria had had no reason to ever consider; it laid a claim on each other's kindly relations every year until 1990; and it laid the foundation of capital flows that were now set to accumulate in a world without end, without phases or fruition, a world made of mere growth, and a "desire for the further expansion of relations," as the phrase went. This meant the introduction and intensified use of financial departments and agents in the conduct of economic diplomacy; they would slowly replace the agents of industry that had governed exchanges when exchanges meant barter.[84] For as the KGB reported of a meeting between Klaus and West German Chancellor Kurt Kiesinger in 1969, it seemed to the Austrian chancellor possible now to develop "a deep economic relationship based on mutual trust with the Soviet Union and the other socialist governments."[85] Depth here was a temporal category rather than a spatial one, and finance would do the drilling.

The deal had another effect that the Soviets had long desired. It finally overcame the inclination of the Austrian state to govern the relationship through account clearing and transition to one based on hard currency. The gas-for-pipe agreement had been negotiated independently of the new five-year trade agreement, per Soviet insistence. And it had overwhelmed it. As the financial configurations of their relationship werereconsidered in order to organize the new infrastructure bond, opportunities among Austrian businesspeople multiplied to participate in the consumption of the future that the intensifying financial flows opened up.[86] And if Austria had literally energized the East–West relationship by becoming the gate through which the energy would flow, did it not follow that financiers would come to flutter around it? A light in the

---

[84] It was at this point that Minister of Finance Vasilii Garbuzov became a regular member of the economic diplomacy between Austria and the Soviet Union, where he casually adopted the phrase quoted above, in RGANI, f. 5, op. 61, d. 265, ll. 41–44. Contrast this with his unusual involvement in 1968 in an eccentric insurance scheme for which the Soviets created a joint stock company in Austria a decade before and which by this time required Garbuzov's involvement to convince the Austrian finance minister to allow that Soviet company to expand the kinds of insurance it could offer, as laid down in RGANI, f. 5, op. 60, d. 230, ll. 59–65.

[85] RGANI, f. 5, op. 61, d. 570, ll. 20–23. Meaningfully, this meeting took place in the midst of Austria's insertion into a special relationship with the common market the Soviets opposed.

[86] RGAE, f. 413, op. 31, d. 3641, l. 1.

night. The Austrian Bank for Foreign Trade, for example, formed just as the ink was drying on the agreements that would make Austria's speculative deal into a driving material future. Despite its name, however, this was to be a private bank attracting capital from West Germany, France, Francoist Spain, and as far afield as the United States.[87] The objective, the bank's organizers announced to the Soviets, was to develop and strengthen relations with socialist countries and finance imports from the socialist bloc and deliveries of large projects that cannot be financed by one country.[88] The pipeline had shown the way, and the banks had financed it. Why wait for ÖMV, VÖEST, or any large industrial concern to organize another chance at rendering material an expansion of the capital they commanded? Bankers everywhere asked themselves: Why not organize the conduit for expanding their social power and international reach themselves? After all, there was no expression of limits or exception in the organizational language of the infrastructure that the Soviets and the Austrians had agreed to cooperate on; there was only growth.

This process of replacement whereby banks took over from industry as organizers of international exchange may have started at this moment, but it took time. Meanwhile, the growing quantities of energy quickly rendering coal and its miners socially immaterial in Western Europe required a buildup of capital in quantities that seemed to outstrip the growth possibilities of material exchange. This contributed to the elevation of finance as the vehicle for economic expansion, just as it regularized finance's ally, the Soviet Union, as a ready solution for what was coming to be understood as an energy crisis. In January 1970 the United States announced to its allies at the Organization for Economic Cooperation and Development (OECD) that, with consumption rising, they would soon lack the spare capacity to ramp up production in case of an oil embargo.[89] This had been precisely the scarcity-making power the Texas Railroad Commission had wielded for three decades, only just frustrating another attempt from the Middle East in 1967 to impose an embargo in the wake of the Six-Day War – or in other words, an attempt to strip off the power to create scarcity that had traditionally been held in the United States, and had generated the possibility for the Bretton

---

[87] See also RGAE, f. 7590, op. 17, d. 268, ll. 20–22, for Bank für Gemeinwirtschaft announcing its participation as early as January 1968.

[88] Ibid., ll. 8–9.

[89] Rüdiger Graf has again reminded us of the fact that the energy crisis was not born all at once in the waning weeks of 1973, but had in fact been anticipated for many years before the oil embargo, in *Oil and Sovereignty. Petro-Knowledge and Energy Policy in the United States and Western Europe in the 1970s* (New York: Berghahn Books, 2018), chapter 2.

Woods regime in the postwar era. A new epoch was coming, and in 1970 its material basis was still uncertain. This was the context within which the Soviets became partners, arbiters, and fixers, commanding liberated capital and a degree of refracted power that inhered in the US dollar they could now accumulate but never produce. The Soviet Union was a moon to the American sun.

The convulsion that produced the energy crisis was not only a matter of postmodern perception; it was material. When ÖMV went to Moscow cap in hand to plead for more oil, the firm did so because it was physically short of supplies for 1970 and failed to secure more than half a million tons of oil and oil products.[90] ÖMV had never pleaded before, and now it was appealing to their decades-long partnership, targeting Osipov directly and bypassing Soiuznefteeksport's (SNE) head V. E. Merkulov because the latter had promised to consider the request only after the next month. ÖMV needed an answer before next week, when they were due to present the country's energy balance to the government. The company came bearing a gift, US cash on the nail; and it came bearing an oblique threat: It was being blamed in the press, as a state company, for not being able to reliably maintain the energy balance in the country. There had long been calls for the state monopoly to be taken down a peg; the Soviets, it was left unsaid, might end up losing a reliable partner were they to remain passive.[91]

The Soviets answered this plea in the usual way, by noting that they could hardly keep up with domestic consumption and would not be able to free up crude for Austria. But they wanted to help, and when they suggested that they could put ÖMV in touch with Egyptian oil authorities and mediate a transaction, two processes suggest themselves. First, the Soviet Union's long-standing commitment to the promotion of international trade during the Cold War years of their US dollar ostracism meant that they had developed – through barter and eventually ruble-denominated debt – an important network they could now activate for the benefit of their dealings in the West. Doug Rogers has suggested the term Petrobarter, for which extensive use in the Perm region in the postsocialist era he traces antecedents in the Cold War period, particularly the 1950s and 1960s.[92] The second process at work here involves the acceleration in the shifts these relations experienced as the energy crisis and its twin in the

---

[90] In a meeting on July 29, 1970, RGAE, f. 413, op. 31, d. 3641, ll. 10–12.

[91] Ibid. The forceful pleading and argumentation seemed to have worked. Osipov promised to give an answer within ten days, though he was sure they would not be able to find the 300,000 tons of crude the Austrians were requesting.

[92] Douglas Rogers, "Petrobarter: Oil, Inequality, and the Political Imagination in and after the Cold War," *Current Anthropology* 55:2 (2014): 131–153. With respect to the Global

financial world began redrawing relations and practices that had barely had time to establish themselves in the back half of the Bretton Woods era. This would not be the last time the Soviets would offer Egyptian oil; it was, after all, a useful way of upgrading Soviet debt into hard currency. And yet it transpired that ÖMV had already been offered Egyptian oil through "other sources," but the company had turned the offer down for technical reasons having to do with the nature of Egyptian oil.[93]

In the end, the Soviets scrounged from under the sofa cushions of its economy 200,000 tons of crude out of the 300,000 tons the Austrians had requested.[94] Within two years, this new energy fixer role the Soviets came to occupy helped transform an older language of commercial ethics concerning reliability and mutual benefit to one that pressured, not for more trade per se, but for more dollar-denominated trade. Years before the emergence of the petrodollar made its global supply abundant, its demand – and the acquiescence with which these forceful demands were met in the context of energy insecurity – was wrecking the financial system as it existed under Bretton Woods. The petrodollar resolved a demand for Eurodollars the energy regime change had both intensified – because of the infrastructure building it required – and itself supplied – because of the intensified lending. Eurodollar money was created with every borrowing of uprooted US dollars, which only ended up creating new deposits somewhere else in the Eurodollar market, contributing to the astonishing growth contemporaries so often noted.[95] The Eurodollar market was not being fed by US deficits and banks drawing dollars out of the regulated US banking system, but rather through processes such as the one the Soviet Bank for Foreign Trade suggested to banker Walter Hesselbach, president of Bank für Gemeinwirtschaft – in a searching discussion for ways of financing part of the $30–50 million US dollar West German tranche of the Fiat deal.[96] Hesselbach would mobilize $3 million to be deposited with the Soviet bank, which would go to pay for whatever machinery the Soviets needed. These German earnings would end up in a second German bank, giving that second bank the chance to make another bout

---

South, the barter aspect of that term was ultimately sufficient for the generation of that extra-dollar exchange network.

[93] RGAE, f. 413, op. 31, d. 3641, l. 11.   [94] Ibid., l. 1.

[95] The classic explanation of money creation by banks is James Tobin, "Commercial Banks as Creators of Money," in Deane Carson, ed., *Banking and Monetary Studies* (Homewood, IL, 1963). This is in contrast to the idea that the Eurodollar market was somehow being fed by US deficits and banks drawing dollars out of the regulated US banking system. A cogent explanation of this money creation process as internal to the Eurodollar market itself is Milton Friedman, "The Euro-Dollar Market: Some First Principles," *Federal Reserve Bank of St. Louis Review* 53 (July 1971): 16–24.

[96] RGAE, f. 7590, op. 17, d. 268, ll. 23–24.

of Eurodollar lending. The Soviet Union's vast energy infrastructure undertakings helped produce the Eurodollar market.

At the center of the financial maelstrom were insistent refusals to deal in anything other than US dollars, refusals like the one Manzhulo dealt the Austrian ambassador in Moscow in October 1971. Acceptance of hard currency exchange had been quickly regretted in Austria. A quarter to a third of transactions with the Soviets were still being carried out in schillings, while the rest were denominated in other hard currencies set to appreciate against the US dollar in the medium term – the deutsche mark foremost among them. Manzhulo's response was in the ironic tone the Soviets had polished to an art form: He politely inquired "whether the Austrian side had raised the issue of switching to payments in Austrian schillings with other partners like West Germany, France, and the United States."[97] The longer explanation the memo of Manzhulo's conversation renders is much more revealing of the issues the Soviets themselves would be dealing with as a consequence of their success in the decades-long efforts for access to liberated finance and the US dollar:

He explained that all trade organizations are autonomous and fully responsible for all the risks associated with the currency terms of their contracts. Therefore, they have the right to conclude contracts in any freely convertible currency. He said that in the context of the ongoing currency crisis, when there was no capitalist currency that would guarantee both parties to a contract against risk, the trade organizations, naturally, cannot experiment with changing the currency of payment. He further pointed to the technical difficulties in translating price quotations, especially with fluctuating exchange rates, and the limited circulation of the Austrian Schilling in international settlements.

He said that in view of the above, the Ministry [of Foreign Trade], and in particular its foreign exchange department, could not recommend the use of the Austrian schilling or any other hard currency in valuations. He suggested that trading partners should decide on a case by case basis which currency to accept as payment. He therefore asked [the ambassador] not to insist on any changes in payments, especially in the midst of a currency crisis.[98]

[97] RGAE, f. 413, op. 31, d. 4394, l. 4.
[98] Ibid., l. 5. Describing the all-union associations that acted as departments of the Ministry of Foreign Trade as autonomous seems disingenuous. In 1969 they offered a French dignitary an interesting rationale for this designation as it related to one of those associations, Soiuznefteeksport. It was, they said, a juridical entity based on the principle of cost accounting (*khozraschet*), and so makes decisions strictly on that principle, in RGAE, f. 413, op. 31, d. 3020, l. 106. What is interesting here is less whether it was true – it mostly was, except when it was not – but in the Soviet appeal to market principles in order to accrue authority for its positions and institutions.

Austria and the Soviet Union were careening toward uncertainties developed in the very realization of their separate ambitions. The Austrians guaranteed for themselves a competitively priced, reliable source of energy with which to continue shifting their energy regime; the Soviets could now press for US dollars almost on demand, limited only by their own sense of diplomacy and neighborliness. And neither party could predict when the values around which they were developing this deeper relationship might suddenly lurch into new configurations. The speculative norms they had jointly liberated in the material form of a long gas pipe seemed to deliver a spatial solidity to a relationship that had, in effect, been rendered temporally fragile. In time, parties other than the states and industrial firms that had executed the project would reap the benefits.

4 West Germany
Betrayal, Stagnation, and the Triumph of Capitalization

In the era before political risk consultancy put a number on sovereign credibility, the Soviets had learned that West Germany was unreliable. The country had been bullied by the United States into breaking contracts that would have transferred large quantities of energy resources from the Soviet Union to West Germany in exchange for the wide-diameter pipes that would be needed for this transfer. The veto would be in place for five years. The West German state had followed that up with restrictions on the number of licenses issued to German companies to import Soviet goods. And, for good measure, it had raised tariffs.[1] So had the relationship gone since 1962, "tied to the conduct of a revanchist political course by the West German government," a later Soviet report explained, filtering outrage through the well-worn language of the World War II experience.[2] And so would it continue for the next half-decade.[3] Illustrative was the operative agreement that regulated exchanges between the two countries through the 1960s: Whereas such agreements had been renewed with every new trade list drawn up between the Soviets and most other European countries, Soviet–West German exchange was

---

[1] See for example RGAE, f. 413, op. 31, d. 71, ll. 3–4, for complaints in 1964.
[2] RGAE, f. 413, op. 31, d. 1667, l. 106. The report dates from June 6, 1967.
[3] The German side of this story is detailed in Angela Stent, *From Embargo to Ostpolitik. The Political Economy of West German-Soviet Relations 1955-1980* (Cambridge: Cambridge University Press, 1981), among other works; the American side is recovered in Bruce W. Jentleson, *Pipeline Politics. The Complex Political Economy of East-West Trade* (Ithaca: Cornell University Press, 1986); and finally, the Soviet side was documented more recently in Oscar Sanchez-Sibony, *Red Globalization. The Political Economy of the Soviet Cold War from Stalin to Khrushchev* (Cambridge: Cambridge University press, 2014). Pace Rüdiger Graf's largely diplomatic, constructivist account in *Oil and Sovereignty. Petro-Knowledge and Energy Policy in the United States and Western Europe in the 1970s* (New York: Berghahn Books, 2018), this first attempt at a pipe-for-oil deal in 1962 shows that the deal was prompted by much more than a sudden change in perceptions of energy security in the 1970s. It is better contextualized within a longer arch of energy regime change and the waning fate of American Cold War hegemony.

still regulated by the first and only agreement and trade list the two ever signed, in 1958.[4]

It is usually said that improved economic relations followed on the heels of a politics of détente and Ostpolitik. There is no reason to believe that it was the political covenant we call détente that spurred economic relations, and one could hold that equation's inverse, that a political settlement followed an economic compulsion, with the same degree of ease with which scholars have given pride of place to the political. The question itself is not philosophical, but empirical, and could probably be addressed systematically to arrive at some nuanced explanation of the historic motor of that development. This study is not concerned with that historic problem, although it aligns with Julia von Dannenberg's conclusion that Ostpolitik was not new under the sun with the 1969 arrival of Willy Brandt and the Social Democratic Party to the chancellorship in West Germany.[5] Crucially, the narrative presented here expands the political actors involved to encompass an influential industrial lobby during Kurt Georg Kiesinger's chancellorship as well as initiatives elsewhere in Europe, and all within the context of an Eastern door that the Soviets had long kept open for all Western comers.[6] But it might be that this is not a useful question to ask. It might be better to analyze, not the terms in which something was politically expedient, but the conditions under which a certain politics becomes economically feasible.

This half-decade stagnation in that bilateral relationship produced two outcomes: a half-decade of complaints from the Soviets that added up to a full-throated promotion of liberal trade, and a radical shift in the power of capital to determine material flows in and out of the Soviet Union and,

---

[4] RGANI, f. 5, op. 63, d. 620, l. 81.

[5] Julia von Dannenberg, *The Foundations of Ostpolitik. The Making of the Moscow Treaty between West Germany and the USSR* (Oxford: Oxford University Press, 2008). Von Dannenberg critiqued this common wisdom, as this book does, mostly from a chronological standpoint, though it remains fairly hegemonic, for example in Tony Judt, *Postwar. A History of Europe since 1945* (New York: The Penguin Press, 2005): 496–503; Carol K. Fink, *Cold War. An International History* (Boulder: Westview Press, 2014): 153–156; Vladislav Zubok, *A Failed Empire. The Soviet Union in the Cold War from Stalin to Gorbachev* (Chapel Hill: The University of North Carolina Press, 2007), 210–215, and along with any other number of textbook tracks, perhaps because the detailed disentanglements von Dannenberg makes are deemed irrelevant and aesthetically muddling of a narrative in which the first social democratic party to take over a major government in postwar Europe is applying ideology to make a political innovation. When economic crisis is made to support this narrative, the reference is to the crises of 1969, when that of 1966 in West Germany is more appropriate, consonant as it is with business anxieties and documentary evidence.

[6] An example of Kiesinger's eager production of and participation in the change of foreign policy are his talks with Soviet journalists in March 1967, RGANI, f. 5, op. 59, d. 360, ll. 73–77.

connectedly, to forge political imaginaries.[7] The world Soviet trade officials argued for with West German state officials and industrialists was one in which license-less, liberalized trade, capitalized thoroughly with West German credit, created long-term commitments to continuous and ever-growing exchange. This was a global vision, so that retreat by any individual country that might decide to politicize this free exchange would simply transfer the site of exchange elsewhere within a competitive international market system. This is to say, the Soviet Union envisioned and struggled for the creation of what we now reify as the world market.

The original sin generating this ubiquitous discourse of the market with which the Soviets threatened their West German partners was of course that embargo of wide-diameter pipe. In September 1964 for example, in the middle of that stagnation in German–Soviet relations, the Deputy Minister of Foreign Trade Mikhail Kuz'min impressed upon State Secretary of the Foreign Office Karl Carstens that other capitalist countries were already providing the wide-diameter pipe the Germans were refusing to sell.[8] Rather less convincingly, the Soviets also claimed that they were producing it themselves, but this too served up a lesson in free-market exchange for West Germans to learn from: Although they could produce the pipe themselves, they wanted to buy the German-made pipe to take advantage of the international division of labor and gain time thereby.[9] For as the head of the ministry's section for trade with Western countries Aleksei N. Manzhulo told a delegation of German experts a month later, the operating principle for their bilateral trade should be the free exchange of whatever each side is interested in buying and selling.[10]

Over the next few years the Soviets continued to perform the market in conversations with state agents of one sort or another.[11] In September

---

[7] What they were up against was a German state that consistently looked to use economic linkage for particular political outcomes, most successfully in the 1955 official establishment of economic relations, which was linked to the release of German POWs and acceptance of its non-recognition of the GDR. On economic linkage as a mainstay of German foreign relations see Randall Newnham, *Deutsche Mark Diplomacy. Positive Economic Sanctions in German–Russian Relations* (University Park: Pennsylvania State University Press, 2002).

[8] RGAE, f. 413, op. 31, d. 71, ll. 18–27.   [9] Ibid., l. 22.

[10] Ibid., ll. 28–33. Manzhulo's statement of principle here follows his brief history of how Germany was at fault for the trade stagnation, which was ritually reiterated to all West German visitors. The line trickled down to the Soviet representative offices in Germany, where officials reiterated the same doleful accusation to prominent German businessmen who had little to do with the situation, for example in January 1964 in RGAE, f. 413, op. 31, d. 277, ll. 29–31.

[11] Only very occasionally did it come with a more generous acknowledgment, as Foreign Trade Minister Nikolai Patolichev observed in a September 1966 meeting with a

1966, for example, Manzhulo performed his well-practiced lecture on German unreliability for a delegation of Bundestag deputies.[12] Manzhulo's pedagogical approach had an overarching message: The market the Soviet Union had carved for itself in Europe was ultimately unmoved by German politicizations, to the detriment of German companies. So even as the German government moved since 1961 to ever stricter licensing of Soviet imports, France had done away with licensing altogether.[13] The German embargo of wide-diameter pipe had done little to slow the construction of the "Druzhba" pipeline, Manzhulo stressed, but it had hurt Soviet–German relations and, more importantly, German credibility as a commercial partner. And what is more, the German state was moving in the wrong direction. It was even then, Manzhulo said, considering the institution of a system that would insure German companies against the risk of a sudden embargo in trade with the socialist bloc. In other words, the German government was looking to encase its geopolitical prerogatives from market pressures, so that it could embargo at will without internal resistance from the German business community. So even though relations with German firms were good, Manzhulo explained, Soviet organizations could not be sure that these German companies could fulfill their contracts, and so they preferred to do business with firms from other countries like Fiat and Renault.[14]

In October 1966, in talks intended to resolve the trade tensions between the two countries – or in the Soviet formulation, "for the creation of normal conditions of trade and the recovery of trust toward West Germany as a trade partner" – the Germans had floated the idea of a partial liberalization of their trade with the Soviets.[15] This was a patchwork solution they had introduced in May of that year in their trade relations with Hungary, Bulgaria, Poland, and Czechoslovakia. But the Soviets regarded this as discrimination and wanted nothing less than the same treatment the Germans extended to their Western partners. When three months later the German ambassador announced that the German government was further liberalizing trade with the East and asked Manzhulo to render a list of goods the Soviets were particularly interested in seeing liberalized, Manzhulo countered with outrage. The Soviets would not stoop to requesting a piecemeal liberalization, he

---

Japanese business delegation, that "Japanese firms are not going to be taught commerce from us; they know it all better themselves." In RGAE, f. 413, op. 31, d. 640, l. 91.
[12] RGAE, f. 413, op. 31, d. 1119, ll. 58–61.   [13] Ibid., l. 59.   [14] Ibid.
[15] RGAE, f. 413, op. 31, d. 1667, ll. 106–108.

fumed. England and France, after all, had already liberalized 95–98 percent of their trade with the Soviets, Manzhulo estimated.[16]

The Soviets' message was clear, insistent, and ubiquitous: The market was inevitable, as was its advance to freedom. And the Soviet Union was its standard-bearer.

Soviet discursive generation of the authority of markets was coherent also with respect to the German business community. Visiting business-men throughout the second half of the 1960s were essentially recruited to lobby the German state through the ritual invocation of the pipe embargo. In September 1965, for example, representatives from Siemens were told that it was important for Soviet organizations to be "certain that the contract will be fulfilled when importing goods, especially complete equipment. However, such actions of the German authorities as embar-goes on exports to the Soviet Union of wide-diameter pipe, and the refusal by German firms to fulfill several contracts for the purchase of Soviet goods, undermined the confidence that German firms are able to fulfill any particular order."[17] In 1965 Siemens had at the very least prepared for this Soviet expression of uncertainty, reassuring the Soviets that groups of industrialists had met with the government to make sure everyone was on the same page on the list of goods that could and could not be sold to the Soviets. Even Kosygin would occasionally answer correspondence from large corporations like Krupp to remind them that the state he led would be happy to cooperate with Krupp and buy equipment for the Soviet chemical industry only if Krupp offered better, more competitive condi-tions than other firms, technically, commercially, and financially.[18] The free-market pedagogical approach to potential cooperation with the West was party line.

The tradesman Otto Wolff von Amerongen heard much the same thing, and here the archives record a case worth detailing.[19] The Soviet organization for the import of ships had contracts for eight fish-processing ships worth fifty-six million rubles, and the steel-maker Zalzgitter AG, which owned the shipyard that received the order, agreed to deliver another order for two factories for the production of high-pressure polyethylene (hard plastics) worth seventeen million rubles. It was stipulated that the shipyard or a related company would buy enough Soviet products to cover those Soviet purchases, including the sale of 1.5 million rubles worth of Soviet gasoil. However, the company refused to honor this last part of the contracted exchange alleging that the German authorities were not allowing the import of Soviet gasoil, which

[16] RGAE, f. 413, op. 31, d. 1690, ll. 59–61.   [17] RGAE, f. 413, op. 31, d. 585, l. 63.
[18] RGAE, f. 413, op. 31, d. 277, l. 55.   [19] RGAE, f. 413, op. 31, d. 585, ll. 78–81.

complicated the whole barter deal and called new ones into question. Barter had been the Soviet Union's bread and butter during the Bretton Woods years of the global dollar shortage that lasted until the end of the 1950s. The dollar glut of the 1960s had allowed for the liberalization and capitalization of ever greater amounts of trade, but with states still able to control financial flows in the mid-1960s, barter continued to be the primary mode of East–West economic exchange. The state's role in international commerce had been receding with the liberalizations of the 1960s, but paradoxically, the state's power of sabotage had grown as barter deals grew in complexity. Only the full monetization of these exchanges could expunge state prerogatives from such deals; as long as barter remained, the state could ultimately determine material exchanges in and out of the country.

One change the German state had actively encouraged within the parameters of Bretton Woods was the wholesale replacement of coal for oil as the basis of industrial society. The move in 1958 to convertible currencies that allowed for some easing of the licensing system for commercial and financial movements internationally had also coincided with the final victory of oil over coal in terms of price competitiveness throughout Europe. Finally conceding to the impetus given by the Marshall Plan at the turn of the 1950s, European states facilitated the energy regime transition to oil with unexpectedly swift results. One way to demonstrate these results is to cite Daniel Yergin's numbers for Western Europe's structure of energy consumption: Coal's provision of three-fourths of total energy use to oil's one-fourth in 1955 virtually flipped around by 1972, when oil provided two-thirds of energy consumed and coal one-fifth.[20] Another way to represent this shift as it happened in Germany would be to trace the choices made there by firms in the internationally leading chemical industry. As Raymond G. Stokes documents, the West German chemical industry continued its coal preference well into the 1950s.[21] The rise of petrochemicals, Stokes argues, was not overdetermined, and the logic for the adoption of related technologies at each of the leading companies differed widely. The adoption of petroleum meant a shift in German reliance on domestic energy resources to a reliance on foreign oil resources secured by the United States.[22] This, however, was a shift the chemical industry was

---

[20] Daniel Yergin, *The Prize. The Epic Quest for Oil, Money and Power* (New York: Simon & Schuster, 1991): 544–545.

[21] Raymond G. Stokes, *Opting for Oil. The Political Economy of Technological Change in the West German Chemical Industry, 1945–1961* (Cambridge: Cambridge University Press, 1994).

[22] The same could be said of gas, of course, which according to a Soviet report amounted to 1.6 percent of the West German energy balance in 1966 and grew relatively fast to 3.2

hesitant to undertake, as it would come under a relation of dependence on foreign trade the industry had never experienced before.

More relevant to the Soviet–German relationship was the timing of the transition, which Stokes narrows to the politically fraught period from 1957 to 1961.[23] Stokes points to the clarifying resolutions to those Cold War crises, with especial emphasis on the wall built in Berlin in 1961.[24] He might have pointed as well to the 1958 transition to currency convertibility as well as the simultaneous end to the US dollar shortage, important evolutions in the financial infrastructure that made the decision to rely on trade much easier for German business. The point is that there was a reason the 1962 pipeline negotiations happened when they did, and it was the same reason the leading American energy companies lobbied Washington to put a stop to it. From the beginning of its commitment to sources of energy other than coal, West Germany had looked to diversify away from the oligopolistic grip of the seven majors. Despite the setback of 1962, West Germany never stopped diversifying. So much so, in fact, that by 1964 they were reporting to the Soviets that Shell and Esso were in a full-scale price war to maintain their positions against upstart oil companies from the United States and Europe.[25] This presaged precisely the disorder the seven majors had met in Achnacarry to forestall in 1928. Well before OPEC took over the reins of oil pricing from the majors, these were the kinds of challenges that began to erode the Achnacarry regime in the 1960s. Bretton Woods, in turn, mitigated this erosion through the market segmentations it enforced, which insured that problems such as these would remain compartmentalized within the rigid boundaries of national economies. Meanwhile, the German energy complex more broadly forged ahead with diversification, so that in 1964, with contracts for US-dominated Kuwaiti oil coming to an end, German oil refineries went straight to Moscow to line up contracts with Soiuznefteeksport (SNE) – where pipelines could not bring red oil and gas, tankers would have to do.[26] As energy provision practices in West Germany – to avoid the market metaphor the Soviets themselves used

percent two years later, on the eve of the famous gas deals. The report from Soiuznefteeksport is in RGAE, f. 413, op. 31, d. 2985, ll. 79–85.

[23] Coal production in Germany in fact peaked in 1956, Per Högselius, *Energy and Geopolitics* (London: Routledge, 2019): 71.

[24] Stokes, *Opting for Oil*, chapter 10.

[25] Two different German oil trading companies reported this independently, which was producing large quantities of unsold oil, including oil from Romania, as well as oil bought in the Soviet Union by ENI. RGAE, f. 413, op. 31, d. 277, ll. 138–141, and ll. 142–143.

[26] Ibid., ll. 77–78. This particular West German refinery was hoping to bring in 100,000 tons of crude oil monthly by the second half of 1965.

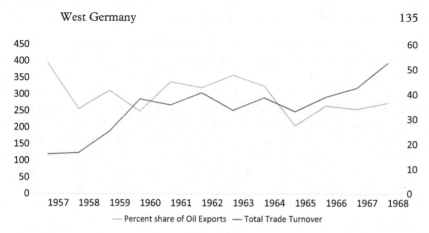

Figure 4.1 Total trade turnover with Germany and share of oil in Soviet export, 1957–1968

misleadingly – became destabilized in the transition to oil, the Soviets finally succeeded in organizing longer-term agreements of five to seven years with the variety of anxious, smaller German firms that presented themselves at their door.[27]

This diversification strategy had actually kept trade volumes afloat during the rancorous stagnation period of Soviet–West German commerce (see Figure 4.1). Without it, the record might have shown a plunge more accurately reflective of Soviet esteem for their West German partnership. The Soviets found West German state agents unreliable in their vision of a liberalized trade system, while companies remained ineffectual in bringing it about. What is more, the long-term trade agreements with which the Soviets operated everywhere in Europe had lapsed in West Germany, and some West German officials exhibited a studied satisfaction with trade as it was, without the possibility for claim-making such a document might produce; having reneged on past promises, the West Germans seemed unwilling to be held to new ones.[28] It was in the merchants of capital that the Soviet Union found ready partners for its vision. The change, it was clear, would have to be internal to the sociopolitical organization of Western countries; the Soviets could cheer on

---

[27] Interestingly a French import/export firm had presented itself in Moscow at this time to see about become an agent of Soviet oil in West Germany, lending further testimony to the fluidity of this transitionary period. That was the pull factor; the push factor, the French firm explained, was the recessionary environment in France that year. RGAE, f. 413, op. 31, d. 299, ll. 29–30.

[28] Commercial relations were "developing not badly even without an agreement," in the opinion of a visiting Bundestag member in September 1967, in RGANI, f. 5, op. 59, d. 360, l. 155.

the sidelines, complain of injustice, and prescriptively perform the market in talks while goading businesses to lobby for regulatory changes in German trade. They had suddenly inexhaustible reserves of energy, but without the infrastructures necessary for a steady supply of energy westward, this energy was of little political value. The Soviets clamored for a future in which Western states would not interfere with their economic interests. The construction of those infrastructures would constitute the realization of a global political economy inimical to the Cold War discipline the US had been able to maintain – partly through Bretton Woods structures of political economy, partly through the global deployment of its military – for two full decades.

★★★★★★★★★★

West German interest rates in the postwar period had never been particularly competitive.[29] In the Bretton Woods world of state control of capital flows, the short-term credit with which the Soviets financed all purchases in German markets, and which were set by the Bundesbank, were often above those of other European countries. Long-term credit, meanwhile, was available only through state-controlled banks.[30] The Soviet reaction was to quickly expand correspondent relations with German banks and diversify their purchases of capital in West Germany.[31] Another reaction was to routinely impress upon West German businessmen that not only were they losing orders to European competitors because of comparatively high interests, but also because of the lack of long-term credit options.[32] This was problematic not only in light of changing credit practices in other European countries, but also because of the increasing complexity of industrial imports – complete factories for example – that required longer time horizons than Bretton Woods finance could customarily support.

---

[29] The constant Soviet grumbling apparent from Soviet documents from the 1960s on this count is borne out by OECD statistical data, which shows Germany to have had the highest interest rates in the leading countries of Western Europe until the late 1960s. Germany's inversion to lower-than-average interest rates happened only in the mid-1970s. The data can be accessed in OECD Data, "Long-term interest rates." https://data .oecd.org/interest/long-term-interest-rates.htm (Accessed on May 1, 2019).

[30] As a Dresdner Bank representative explained in 1962 to the deputy chairman of the Bank for Foreign Trade (VTB), in RGAE f. 7590, op. 17, d. 268, l. 6.

[31] In ibid., to the chagrin of Dresdner Bank, whose weight by 1962 in the financing of Soviet trade fell from 30 percent to 14 percent in a few years. German interest rates remained uncompetitive almost a decade later. See ibid., ll. 34–35.

[32] For example, they formed part of the complaints in the cited meetings with Siemens and Otto Wolff in RGAE, f. 413, op. 31, d. 585, ll. 63–65, 78–81.

These temporal disparities between the requirements of physical capital formation and the organization of capital flows under Bretton Woods
was precisely what Fritz Brennekemper, vice-director of Imhausen chemical group, was trying to resolve with the German state in the mid-1960s.
The company wanted to sell oil refinery equipment to the Soviets. The
technical provision of equipment was not the problem, but the German
company could simply not offer the long-term credits necessary for such
an undertaking – specifically the construction of an oil refinery with a
capacity of twelve million tons a year with a 600 million deutsche mark
price tag. The group of German industrialists that were to provide for the
undertaking, a group that included Otto Wolff and Zalzgitter AG, used
the large order to put pressure on their government to change the
organization of credit with respect to the Soviet Union, repeatedly meeting with the ministers of foreign affairs and the economy and taking the
issue all the way to Chancellor Ludwig Erhard. In June 1965 they were in
Moscow to announce that they had created a consortium that added
Siemens, Krupp, and others to this political endeavor, and that they had
extracted from the government a guarantee for a ten-year credit.[33]

While the large industrial concerns of West Germany united to resolve
issues of international lending on an ad hoc basis, the government
continued to tantalize and delay moves toward trade liberalization with
the Soviet Union.[34] In November 1966, as negotiations with Italy over a
groundbreaking gas-for-pipe deal were reaching a first crescendo, the
West German ambassador decided to approach the Soviets "unofficially"
to see whether the Soviets were amenable to including Bavaria as a client
within the Italian gas pipe deal that had recently incorporated Austria
and France. If gas prices were acceptable, the ambassador proposed, "the
West German chemical industry would also be interested in procuring
that gas."[35] The buyer would be the Bavarian government in partnership
with a consortium of German firms that had already been formed to
negotiate gas deliveries from Algeria. The Germans were finally breaking
the impasse of 1962; after half a decade of griping, Manzhulo did not
have to spell out for the ambassador what the conditions would be were
he to inform the Kremlin about this unofficial inquiry. "The conditions
were well known in West Germany," the German ambassador winked.
Furthermore, the Austrian firms involved in the project would be buying

---

[33] Brennekemper tells the story to deputy head for trade with Western countries A. I.
Kurepov in RGAE, f. 413, op. 31, d. 585, ll. 47–48.
[34] They alleged fears among German farmers that feared competition from Soviet
products – notwithstanding the state of the Soviet agricultural sector in the mid-1960s.
In RGAE, f. 413, op. 31, d. 1119, ll. 121–122.
[35] Ibid., l. 123.

the pipe from the Germans in any case, since pipes of 48 inches and a pressure of 80 atmospheres were produced only in Germany, the ambassador told the Soviets. West Germany would be involved anyway; the country was finally ready, eager even in light of its neighbors' initiative, to establish a long-term energy relation with the Soviet Union.[36] The capital restructurings the Soviets had long hoped for were on the horizon, and they had come on the heels of the restructuring of the energy regime in a European continent that was quickly moving away from coal and the radical politics it had historically produced.[37]

In the history of international political economy, the late 1960s, and particularly 1969, was a harbinger of the collapse to come, a time of half measures. Viewed from a strictly financial perspective this was indeed so. The year 1969 was marked by a reevaluation of the deutsche mark in October as a late effort to reverse the imbalances that had been ushered by the dollar glut at the beginning of the decade. Viewed from the Kremlin and the immense reservoir of energy it controlled, however, this period looks like a much more positive inflection point in the political economy of Europe. The German ambassador had followed up his unofficial 1966 inquiries about deliveries of energy with more concrete, official ones in 1967, after the expiration of the US veto. By July he could report to the Soviets that a German company was ready to enter into a long-term contract with the Soviet oil-exporting organization under the Ministry of Foreign Trade (SNE). This particular company's twenty-year contract with Texaco was expiring, and it was now looking east for oil.[38]

Two sets of infrastructural absences are evident in this exchange, and it is important to take a minute in order to historicize them into visibility. On the one hand, the physical infrastructure that would later be at the core of the Soviet–German relationship, the network of pipelines built from the 1970s, was absent. The Soviets were finishing an oil pipeline to the Baltics, where the German company that the ambassador was recommending could pick up the Soviet oil as it once had done Texaco

---

[36] Ibid., ll. 123–124.

[37] For the undemocratic influence this change in the energy regime exerted see Timothy Mitchell, *Carbon Democracy. Political Power in the Age of Oil* (New York: Verso, 2011). See also Laleh Khalili, *Sinews of War and Trade. Shipping and Capitalism in the Arabian Peninsula* (New York: Verso, 2020), who incorporates tankers as a technology for sidelining organized labor at the docks, preceding and heralding the transformative, labor-union-undermining technology of containerization, whose useful if uncritical history is told in Marc Levinson, *The Box. How the Shipping Container Made the World Smaller and the World Economy Bigger* (Princeton: Princeton University Press, 2006). The crucial role the Soviet Union played in this change is not incidental to the political forces at play, nor to the political outcome.

[38] RGAE, f. 413, op. 31, d. 1690, l. 28.

oil, on a long-term contract.[39] Momentary constraints on their oil resources meant the Soviets were in no hurry to finalize this particular deal. But they also made it clear to the German ambassador that finding "the possibility of delivery is always possible, if we receive an interesting proposal regarding the price, conditions, etc."[40] The other absence is presaged by the fact that this was being negotiated by the German ambassador, who self-consciously acted as go-between. In other words, the infrastructure we usually denominate as the "world oil market" put simply did not exist. Timothy Mitchell has argued that this was very much by design.[41] Despite analysts' careless use of the metaphor of the market to describe the international exchange of oil, the fact is that the major oil companies that had governed this international exchange since the Achnacarry agreement of 1928 had done so through cartelized practices of quotas and instituted geographical monopolies.[42] They did everything in their power to forestall the market. This form of governance had stabilized the price of oil for three decades. Energy reconfigurations like the one the German ambassador was proposing, and which would ultimately require a pan-European infrastructural construction, was precisely the kind of micro-decision that would tear down this 1930s institution. It would not, however, usher in a world market for oil – this can only be said to have its origins in the futures markets constructed in the 1980s in New York. The managers of the cartel would simply change with the rise of OPEC.

It is not surprising that the German state, through its ambassador in Moscow, still played the role of commercial facilitator in international exchange. Within existing physical energy infrastructures, this was still a Keynesian world of trade and financial controls. Reconfiguring that physical infrastructure would require a vastly different financial architecture than the one Bretton Woods had put in place. It is this latter project, one

---

[39] Ibid.   [40] Ibid., l. 29.   [41] Mitchell, *Carbon Democracy*, chapter 2.
[42] Geographers have generated the most convincing critique of the simple demand and supply view of oil price setting. They suggest instead that scarcity is often operationally instituted and bolstered by narrative constructions of scarcity directed at managing market-driven oil gluts. See for example, Philippe Le Billon and Alejandro Cervantes, "Oil Prices, Scarcity, and Geographies of War," *Annals of the Association of American Geographers* 99:5 (2009): 836–844; and Mazen Labban, "Oil in Parallax: Scarcity, Markets, and the Financialization of Accumulation," *Geoforum* 41:4 (2010): 541–552. Taking his cue from a neoclassical economics stress on competition and the indocility of markets, Daniel Yergin tells a Schumpeterian tale of entrepreneurial heroics in *The Prize*. Equally engaging accounts that are much more accurate descriptions of power in the global oil industry are Anthony Sampson, *The Seven Sisters. The Great Oil Companies and the World They Made* (New York: Viking Press, 1975), and Antonia Juhasz, *The Tyranny of Oil. The World's Most Powerful Industry – and What We Must Do to Stop It* (New York: William Morrow, 2008).

the Soviets had been fighting for through the 1960s, that the Germans were only belatedly beginning to perceive and react to. The undertaking would require a political coalition of powerful economic actors. Among the first to recognize this were the German firms that would provide the steel and pipe technology for this vast energy restructuring, Mannesmann and Thyssen. Not coincidentally, the industry was generally suffering from low demand. Capital goods were often the first to suffer in an economic downturn, and it has long ago been noticed that exports of such goods to the socialist world rose during recessions, and subsided, relatively speaking, during boom times.[43] The industrial giants were once again looking to Eastern markets to keep afloat a production complex that would soon sink beneath the globalizing tide.

But more immediately, the Austrian firm tasked with creating the transalpine link between the Bratstvo gas pipeline in Czechoslovakia and the consumers in Austria and Italy, VÖEST, was already in talks with the two German firms for the supply of the pipe in the spring of 1967. When all was said and done, of the $110–$114 million US dollars of gas deliveries the Soviets had committed to Austria, the Austrians had estimated that only $30–$35 would be used to pay Austrian costs and profits, the rest would go to West German companies.[44] And still, on April 1, these West German industrial giants made a direct overture to the Soviets through their trade representative in West Germany, Ye. P. Volchkov, as part of the coalition-building efforts that would guarantee a prominent role for Mannesmann and Thyssen.[45] The Mannesmann representative, speaking also on behalf of Thyssen, explained to Volchkov that the credits necessary for the pipe could not be offered to VÖEST; according to German law, it had to be offered to the end consumer of the pipe, the Soviet Foreign Trade Ministry. Although this was not always followed in practice, the immensity of the deal meant that the German authorities would be very careful about the solvency of the debtor. It seemed to the Germans that the Soviet foreign trade organizations were more solvent than VÖEST, itself a state company. And yet the initial numbers for the credit could not have been very promising for the Soviets: Mannesmann's informants had the loan at 7 percent for four years, which meant repayments in cast iron, oil products, cotton, and perhaps other raw materials. This, of course,

---

[43] André Gunder Frank, "Long Live Transideological Enterprise! The Socialist Economies in the Capitalist International Division of Labor," *Review (Fernand Braudel Center)* 1:1 (1977), 108. Global South commodity production worked similarly, only to the rhythms of their commodity prices.

[44] RGAE, f. 413, op. 31, d. 2293, l. 4 and ll. 13–14.

[45] The following discussion is based on the Soviet trade representative's report of this meeting in RGAE, f. 413, op. 31, d. 1690, ll. 46–49.

compared quite badly with the gas-for-pipe deal the Soviets thought they were getting from VÖEST.

Mannesmann seemed to want above all to sow uncertainty among the Soviets that the deal, negotiated within its current political configuration, could maintain the kinds of conditions the Soviets preferred. At the time of Austrian Chancellor Klaus' visit to the Soviet Union, the Soviets had said in no uncertain terms that Bavaria, which had entrusted Klaus with asking the Soviets about possibly diverting two to three million cubic meters of gas a year its way, was to be denied any of the Soviet gas flowing west. These were the conditions that would necessitate an ad hoc set of Soviet raw materials to be exported to West Germany within a very short four years. Left unspoken was the obvious alternative: Paying the credit back in gas through the Bavarian extension of the pipeline. Mannesmann wanted the Soviets to know that gas was needed in Germany, but that given the system of private enterprise in the country, no organ had been organized to work on getting Soviet gas. Interested German firms, however, were beginning to organize themselves. In the absence of this coalition, an American engineering company had been engaged to do the prospective work and had suggested that the pipe needed was of the 36-inch variety – rather than the 48-inch diameter pipe the Germans could produce – which would guarantee that gas export capacity was enough only for Austria and Italy. Germany would then be at the mercy of Dutch and American supply. The fact that German companies had yet to organize meant that all they had was a few representatives within the VÖEST delegation talking to the different sides of the deal.[46] The petition from Mannesmann was clear. The elements for a coalition that could widen the already robust gas deal and reshape the energy and financial landscape in Europe were in place; the Soviets needed only to activate them.

At this moment of inflection, 1968, the great year of revolution, meant a delay. In their talks with German industry, the Soviets put pressure on their partners to create a gold proviso that would insure their deals against a deutsche mark revaluation.[47] In their talks with German banks, on the other hand, the Soviets expanded the networks that would help

---

[46] Ibid. The Mannesmann representative ended with a proposal for a smaller, more symbolic deal. Ten years earlier Mannesmann had gone 50/50 with the Comptoir Français de Pétrole to supply oil products in German territory bought from oil supermajors like Shell and Esso. Rather than renewing the contract, they wanted to change suppliers, and were proposing the import of 400,000–600,000 tons of oil products from the Soviet Union a year.

[47] Most bilateral meetings with West Germans in 1968 took up this issue, although the Germans usually met the request with refusal. See RGAE, f. 413, op. 31, d. 2308.

promote an international capital market and its ultimate temporal liber-ation. In the absence of pipelines and energy flows, the material vehicle in place around which the Soviets fashioned and deepened capital markets would be a Fiat. Here too it was the Italians who had broken ground with a large and complex turnkey project: a Fiat factory in Togliatti, by the Volga River. When the deal had been struck in the summer of 1966, it represented an apotheosis of the kind of industrial relations that had helped the postwar world recover from the 1930s.[48] The car factory's estimated cost of $642 million was to be covered by borrowing money from banks from the different nations that were to provide for the plant, so that only about 40 percent of it would come from Italy.[49] The rest was to be financed by West Germany, France, the United States, Belgium, Great Britain, and even Switzerland. Governments would be on hand to help lower interest rates and smooth transactions. The Fordist world that Bretton Woods nurtured had come of age.

The deal, however, also allowed the Soviets a set of claims they could make all over Europe that set the diverse money market conditions in different countries against one another. In their first approach in Germany, for example, they asked Deutsche Bank for a $90 million loan to buy equipment for the Fiat factory, but on terms no worse than the subsidized conditions of the Italian loans.[50] The terms the Soviets received for the $300 million loan from the Istituto Mobiliare Italiano (IMI) were at 5.6 percent interest for eight and a half years after the start of production at the plant. The Germans explained they could not go over eight years, and that the interest rate would have to be determined by the domestic money market, since their government was not in the habit of compensating the difference. But they had other ways to make up this difference, for example, by negotiating lower prices from the German suppliers. Half a year later, however, Deutsche Bank had to explain that the success of German finance was not in the cost of its money, which was higher than elsewhere in Europe, but in the low cost and high quality of the country's production. If the Soviets wanted to import German products, they explained, they would be better off

---

[48] "With Vaz, the long history of Soviet efforts to import American Fordism came full circle," in the words of Fordism's biography in the USSR, Stefan J. Link, *Forging Global Fordism. Nazi Germany, Soviet Russia, and the Contest over the Industrial Order* (Princeton: Princeton University Press, 2020): 214.

[49] A thorough account from the Fiat archives is in Valentina Fava, "Between Business Interests and Ideological Marketing: The USSR and the Cold War in Fiat Corporate Strategy, 1957–1972," *Journal of Cold War Studies* 20:4 (2018): 26–64.

[50] Record of conversation between Vneshtorgbank and Deutsche Bank, July 5, 1967, RGAE, f. 7590, op. 17, d. 268, ll. 12–14.

accepting bank credit rather than firm credit, which was still higher.[51] More immediately, however, the Soviets would seek competitive offers that would put pressure on Deutsche Bank, German exporters, or both in order to achieve rates that were at least nominally similar to those in other countries – which would help them in still further negotiations both in Germany and around Europe.[52]

****

Per Högselius' *Red Gas* has laid out the ups and downs of Soviet–German talks over the gas pipeline in fairly definitive detail.[53] Despite the Fiat deal's reputation as the "deal of the century," the initial 1.2 billion deutsche mark investment deal with Germany easily matches Italy's financial commitment to the Fiat plant. Commitments from other European countries and subsequent gas pipe extension deals would come to dwarf the more famous turnkey projects that European countries assembled in the Soviet Union. In fact it is difficult to imagine so many of these latter projects would have been possible without the underlying energy/capital exchange that underwrote them. Högselius' fascinating geopolitical and technopolitical account of the negotiations, largely reconstructed from German archival documents, tends to reflect German concerns, which revolved around the issue of price. With demand for gas only then ramping up, the Germans wanted to manufacture price competition so as to reduce possible monopolistic abuse by Dutch gas, and to lower imported gas prices. As Högselius documents, negotiators made continuous reference to Dutch gas, successfully bringing down the gas price the Soviets initially proffered, and eventually the price that had been negotiated with the Dutch. Soviet documents also show Germans to have this overriding concern, but they reveal two other important elements.[54] The first complements Högselius' stress on the technopolitical accretion of stakeholders that produced the pipeline,

---

[51] Record of conversation between Vneshtorgbank and Deutsche Bank, January 17–18, 1968, Ibid., ll. 15–19. The Soviets further complained about the insurance markup, which added another percentage point to the price and was much higher than in the rest of Europe.

[52] They approached at least one other bank, Bank für Gemeinwirtschaft (BfG), to get to that 5.6 percent interest mark, especially at the cost of German exporters subsidizing higher prices by taking on debt at a higher interest rate. In talks in February 1968, in ibid., ll. 20–22, 23–25.

[53] Per Högselius, *Red Gas. Russia and the Origins of European Energy Dependence* (Basingstoke: Palgrave Macmillan, 2013), mainly in chapter 7.

[54] Made with increasing stress, for example, just over a week before the start of negotiations to Soviet Ambassador in West German Semen K. Tsarapkin in RGAE, f. 413, op. 31, d. 2985, ll. 93–94.

which we have already seen included more than just regional and federal political agents and energy companies, encompassing also the large business interests from Mannesmann, Thyssen, and others that had, to a large extent, laid the groundwork earlier on.[55] The second moves us into the more important Soviet political calculation, one they stressed as assiduously as the Germans fixated on price – sometimes to German bewilderment. It is one Foreign Trade Minister Nikolai Patolichev once again called attention to on the day of the signing in Essen on February 1, 1970, where he expressed his view that the importance of the contract laid in both its "volume as well as the length of its validity."[56]

This, in effect, was a question of credit, and the reason the Soviets insisted so assiduously that bankers be an integral part of the negotiations. "Basically [the talks] will be arranged according to the Austrian model," Soviet trade representative Volchkov told State Secretary Klaus von Dohnanyi as the latter prepared to organize the German negotiating team in June 1969, "when ÖMV [the Austrian Mineral Oil Administration] and VÖEST discussed the delivery of pipes, and the linking nexus (*sviazuiushchem zvenom*) was the bank."[57] The day before, the minister of the economy of the Bavarian government, Otto Schedl, who had been key to the start of negotiations with the Soviets, had been somewhat baffled at the Soviet insistence that bankers be part of the negotiations.[58] During these heady June days, Patolichev in turn had stressed the dominating effect of the length of the contract itself, upon which lesser determinations like price would be based. For Patolichev, the significance of the deal was in the fact that "gas contracts are concluded for a long time, often no less than for 15–20 years." This implied not only the necessity of credit arrangements that could cover this new energy relationship, but also, and relatedly, "it must be borne in mind that gas supply arrangements create a stable trade relationship."[59] Or as Deputy Minister of Foreign Trade Nikolai G. Osipov pointedly told von

---

[55] One can contrast this much broader approach that views economics as politics to narrower assessments of diplomatic history that view complex and dynamic economic relations as the personal statecraft of leaders, usually referred as an "economic dimension," for example, Stephan Kieninger, "Diplomacy Beyond Deterrence: Helmut Schmidt and the Economic Dimension of Ostpolitik," *Cold War History* 20:2 (2020): 176–196.

[56] RGAE, f. 413, op. 31, d. 3652, l. 55.

[57] RGAE, f. 413, op. 31, d. 2985, l. 91. The meeting took place on June 10, ten days before the official start of negotiations in Vienna.

[58] Ibid., ll. 87–89. Schedl: "Are representatives of the banks needed for the negotiations in Vienna?"

[59] In ibid., ll. 70–72, in talks with von Dohnanyi on June 23, 1969. Patolichev was of course answering to the German's concerns over price. The document goes on to underscore that "Dohnanyi again stressed that the fundamental question for them is the price of the gas."

Dohnanyi as he tried to undermine the German's position for a low gas price in the midst of the ongoing negotiations in July, "the revenue from the sale of gas will at first be spent to pay off the purchase of West German pipes, and then to pay off a variety of German goods, and consequently this will make possible the development of exports from West Germany to the USSR on a long-term basis."[60]

The materiality of the gas itself was the critical aspect sustaining the Soviets' political goals in this venture. The comparatively large-value amount the Soviets aimed for was important, of course, and the fact that the infrastructural ambitions the Soviets had for their Siberian fields would be matched with Western piping technologies well ahead of Soviet capabilities was likewise a real benefit. But Soviet handling of Mannesmann's mutually beneficial proposals shows why the kind of relationship the Soviets were seeking could not be met simply by escalating trade volumes. Mannesmann had, in the first instance, tried to circumvent VÖEST a year earlier and appropriate the profits of a deal they would ultimately be responsible for anyway.[61] However interested in the advanced technology Mannesmann represented, or the lower prices they offered, the Soviets were more interested in establishing a template for the relationship they wanted with Western Europe: a financial flow that would take on the constancy and unidirectional motion of gas in a pipe. On May 1, on the eve of the start of the gas-for-pipe negotiations later that month, Mannesmann wanted to know what contingency plans the Soviets had for the Mannesmann pipe should the larger deal fall through. The Soviets unquestionably wanted the pipe, but were the deal to go through in its financialized barter mode, as Mannesmann was prepared to offer, it would be greatly impoverished in the eyes of the Soviets. At that point in the Bretton Woods order, banks did not even have to request a state guarantee for credit lasting less than four years, which would likely cover this medium-term exchange; and Mannesmann was ready to offer an even lower price for the pipes than the one the Soviets negotiated with the Austrians.[62] A week later Mannesmann added the full strategic panoply of the average salesman, asserting that demand was coming from the United States, from Iran, from Argentina, all willing to pay more than the price the company was offering the USSR. "He added that if it is the length of the credit that doesn't suit us," the Soviet memo records the German company recognizing, "then it

---

[60] Ibid., l. 125.
[61] As the Soviet representative in West Germany reminded his interlocutors, in RGAE, f. 413, op. 31, d. 2985, l. 14.
[62] Ibid., ll. 13–15.

is technically possible to make it so that after three years and ten months from the date of completion of pipe delivery, Vneshtorg [*sic*, probably the Bank for Foreign Trade] transfers the amount of the debt to the bank in Germany, and the latter returns it back, and the repayment deadline is pushed back another 47 months."[63] But the Soviets were resolute; the pipe was linked to the gas, to its much longer delivery schedules and its underlying technopolitical infrastructure, all of which made the venture politically intelligible for them. The Soviets would have had an easy time accommodating a simple pipe deal within the annual trade lists – more the financialized barter of yesteryear rather than the value in motion of the future the Soviets envisioned. Soviet ambition extended well beyond German pipe technology.

The spark to the negotiations was Patolichev's visit to Hanover at the end of April 1969. The Austrians had been trying since that winter to pile on greater mass to the speculative deal they had arrived at with the Soviets, and ENI was that very month trying to restart its stalled talks, afraid the window was closing on the ever more remote possibility of extracting from their Soviet partners the stringent terms they had pursued for two years. And France too had expressed interest that spring to move forward with its bid for Soviet gas. Importantly also for the West German state, an accretion of domestic interests had now reached critical mass, prompting German Minister of Economy Karl Schiller to approach Patolichev in Hanover and set the negotiations in motion. First in line was Mannesmann, as we have seen, which waited all of three days to confirm that they could indeed provide thousands upon thousands of tons of pipe even before the year was over.[64] And if only the Soviets would permit them to withdraw from their promises to Austria's VÖEST, they could follow that up with hundreds of thousands of tons sold directly to Moscow, rather than through the Austrians, over the next few years. A flurry of consultations between these assembled interests and the Soviet trade representation in Cologne lasted throughout May; State Secretary von Dohnanyi followed this at the end of that month in Moscow; in June the Soviets sent an official delegation to Vienna; and after several rounds, the deal was all but closed by the end of the summer. Here again the Soviet archival records closely reflect Per Högselius' detailed, technical narrative of the negotiations recreated from German archival sources.[65] But they also validate the conclusion presented at the Politburo on December 1 (a few days after terms were agreed to and a month after Brandt had been voted into office) that the great industrial

---

[63] Ibid., l. 23.   [64] Ibid., ll. 13–15, in a meeting on May 1.
[65] Högselius, *Red Gas*, 112–118.

concerns that had historically "gravitate[d] toward the markets of Eastern European countries" would support and pull Brandt in that direction.[66] Brezhnev knew first hand that the technopolitical coalition redrawing the energy map of Europe was wider than state administrators and gas companies.

The Germans, like the Austrians, were explicit from the beginning about the primacy of price in their approach to the deal. But so were the Soviets explicit about their goal for this deal, a goal that had clarified over the last four years since Italy first broached the idea of a gas pipeline. Even if it had only crystallized over the previous year as the ink dried on the contract with Austria, the positions were clearly delineated from the first day in late May as soon as von Dohnanyi met Patolichev. That day, the Soviet minister moved quickly to assuage von Dohnanyi's anxiety over the price – "the fundamental issue" for them; Patolichev was confident the experts could easily arrive at one that reflected the complexity of "factors that influence the market."[67] But the main thing to keep in mind even with respect to price, Patolichev wanted his interlocutor to know, was that the arrangement "creates stability in commercial relations, since contracts for gas are concluded for a long period of time, often no less than 15 to 20 years."[68]

If there is a whiff of the inevitable in the deal in hindsight, the fact was that just a couple of weeks before the start of negotiations, success seemed precarious. The head of the German oil trading firm Bochumer Mineralölgesellschaft (Bomin), who had for many years acted as intermediary of Soviet oil in West Germany and knew the country's energy landscape as well as anyone, could not say with any certainty whether the gas deal would succeed; "the current opposition to these plans, primarily from companies like Shell and Esso, is very great given their vital interest in promoting Dutch gas," he advised.[69] The political weight of the big oil majors had, after all, sunk the 1962 deal, and at the end of the decade they still provided 90 percent of the oil and gas to West Germany.[70] Moreover, the German press did not take kindly to Soviet gas, which seemed more threatening than the monopolized gas coming from Holland. Or perhaps this was merely the monopolist's despair. Mannesmann executives counseled the Soviets not to pay attention;

---

[66] RGANI, f. 3, op. 72, d. 304, l. 10.
[67] RGAE, f. 413, op. 31, d. 2985, ll. 70–72. The meeting took place on May 23, 1969.
[68] Ibid. With apologies to the readers for the repetition, but repetition was the point for Brezhnev.
[69] Ibid., l. 39, in a meeting on May 9, 1969.
[70] Ibid., l. 20. The numbers are Jos van Beveren's, the Belgian-born commercial director at Mannesmann, who used the numbers in a meeting on May 8 to likewise express how difficult it would be to elide the influence of the two companies.

this was merely international monopolies doing their best to confuse public opinion.[71] For the fact was that changes since then had gone a long way in undermining the structural power of the oil majors and the governments that served them. The world of oil they had ushered in Europe with the Marshall Plan increased consumption and profits in the same measure as it prompted consumers to undermine the suppliers' monopoly power. Still, the very start of the negotiations was threatened by a strange coyness on both sides, as each urged the other to make the first approach.[72] The matchmakers to overcome this Cold War bashfulness, however, were the who's who of West German industry and banking.[73]

It is not surprising, then, that when the Soviets finally touched base with the crucial Bavarian minister Otto Schedl, they did so at Mannesmann's Bonn headquarters, with the intermediation of its commercial director, Jos van Beveren.[74] As the two parties prepared – themselves and each other – for the upcoming negotiation, trade representative Volchkov wanted to make sure the Bavarian government understood that the deal was to be holistic, including pipes, gas, and finance; it could not be parceled out piecemeal. Volchkov insisted on this point because of its sheer novelty: "These transactions can only be considered as a single operation."[75] Schedl, predictably, moved immediately to the question of price, while daring a prediction: Imminent gas import needs in the region would reach 7 bcm. This was a prediction well above the operative numbers that Ruhrgas had felt and would feel like proffering the Soviets, lest it become a claim-making tool for the socialist suppliers.[76] Schedl would keep on the issue of price like a broken record, insisting that no permissions would be granted from the Free State of Bavaria until the price was clarified and acceptable to Bavarians. Schedl's insistence highlighted another German organizational problem; the Soviets remained puzzled on the question of who would drive this holistic deal. Large conglomerates had in the past been able to handle complex barter deals of this sort on the basis of their sheer capacity. But the financial and productive capacity here, as ENI had found earlier, was well beyond that

---

[71] Ibid., l. 21.

[72] Ibid., ll. 28–30, in the main exchange of a May 21 meeting between Volchkov and von Dohnanyi. It was also Bomin's main piece of intel, in ibid., l. 36, reported by telephone to trade representative Volchkov just before the latter met with von Dohnanyi on the eve of his departure to Moscow, at which time the German state secretary in turn had yet to receive a visa.

[73] Ibid., ll. 31–35, in the flurry of excitement before von Dohnanyi's visit included Ruhrgas and Mannesmann directors serving intel to Volchkov on May 20 and offering to broker a meeting with key Bavarian minister Otto Schedl. Mannesmann had gone so far as to arrange its own financing already with Commerzbank, in ibid., l. 76.

[74] Ibid., ll. 74–78, in a meeting on June 4, 1969.   [75] Ibid., l. 74.   [76] Ibid., l. 75.

of any single conglomerate. Meanwhile, the Soviets had difficulties to think beyond the state; only state agents could have the coordinating capacity to pull this off. The Germans, however, sent contradictory messages hinting that private actors would do much of the talking. Volchkov wanted to know "who is going to be our partner in the negotiations, considering the need to discuss the issue as a whole, that is to say, the purchase of pipe and equipment, credit, and its repayment with gas."[77] In June, Schedl had every intention of playing this role; after all, he explained, no construction in Bavaria could be initiated without the permission of his administration. Later events proved otherwise, and the confusion itself would prevail all the way to the beginning of negotiations in Vienna on June 20 and beyond.[78] Only in the final stages of the negotiations later that year would Ruhrgas's chairman Herbert Schelberger agree to limited interventions by different state ministers on his (gas) side of the negotiations with the Soviets, which he handled mostly on his own.

When everyone met in Vienna, the Soviet delegation was forced, against its wishes, to meet Schedl and Schelberger on parallel tracks. In this context, Schelberger's first instinct was to shield his own negotiating lane from any possible failure on the pipelines track the Bavarian government handled.[79] They wanted a deal, Schelberger told the head of the Soviet delegation Nikolai Osipov; whether or not Schedl approves of it, Ruhrgas would carry on faithfully with its commitments at its own risk and could even serve as a crucial connection to Gaz de France, he offered. West German companies were hungry for business from the East, in other words. The Soviets knew as much. But West Germans remained uncommitted to the holistic approach the Soviets envisioned – and its politico-financial meaning. And as many analysts have done since, Schelberger mistook Soviet intentions. The Soviets were not merely looking to earn hard currency, not even primarily to do so; they were looking for a new relationship to financial time through infrastructure building; they were looking for a delay to reposition the country in the global economy; they were looking for a means to help private banks generate new international money that could no longer be denied them, and with which they could better control future international allocations of labor and energy, what economists often abstract with the term "investment." This could not be constructed through institutional mechanisms as they existed then. However, the ongoing redeployment of energy that concentrated political power and insulated it from labor demands gave the Soviets the political window they needed, even as this

---

[77] Ibid., l. 76. [78] Högselius, *Red Gas*, 113–114. [79] Ibid., ll. 95–98.

purpose was obfuscated through the very material task of constructing new, resilient infrastructure. The resilience of the infrastructure under negotiation was as much a physical quality as it was political. Moreover, all of it was subsumed under ideologies of growth and binary distinctions between the material and immaterial that obscured and confused ends and means, such that finance appeared as means, while consumption and trade growth seemed its purpose.[80] And this is how, despite all the preparatory excitement, the perplexed and perhaps somewhat deflated Osipov had to ask on the very first day of talks whether Schelberger understood the full spectrum of the deal, which went well beyond gas and included pipe and an emphasis on credit: "The more gas is sold, the easier it will be to pay for the loan and lower the transportation costs of the gas," Osipov tendered.

The next evening, it was Schedl's turn; that meant discussing the gas price.[81] In fact, it took this first ten-day round of negotiations, and the next one in Cologne in July before real progress on the question of price was achieved, while everything else took a backseat. The Germans complained bitterly to one another that this should be so. Per Högselius has recovered from the German archives the self-righteous tone of their irritation, drawing as it did from a well of Western self-conceptions produced by binary Cold War thinking, rather than even minimal self-reflection. It was in this mood that von Dohnanyi reported to Economic Minister Schiller that it had "not yet been made sufficiently clear to the Soviets that they arrive with their natural gas in an intensely competitive market and that the price conceptions presented by the German side are justified."[82] In fact, as with all European partners, the common discourse around which the negotiations revolved was that of the market. This insistence on market discourse was not produced because "the market" framed the kind of objective reality that could serve as a linchpin in the negotiations, but precisely because no market existed to anchor this prospective material relationship. Rather than sound "price conceptions," the Germans had spent the lead up to the negotiations stressing the fact that they wanted Soviet gas to flow into West Germany to initiate the creation of a market that could discipline the monopoly of Dutch gas and the Anglo-Saxon oil majors that stood behind it. Or as Schelberger had explained more openly on the first day, "Dutch gas had already

---

[80] On the relation between infrastructure and finance, and the way infrastructure renders the delay finance needs to bring future values forward into the present, see Timothy Mitchell, "Infrastructures Work on Time," in New Silk Roads, *e-flux Architecture* (January 2020), www.e-flux.com/architecture/new-silk-roads/312596/infrastructures-work-on-time/.

[81] RGAE, f. 413, op. 31, d. 2985, ll. 99–100.   [82] Quoted in Högselius, *Red Gas*, 115.

reached the southern regions of West Germany, and in the presence in northern Bavaria of a gas distribution company under their control, Ferngas Nordbayern GmbH, will make it possible to obtain gas from two sides."[83] Their more immediate task now, however, was to discipline the Soviets, which no doubt had been the reason for stressing the Dutch presence in northern Bavaria. It was also the reason for insisting that heating oil was the real market-maker in Bavaria, and that this was the natural benchmark for Soviet natural gas.[84] German market sanctimony notwithstanding, the Soviets in fact understood market discourse as well as anyone, and countered the Germans by pointing to Dutch gas prices in West Germany and Soviet gas prices in Austria. Market discourse was capacious.

To state agents, on the other hand, the Soviets complemented their insistent adherence to market discourse with other discursive tools. The strict and quintessentially Soviet separation of economics and politics, performed discursively as much as institutionally, was one they used when confronted with highly politicized negotiations on trade and finance, as had often been the case over the course of the 1950s and 1960s.[85] By the late 1960s, routine economic intercourse had more or less obviated earlier sanction regimes tied to economic linkages, and the Soviets relished the chance to make more positive linkages to interlocutors who could be motivated by them, that is, state officials like Schedl. In talks between him and Osipov, the Soviets stressed not only the greater independence from Dutch gas that would accrue to the region, but also the extent to which the proceeds from the gas would purchase German goods, which would have a "colossal economic effect."[86]

As positions grew closer through July and August and this movable feast of technocrats traveled to Cologne and then Moscow, claim-making grew more technical, but always ultimately commoditized within the monetary sovereignty of the US dollar that ruled over the prospective transformation of the Soviet–German relationship. The translation of all

---

[83] RGAE, f. 413, op. 31, d. 2985, ll. 95–96.

[84] Ibid., l. 113. Shelberger had a system: If heating oil's price went up or down 3 percent, the price of gas remained the same; if 3.5 percent, then there would be an automatic change to the gas price; anything over that would prompt new negotiations. These, he offered, concerned 80 percent of the price, while 20 percent would remain unchanged according to whatever price was established then..

[85] A prime example is the negotiations for the first long-term trade agreement with West Germany in 1957, in Sanchez-Sibony, *Red Globalization*, 96–101. The German side of the deal was covered in Robert Mark Spaulding, *Osthandel and Ostpolitik. German foreign trade policies in Eastern Europe from Bismarck to Adenauer* (Providence: Berghahn Books, 1997).

[86] RGAE, f. 413, op. 31, d. 2985, l. 105.

qualities into US dollars and its subsidiary, the deutsche mark, was unremitting. Kilocalories, which it turned out Soviet gas had too much of, requiring conversion to less calorific gas, were transmogrified and made part of the price. Atmospheric pressures were translated into cents per cubic meter, while arcane links to heating oil subdivided price values so that half of the gas price could oscillate around it while the other half moved up and down according to prices of gas negotiated elsewhere in Europe.[87] Transport costs and possible gas transmission volumes were similarly mobilized. And all the while the Dutch company NAM, and the practices it had invented to navigate the non-market environment within which it had established its production and delivery systems, served as authoritative reference as it suited one side or the other. This, then, was "the market" before which all agents genuflected, and through which all struggled to develop authority.

This intense international collaboration to engender the commodification of Soviet gas slowly generated a numerical value amenable to interpretation by financiers and the social substance they produced: US dollar-denominated debt. The fact that finance today works in strictly hierarchical fashion is somewhat masked by the ease with which people can exchange currencies or draw them out of automatic teller machines, rendering horizontal what is in fact a power vertical.[88] In this the Bretton Woods era was more straightforward; a nation's money exchangeability, a national money's ability to interface with societies outside its own, rested on the extent to which there was a large enough reserve of US dollars behind it. And in this global hierarchy of power, few currencies had attracted as large a reserve as the deutsche mark, which in fact had undergone a revaluation in an attempt to slow down the accumulation of US dollars in the country. Unlike Austria or Italy, in other words, West Germany had the capital resources and the productive capacity to render

---

[87] Much of this was covered in ibid., ll. 107–117, covering the Cologne round that took place over a week in mid-July. The 50/50 link to heating oil and gas, in ibid., ll. 115–116, represented a change from a month earlier, when Schelberger had offered 80/20 respectively. On the issue of calorie values, Soviet gas had a calorie value of 9,200 kilocalories, while the German gas network functioned on 8,400 kilocalories, as discussed in ibid., l. 111. Ruhrgas also wanted consumption and payment to be assessed monthly and paid biweekly, as was the practice with NAM, in ibid., l. 112. Since Vienna, the Germans had also raised the pressure of gas circulation from 40 to 50 atmospheres, but without any offsetting change in price, despite the increased costs for the Soviets, discussed in ibid., ll. 113–114.

[88] On the hierarchy of international money and the hybridity of its power in the nexus between state and private banking see Perry Mehrling, "Essential Hybridity: A Money View of FX," *Journal of Comparative Economics* 41:2 (2013): 355–363, and Katharina Pistor, "From Territorial to Monetary Sovereignty," *Theoretical Inquiries in Law* 18:2 (2017): 491–517.

the financial delay and the spatially ambitious mobilization of energy the Soviets sought from the pipeline infrastructure. I mention this in part because there is no archival evidentiary trail available at the moment to understand why, as the parties moved to Moscow to negotiate two weeks after Cologne, the Soviets suddenly acquiesced to German prices that were well below those they had negotiated with Austria, and those they had maintained for almost two months.[89] Despite all the West German grumbling, they were also below those that Schedl felt Bavarians could accept and still find profitable.[90] So perhaps it has to do with that power of West German capital to make real what the capital of other nations could only render prospective, a synchrony of mobilization and delay. Faced with the power that inhered in West German capital, reflecting like the moon the sunrays of the US dollar, the Soviets opted for realization over profit, for the actuation of a system that would open access to the American world of global money creation rather than risk it on the insistence of a larger trickle of hard currency.

Or perhaps what was being realized for the first time was that market of German design, yielding market discipline years before the product could even be consumed. "Our aim is to sell gas at a fair market price," the weakening Osipov told von Dohnanyi in between bouts of negotiations while again pitching as large a deal as possible.[91] Or perhaps it was the disciplined and effective teamwork with which Schelberger and Schedl learned to collaborate that disarmed the Soviets.[92] For Schedl kept insisting to the Soviets that the price Ruhrgas was offering – and which Ruhrgas would later increase – was much too high and "rendered Soviet gas impossible for an array of Bavarian consumers" – even as he told his fellow Germans that the Soviet asking price, then 15 percent

---

[89] RGAE, f. 413, op. 31, d. 2985, ll. 118–119 and ll. 129–133.
[90] Högselius, *Red Gas*, 115.
[91] RGAE, f. 413, op. 31, d. 2985, ll. 123–126, Osipov: "5 bcm a year should be considered the optimal quantity, with a smaller amount it would hardly be reasonable to build such a long gas pipeline."
[92] Per Högselius seems of two minds on this count. In his collaborative writing, in Per Högselius, Anna Åberg and Arne Kaijser, "Natural Gas in Cold War Europe: The Making of a Critical Infrastructure," in Per Högselius, Anique Hommels, Arne Kaijser, and Erik van der Vleuten, eds., *The Making of Europe's Critical Infrastructure. Common Connections and Shared Vulnerabilities* (Basingstoke: Palgrave Macmillan, 2013), 35, Schedl is said to have been on the losing end of a power struggle against Ruhrgas that sidelined him; however, in *Red Gas*, 116, Schedl remains integral to all negotiations and even learns to collaborate with Ruhrgas's Schelberger. This last interpretation makes better sense of the negotiations' reflection in the Soviet archives. However, even if Schedl did not share the same fate, Högselius, Åberg, and Kaijser's collaborative narrative seems accurate in noting the extent to which Bayerngas lost and was sidelined in its confrontation with its powerful northern rival.

higher, was perfectly acceptable.[93] Whatever the case, the Soviets conceded to German price pressure in August, leaving a gap in the asking price and the offering price only big enough to contain a sliver of Soviet pride. It took three months to overcome that fissure of Soviet dignity, a 1 percent difference, fulfilling a frustrated Osipov's prediction at the end of August and echoing the bizarre, prideful process in the spring of waiting for the other side to take the decisive step through which both parties came together.[94] These – admittedly more than – forty days in the desert were not free from revelatory temptation. The politics in West Germany had been such that the northern and much larger Ruhrgas had been brought into Bavaria to negotiate with the Soviets, in the process sidelining Munich's Bayerische Ferngas GmbH (Bayerngas), the region's distributor. During that final contest for dignity between Ruhrgas and the Soviets, the Bavarian firm had offered a smaller but ready deal to the Soviets: They had talked with ENI's subsidiary, Snam, about building a pipeline from Austria, through West Germany to Milan and the Swiss border. The German part of the pipeline would cost $230 million US dollars, of which the two gas companies would pay $30 million while the rest would be financed by Bavaria's banks. Capacity demand would be 2 bcm for Ferngas, 6 bcm for ENI, and 0.5bcm for Switzerland, and they would pay the Soviet price Ruhrgas was refusing.[95] And then the same misconception Schelberger had fallen into back in June: If a deal with ENI does not work out, Bayerngas suggested, then the pipe could still go to Munich and they could all save a great deal of money, and economize on the diameter of the pipe in the bargain. Bayerngas promised to wait in the wings, misunderstanding Soviet intentions while confirming that a deal of this sort had gone from uncertain in the summer of 1969 to almost inevitable by winter. On November 28, the Soviets accepted the German gas price for 3 bcm per year, a volume likewise lower than the one they had worked for.[96] This was disappointing but ultimately fleeting from a Soviet point of view. The Soviets knew that the ongoing energy regime change toward gas would take care of it. They were right.

---

[93] Ibid., ll. 127–128. He also aligned with Schelberger in talking up the possibility of using Ruhrgas to link up with France and Italy, to which Osipov countered that the Italians had other ideas and that Dutch gas would be much more expensive in Bavaria. Osipov was not exactly fooled in July, but then two weeks later he dramatically acquiesced anyway.

[94] Ibid., ll. 140–145, for the late August round in Moscow.

[95] Ibid., ll. 146–147, in a meeting on October 21, 1969. It seems Bayerngas had offered an even higher price earlier.

[96] Högselius, *Red Gas*, 121.

It is no surprise and no great insight to understand that West German companies were thinking about the near term and the bottom line, and that this contrasted with the Soviet state and the political work they expected this infrastructural deal to perform. A report discussed at a Politburo meeting on Monday December 1 had not anticipated the conclusion of the deal the previous Friday, but it had laid out precisely what that political work entailed:

We are talking about the conclusion of a contract that would be valid for two decades and would, to a certain extent, render dependent on the Soviet Union such an important area of the West German economy as energy. The supplies of the Soviet Union would also involve the reconstruction of some West German chemical industries to exploit new sources of raw materials, which would require large investments. As a result, the West German monopoly circles that will benefit from the gas contract (powerful firms like Ruhrgas, Thyssen, Mannesmann, etc.) are likely to put pressure on the Bonn government in terms of keeping away from steps that involve the danger of aggravating relations with the Soviet Union.[97]

The alliance with "West German monopoly circles" was a political objective, not a predicament or an ideological compromise. The Soviets wanted interdependence, time, and a change to their political relationship to Western industry, which would itself occasion energetic reorganizations of capital over there. And they paid the German price for it.[98]

****

By the time the deal had been wrapped up, the financial ecosystem in West Germany had changed.[99] In October 1969 the deutsche mark was revalued, and the Soviets were left to pay for it in higher relative prices for pipes, which were now less competitive internationally but whose volume remained on the contract. When Osipov brought this up with Economy Minister Schiller, the response was one the Soviets had heard many times: The government – which had otherwise facilitated all aspects of

[97] RGANI, f. 3, op. 72, d. 304, l. 20.

[98] The final credit, lent by a consortium led by Deutsche Bank, was for 295 million rubles for over ten years, more or less in line with what the Soviets received from the Italians on the Fiat deal, which was about half the cost of the Fiat factory in Tolyatti. They expected some 614 million rubles in revenue over twenty years just from Germany, twice as much, or about the cost of the whole of the Tolyatti plant. Of course, to this Italy, Austria, and France added their own purchases, and more importantly, on the basis of the flow, over the next few years these numbers were compounded as new demands for gas and new extensions of the pipe network piled up. For numbers on the initial deal, see RGANI, f. 5, op. 63, d. 620, l. 84.

[99] Although the agreement was officially signed on February 1, 1970, the contract had been initialed on November 29, 1969, in RGAE, f. 413, op. 31, d. 3059, l. 2.

the deal – could not put pressure on private firms to change their price.[100] This rang hollow to the Soviets, although it was a stubborn bit of German self-presentation and quite likely self-understanding; whatever else, it was useful as a strategic discourse. As even Deutsche Bank representatives often reminded their Soviet clients, the objective fact of the uncompetitive interest rates they offered was a function of this separation of state and business. Other states may routinely subsidize their banks on the kinds of big deals they occasionally struck with the Eastern Bloc, they admitted, but they could not offer low interest rates because they had to keep large sums of their reserves with the Bundesbank – never mind all the previous occasions in which the West German state had done just that.[101] According to Deutsche Bank bankers themselves, unlike British finance, German finance was not attractive for its own sake, but for what it could buy under Bretton Woods' national compartmentalizations: the best technology at relatively low prices.[102] Rather than state subsidies, West German banks in fact routinely suggested that German exporters draw from their profits in order to subsidize the interest rate to bring it down to the levels the Soviets demanded.[103] Still, they were not wrong, German banking thrived on the country's industrial competence.

This equation was precisely what the revaluation had undercut, setting the Soviets to grumbling again. And the unlucky timing of the deutsche mark revaluation only exacerbated their sulking. Just as they had successfully organized the energy and – soon – financial infrastructure that would compel West Germany into a long, voluminous material relationship with the Soviets, all German goods became more expensive and less competitive, while Soviet products purchased less German know-how and technology domestically. To console them, however, was a much more important achievement: With this deal, the Soviets had radically

---

[100] RGAE, f. 413, op. 31, d. 2985, ll. 158–160, in a meeting on November 28, 1969. Despite the deeply constructivist and historicized analysis in many other facets of the history he tells, Rüdiger Graf in *Oil and Sovereignty* accepts this misleading self-presentation of German actors at both the state and business levels, which is belied by all the ways documented here in which the German state in fact mediated for the profit of its corporations and facilitated financial arrangements, the sine qua non of energy imports, and ultimately the object of its politics. The discourse of separation was as useful for the Germans as it was for the Soviets, to be deployed when suitable.

[101] For an example of this well-practiced speech, see the talks in January 1968 in Frankfurt in RGAE, f. 7590, op. 17, d. 268, ll. 15–19.

[102] Ibid., ll. 15–16.

[103] Ibid., ll. 23–24. Speaking in the context of financing the Fiat deal: "In fact such a loan in Germany costs more than 7 percent, therefore German exporters will have to take on the 1.25 percent difference by reducing their share of the profit." Deutsche Bank had made the same suggestion in ibid., l. 17.

changed their financial prospects within Germany, Europe and ultimately the capitalist world the dollar was about to transform, or, simply, the world. A year later a triumphant Patolichev was still crowing that the gas-for-pipe deal signed a year earlier along with the ongoing support of "West German business circles" would "provide the basis for long-term cooperation between the two countries," this to visiting Germans like Gerhard Schröder – the Christian Democrat former interior, foreign and defense minister in sequential order, and on that day in January 1971 consigned to the Bundestag government opposition to the Social Democratic government.[104] In the hour of his triumph, Patolichev could not resist reminding Schröder, who had been Minister of Foreign Affairs in 1962, of the "famous embargo" that year.[105] A decade had passed, and the world had turned.

When it came down to business, however, Patolichev was back to his usual dissatisfaction. "The economic possibilities of both countries for the development of trade relations are still far from full capacity," he told Schiller on the very day of the signing in the coal and steel town of Essen in the Rhur on February 1, 1970.[106] West Germany was still artificially limiting trade, even as it had almost fully liberalized trade with Western countries, he protested. Schiller, meanwhile, returned to prospecting for Soviet oil. And so they each went back to their favorite preoccupations and expectations of each other. The agreement, with its promise of a long-term material bond between the two countries, had certainly done much to bring about the signing of the Moscow Treaty in the summer of 1970, an accord of great symbolic power that validated postwar borders in Eastern Europe and gave meaning to Chancellor Willy Brandt's détente policies.[107] The treaty in turn spurred a further West German impetus to liberalize imports from socialist countries.[108] This, Yuri

---

[104] Not to be confused with future Social Democrat Chancellor Gerhard Schröder, still only a student then. RGAE, f. 413, op. 31, d. 4407, ll. 69–71.

[105] This was a well of grievance Patolichev came back to again and again, for example, with CDU's leader Ranier Barzel in December 1971, in RGAE, f. 413, op. 31, d. 4407, l. 3.

[106] RGAE, f. 413, op. 31, d. 3652, l. 55–57. Patolichev's answer to Schiller's request for the import of five to six million tons of Soviet oil a year was equally played out, laying on Schiller the old mantra about having difficulty supplying everyone, but promising in the same breath to look for the extra oil from somewhere in the plan.

[107] A discussion of the treaty is in M. E. Sarotte, *Dealing with the Devil. East Germany, Détente, and Ostpolitik, 1969–1973* (Chapel Hill: The University of North Carolina Press, 2001): 65–71.

[108] RGAE, f. 413, op. 31, d. 3652, ll. 22–23. As per Schiller in his third meeting with Patolichev on September 25, 1970, where they also broached the creation of a joint commission that would cement and institutionalize the new, intensified economic relation. It also spurred German business to seek deals in the East, as per the August 1971 report in RGANI, f. 5, op. 63, d. 620, l. 85, which noted that the proof was that

Andropov noted from his chair at the KGB – perhaps with a certain glee – unsettled Henry Kissinger and the US State Department, who, together with some European leaders, feared the treaty would render West Germany more independent, and increase its political and economic influence over Europe as well as its economic relations with the socialist world – the very thing the United States had been able to temporarily sabotage only a half-decade before.[109] "According to Western experts," Andropov reported, "as a result of expanding economic relations between West Germany and the socialist countries, the competition between Western firms for the markets of these countries will intensify, which will also give the Soviet Union additional opportunities to exert political and economic pressure on the Western powers."[110] But the intensification of international competition was not the outcome of symbolic political reorganizations, nor did it follow greater West German involvement in the Eastern Bloc. Competitive market development was inherent to the liberalization of commerce as well as its financialization, both of which were inherent to the Bretton Woods and the Common Market projects. And it was the outcome of the work and increasing sociopolitical authority of the bankers and corporations that pushed it forward. And although it was a Western fantasy that the Soviets would use this increasing interdependence to exert political pressure, the Western analysts the KGB monitored were right to point to the fact that competitive market development was something the Soviet Union welcomed and promoted.

What these developments could not do was to improve interest rates, which were rising in Germany as Bretton Woods began to enter its terminal phase. This worried the Soviets, who saw in the creation of debt the best guarantor of long-term cooperation. As Patolichev told Schiller in September, "major deals will occupy an increasingly significant place in our relations and therefore we'd like to stipulate in the [trade] agreement the creation of credit opportunities that would be no worse than is the case in relations with other countries."[111]

The Soviets were not without strategies for circumventing the restrictions the German government applied to the finance it sponsored. Back

two large delegations of West German businessmen had been received that year by Kosygin.

[109] RGANI, f. 5, op. 62, d. 695, ll. 98–100, in a September 14, 1970, KGB report to the Central Committee. The British, the KGB informed, saw this as both a normalization of relations with the Soviets as well as West Germany's emancipation from its post–World War II constrictions as vanquished country. The French feared the Germans were trying to usurp France's position as the main Soviet partner in the West.

[110] Ibid., l. 100.   [111] RGAE, f. 413, op. 31, d. 3652, l 24.

in Germany on the day after signing the Moscow Treaty, officials from the German Ministry of Economy called Volchkov in to complain that the Soviets had been somewhat expansive in their interpretation of what constituted accessorial elements of the gas-for-pipe deal.[112] The 1.2 billion deutsche marks in credit were to be spent mostly on pipes, with only 5 percent of it dedicated to auxiliary materials and equipment necessary for constructing the pipe network. The Germans were now saying that with the last quarter of the loan still to be committed, the Soviets had in fact used 50 percent of it on these accessories, and that some of these purchases – the truck cranes or the Caterpillar pipelayers – could not even be considered accessories. In an interesting acknowledgment of the extent to which this was a continental effort, the Germans explained that the goods that fell within the accessories category had to be negotiated with their partners in the European Common Market. Another concern was that the Soviets might negotiate purchases with foreign companies like Caterpillar that had representation in Germany but did not produce there; the deal's main beneficiaries were supposed to be Germany's grand industrial corporations like Mannesmann. Even in their twilight, the agents of Keynesian finance cared for their polity. And yet the Germans were willing to be flexible. They had already "made their peace" with the Caterpillar deal and wanted to know from Volchkov whether there were instances in which the Italians had agreed to the use of its credit for the purchase of auxiliary goods like the truck cranes that the Soviets were proposing.[113] Precedent could help their negotiations with their partners, they said.

Volchkov was never likely to know much about what was happening in the Soviet trade representation offices in Italy. And he proved to be much less flexible than the Germans, prompting a wonderfully circular conversation. "Without those accessories the existence of the pipeline is impossible," declared Volchkov. This in turn provoked Helga Steeg, then head of the ministry's foreign trade department, into a third iteration of the deal's stipulations regarding auxiliary purchases, and how the preeminent item should be pipe. Volchkov requested that the German side give a list of what could and could not be bought with that credit. At this, a heated Steeg answered simply: pipe. A German official quickly stepped in to defuse the tension by repeating for the nth time that the credit was extended for the purchase of pipe, materials, and accessories for the construction of the pipeline. With a willful innocence, and, one wants

---

[112] Ibid., ll. 32–38. The meeting took place on August 13, 1970, on the ministry's premises.
[113] Ibid., l. 33.

to presume, comic timing, Volchkov: "The cranes fall under that last one."[114] The Soviets, in other words, sought as much financial elasticity as the Germans would tolerate – and then a little more – from a credit that would be paid back in gas and many years hence. Should there be a need for more pipe after the credit was exhausted, new deals could be struck. The Soviets were attempting to move away from discreet, project-based credit making and toward a revolving and ever-expanding debt relation, energy made capital, in motion.[115]

And just in time. For the Common Market was lying in wait, ready to create new exclusionary practices the Soviets thought they were over-coming through the transformations of finance and energy. In 1971 the Soviets and their allies in the CMEA had not yet decided whether they would even acknowledge, diplomatically speaking, the existence of the European Commission. This faintly ludicrous posture emanated from Soviet fears that the Commission threatened socialist countries' hard-won and growing access to the domestic markets of Western Europe.[116] The Commission itself had arisen in 1967 out of a merger of three previous executive bodies of the European Economic Community (EEC), but it took the Soviets until 1972 to acknowledge its existence, and they did not deign to negotiate directly with it until 1975.[117] The consolidation of the EEC, Suvi Kansikas has shown, frayed relations and created dissension among the ranks of the Soviet bloc, forcing Brezhnev in 1972 to change course in order to reestablish authority in the East.[118] While the Commission slowly integrated the conduct of commerce of EEC members, the Soviets feared the combined power of a Western bloc would extract even more concessions from the Soviets, when not vetoing certain deals altogether. This is the fear Patolichev was channeling in 1971 when he told the visiting Schröder:

---

[114] Ibid., ll. 34–35.
[115] In ibid., ll. 16–18, as early as November 1970 Mannesmann and the Soviets were negotiating contracts that would run within and complementary to the February deal. The Soviets enlisted Mannesmann's help to get Deutsche Bank to extend an extra 100 million deutsche marks should a new holistic deal not be reached by March 1971.
[116] The history of CMEA deliberations on the matter is Suvi Kansikas, *Socialist Countries Face the European Community. Soviet-Bloc Controversies over East-West Trade* (Frankfurt: Peter Lang, 2014).
[117] The fact that the Soviets finally met with the Commission in 1975 followed an EEC institutional timeline; this was the year that its members planned to usher in the Common Commercial Policy, as Europeans informed the Soviets years earlier, for example, in September 1971, in RGAE, f. 413, op. 31, d. 4407, ll. 19–23. Though the Soviets fretted about this for years, in practice the EEC turned out to be flexible, delaying deadlines and continuing to allow a broad bilateralism.
[118] Kansikas, *Socialist Countries Face the European Community*.

We believe that the interests of the people are better served by strengthening and developing bilateral relations. In our opinion, the transfer of more and more rights to the "Common Market" over national authority is not conducive to the successful development of trade and economic relations between individual countries. Had the "Common Market" had full economic power, it is not clear how such major contracts as the gas-for-pipe and Fiat contracts would have been concluded.[119]

In the context of the financializing push the Soviets were undertaking, however, it is clear that bilateralism was not necessarily what the Soviets were after, but rather access and time.[120] A lingering loyalty to bilateralism remained, consequence to the success the Soviets had had in the compartmentalized world of Bretton Woods, but the very examples Patolichev picked out belied the point; both projects were impressively international, one put together smoothly by Fiat with its international partners, the other more awkwardly through bilateral means. This is all to say that amalgamations of business through finance rather than a supra-state were perfectly fine, preferable, and even necessary.

In fact, they did not wait to exhaust the first gas-for-pipe credit, had barely even started drawing from it, before they struck a second in April 1971.[121] This one, however, was not formally signed until July 1972. Ruhrgas alone, no longer shy about taking the first step to approach the Soviets, wanted 10 bcm more gas per year, while Mannesmann and Deutsche Bank stood on the wings to replay the old 1969 hits. Despite the suddenly intense competition for Soviet gas, the Soviets were happy to prioritize Ruhrgas and Mannesmann's entreaties in view of their previous role as architects of the great breakthrough in 1969.[122] This time around, however, the West German state was concerned that Ruhrgas would strengthen its monopoly, and were asking the Soviets to

[119] RGAE, f. 413, op. 31, d. 4407, ll. 70–71. As with all such positions, they were expressions not of individual rogue actors, but of the Soviet state, repeated almost word for word elsewhere up and down the bureaucratic ladder, for example in ibid., l. 22. See also Brezhnev's representation of this line to Brandt in September 1971 in RGANI, f. 3, op. 72, d. 476, l. 192: "I think, L. I. Brezhnev noted, that it would be better to prefer an inter-governmental basis rather than a meeting of blocs, so that each state could decide the issues arising at the meeting independently."

[120] In fact, although the Soviets remained opposed to the Common Market for all the reasons Patolichev expressed, by the early 1970s they had developed their position and no longer thought it the impossible obstacle they once feared it to be. In talks with the British, who in 1971 were preparing to join the Common Market, the Soviets no longer were in the business of trying to dissuade or of expressing strong reservations, stating simply that this was "England's domestic affair" and that "this should not be detrimental to Soviet-British trade relations," in RGAE, f. 413, op. 31, d. 4396, l. 26.

[121] Högselius, Red Gas, 131. The Soviet documents can be found in RGAE, f. 413, op. 31, d. 4407, ll. 48–56.

[122] RGAE, f. 413, op. 31, d. 4407, l. 48.

distribute their gas to other German suppliers.[123] Demands for monopoly rights were not something Ruhrgas had been shy about during the negotiations.[124] Ultimately, agreeing on price, volume, and timeline came easy for the Germans and the Soviets. Agreeing on the financial conditions proved harder.

This was so despite the fact that Mannesmann had come to the table with ready credit from West German banks. In the context of the financial turbulence of 1971 that would end in the termination of the dollar-gold nexus, however, bankers were now less eager to lend money for even ten years. They were going back to higher interest rates and shorter time horizons of five to six years, which in turn prompted Ruhrgas to ask for speeded up increments of annual gas deliveries that had seemed to the Germans so inadvisable just two years earlier, from 1.5 bcm in 1973 to 8 bcm by 1978 – all supplementary to the first deal. In time both partners would learn that energy and finance were alternating aspects of the same revolutionary flow concentrating social power in ways that old institutional forms could neither harness nor contain

★★★★★★★★★★

One such emergent center where dollar-fueled allocative power was concentrating was the Soviet Union. As money continued to liberate itself from strict payments balancing, the Soviets were becoming less inclined to accept deals that bounded what they could do with their US dollars. In December 1970, for example, the West German chemical company Hoechst offered a deal the Soviets would have welcomed at any point in the 1960s: an exchange of gas for chemical equipment. In the new context, however, it made little sense. As the head of raw material export department E. V. Levit explained, they now "receive many requests for deliveries of natural gas from Western European countries above those already being sold .... After repaying the loans with gas

---

[123] In ibid., ll. 42–43, State Secretary of the Ministry for Economy Detlev Karsten Rohwedder expressed this request in talks at the end of negotiations on April 15, 1971 to Osipov. The request seems to have been somewhat ineffective, at least at the beginning, since later that year Bayerngas came to ask the Soviets again for a direct relationship because Ruhrgas was cutting them out of the redistributive commitments Ruhrgas had made. Interestingly, Bayerngas tried this circumvention of Ruhrgas monopolistic show of force at the Soviet trade representation in Austria, rather than in Germany, in RGAE, f. 413, op. 31, d. 4394, ll. 2–3.

[124] Specifically in the administrative region of Giessen, RGAE, f. 413, op. 31, d. 4407, l. 53, although increasingly elsewhere as the negotiations continued, ibid., l. 54. They were also willing to accommodate Soviet demands to obtain the right of first refusal in the whole of West Germany, which of course the Soviets, valuing demand-side competition, were unwilling to grant.

deliveries, gas payments will be carried out in cash. And moreover, we have requests for deliveries of gas in exchange for cash."[125] Hoechst had to catch up to the new dispensation. The Western European rush to Soviet energy in fact collapsed Soviet capabilities by the end of 1971. Before negotiations began in earnest in 1969, West German state authorities had calculated that the country might be able to absorb up to 2–3 bcm of gas by 1975, and that they would only get there through forcing sales. Two years later there were orders for 12 bcm of gas throughout Europe, and the Soviets had by then to routinely turn down massive requests for more oil and gas, even when offering payment in pipe and cash.[126] One of the reasons was a simple extension of the reasons that had brought Ruhrgas to the table: Gas supply companies were busy using the Soviet Union to create the gas market that had eluded them until then. Less than two years after the initial deal, requests were already coming from the Dutch-supplied northern regions of West Germany, where, in the new world of energy the Soviets had created, it had become very important for gas suppliers to have "at a minimum two sources of gas supply," a Hannover-based gas firm explained.[127] Demand had transformed from a political problem into a technical one of fulfillment capacity. But just as the Soviets were resolving the problem of energy demand through a financial fix, finance itself began its decade of turmoil as its increasing strength, nourished by the socialist world among other global parties, decoupled it from old Bretton Woods guarantees and thrust it into an uncertain future. Because as far as the Soviet Union was concerned, those "improved credit conditions" they so persistently demanded were better than cash. These, however, were not forthcoming as the new decade dawned.

---

[125] RGAE, f. 413, op. 31, d. 3652, ll. 6–8. Hoechst's accommodating suggestion that the Soviets need not balance the exchange by spending all their gas earnings on chemical equipment was also met with some derision. After all the Dutch, Levit suggested, did not have to make matching purchases for their gas. The Soviets confirmed this when Hoechst attempted again to break Ruhrgas's monopolistic hold over Soviet gas during the second round of negotiations in April 1972. In RGAE, f. 413, op. 31, d. 4407, ll. 46–47.

[126] See, for example, requests by the oil trading firm Bomin, a Soviet customer in long, good standing, who wanted 10–15-year deals that included an extra 1.5 bcm of gas and a million tons of oil and was interested in facilitating the creation of a joint Soviet–West German company to sell Soviet oil directly in Germany – with Bomin as a shareholder. In RGAE, f. 413, op. 31, d. 4407, ll. 14–16. The state projection is in Högselius, *Red Gas*, 109; Mannesman representatives confirmed a 1.5–2 bcm West German objective for the Soviets as late as May 1, on the eve of negotiations later that month, in RGAE, f. 413, op. 31, d. 2985, ll. 13–15.

[127] RGAE, f. 413, op. 31, d. 4407, ll. 44–45.

This was the message Deutsche Bank representatives brought with them to the Moscow offices of the Soviet Bank for Foreign Trade in July 1971. Just as the Soviets had broken down old Keynesian practices of international lending, in West Germany tight money policies were making money more expensive and debt relations more short-term. Bankers' sentiment was against the longer and bigger credit the Soviets so single-mindedly worked to obtain. The Bank für Gemeinwirtschaft (BfG) had told them much the same thing a few weeks before, to which the Soviets had responded with a request for a ten-year loan untied to deliveries, although still nationally bound (i.e., the money had to be spent in West Germany only).[128] BfG had come asking for more business, as Deutsche Bank had left it out of the eleven-bank consortium that had negotiated the financing of the second, 1.2 billion deutsche mark gas-for-pipe deal. Deutsche Bank, on the other hand, had come to negotiate the Soviets down to five years, compared to the eight years they had allowed in the first deal the year before.[129] Market rhetoric in this context ran against Soviet purpose; so the Soviets would drop the discursive pretense of market inexorability. It turned out now that "the gas-for-pipe deal had independent meaning and could be tied to the market only indirectly." They were particularly distressed with the temporal conditions. Shortening the time made no sense to the Soviets, since they would not be having any uncommitted gas revenues until 1975. Such short terms would mean the deal would lose its compensation character altogether; lending in those terms would mean they would no longer be exchanging gas for capitalized pipe. The Soviets' objections and general characterization of these dealings had the virtue of being more accurate than earlier attempts at performing the market. The point is not that they were disingenuous before, or that they were taking off their masks now; the point is that the evocation of the market is often a rhetoric of power – an essentializing discourse – for negotiating exchange. Another point: Even this surface inconsistency, this denial that the market had organized anything after all, underscored the extent of its authority as a centripetal instrument for integrating global political economic practice – when its logic worked against Soviet purpose, the Soviets did not reject its authority, but were compelled instead to deny its association with the deal.

---

[128] RGAE, f. 7590, op. 17, d. 268, ll. 46–47. "This would give Vneshtorgbank the possibility of using the credit more flexibly for specific contracts," the Soviets justified.

[129] Ibid., ll. 42–45. In exchange they offered to keep the same interest rate. Deutsche Bank also offered to take over the full financing amount, rather than just the third it had committed to, but it would then charge a higher interest.

East and West struggled and cooperated with each other according to the same structurally produced economic coordinates and ethical discourses of impersonal market exchange and reputational merchantry. The vectors were accumulation and profit. The methods: trust, persuasion, and whatever came to hand when navigating the fluid global structures of the moment. The positions state agents performed in this struggle to cooperate were redolent, not of a unified ideological positioning in a binary struggle, as so much Cold War literature insists, but of the position in the hierarchy of power that organized the global economic life of nations. Consider the following minuet Patolichev and Christian Democrats' 1972 candidate for chancellor Ranier Barzel performed in December 1971. This was a time when both countries took stock of their new relationship and looked ahead at a future whose outline and meaning were becoming discernible, as one might slowly make the contours of an odd sight at night. After Patolichev's oft-repeated complaints, Barzel took it upon himself to summarize Patolichev's concerns about the difficulties facing the Soviet–German economic relationship. Barzel did so like this: "There is no confidence in West Germany as a reliable trading partner. This could be corrected by providing a reliable legal basis for trade in the form of a long-term trade agreement. Then [trade] liberalization, which could be done in stages. Finally, the problem of credit."[130] Generally speaking, things went fine when the West German government supported its businessmen, Patolichev wanted the possible future chancellor to know, but the mere doubling of trade volume over the previous five years could not satisfy either side. This was an old rhetorical form emphasizing the growth imperative that organized their respective polities, but Patolichev was by 1971 trotting out new rhetorical usages and business opportunities that would become standard over the decade ahead, mixed with older oratorical standbys.[131] One was Siberia, which Barzel had interested himself about:

Its wealth is being gradually exploited in step with our capacity. New cities are growing there, and new industries are being created. The richest subsoil in the USSR is probably in Siberia and Kazakhstan. In the West it is sometimes believed that without foreign loans we will not develop Siberia. This is not true. After the war we increased industrial production 13 times. If there had been loans, maybe

---

[130] RGAE, f. 413, op. 31, d. 4407, l. 5.
[131] This more or less resembled Brezhnev's talk with Brandt just three months earlier, including the emphasis on signing a new trade agreement. In RGANI, f. 3, op. 72, d. 476, ll. 184–185.

we might have increased production 14 times. But we gave more credits than we received. When we talk about credit, we do not need them to fulfill our economic plans. We rely on our resources. Of course, if we can speed up the implementation of plans and overfulfill them, we can make use of credit.[132]

They would not beg, in other words, and more importantly they would not accept just any conditions for that finance. It was in this same spirit that they had been so shy of approaching Ruhrgas years before and had demanded that the Germans be the ones to ask for a dance. But along with that statement of pride and dignity, there was another: There was much to finance in Siberia. The development of that unspoiled vastness had the potential to work for everyone's profit, if only it could be brought into the global flow of credit production and commodity circulation. Siberia would soon become for the Soviets, if only ephemerally during the 1970s, what the frontier had been for the United States, the depository of a vision of endless growth and expansion that would re-energize the older, sagging prospects of the European side of the Soviet Union. The Soviets would not beg, but they would peddle Siberia relentlessly to bankers, industrialists, and politicians in Japan, West Germany, France, the United States ... to international capital *tout court*.

International capital was welcome. But nowhere in the world in this historic moment was it welcome as it pleased. Institutions everywhere had been set up beginning in the 1930s to make sure international capital, though mostly scarce, worked in tandem with national purpose. The main Soviet iteration of these institutions was the monopoly of foreign trade; but this was far from enough, they felt. The way the Soviets hoped to both reach and tame a potentially dangerous influx of international capital in the context of a late 1960s international political economy was through the establishment of international markets and market-like competitive pressures. The Soviets lacked the kind of institution-building power internationally that had instituted global Euro-American hegemony, but in as far as global business interests were funneled through Moscow, at least an ambient of competition could be reproduced with every business meeting, every potential deal. And alliances could be constructed with business elements everywhere to enhance lobbying efforts that undermined a global hegemony steeped then in Cold War opposition. The liberalization of Western commerce was a first step – even if, they disingenuously stressed, "this is not our request; we are not asking for anything."[133] But the West Germans had to understand that "when West Germany wants to sell us some product,

---

[132] RGAE, f. 413, op. 31, d. 4407, l. 6.   [133] Ibid., l. 4.

the US, Italy, Japan, and East Germany want also to sell us that same product. If the conditions of the deal with a firm from one of those countries is more profitable, then we will sign the contract with that firm." Liberalization was just a matter of remaining competitive.[134]

But it was that term, "conditions," that Soviet market simulacrum most stressed. And credit was its most important component; certainly the one the Soviets almost always singled out: "Credit terms are part of the commercial terms. A country that does not offer good conditions to its partners will put itself at a disadvantage and become uncompetitive."[135] So went the mantra, so well-practiced by the early 1970s. "We receive credit on terms that suit us from Italy, France, and other countries. If credit terms don't suit us, for example because of high interest rates, we don't take such credits. In the USSR the situation has not reached the point where we have to take credit on any condition. We take credit on competitive terms."[136] This prompted Barzel to ask whether West Germany had become uncompetitive; Patolichev must have been pleased. Barzel had been made to think beyond the bilateral relationship, and beyond the borders of his country. A small victory for the market global-ization the Soviets advocated so assiduously.

On the eve of the crises that would reshape global capitalism, the Soviets and the Germans were looking confidently forward. The single, most important Soviet relationship in the capitalist world was even then being literally cemented in place and made nigh irrevocable. A series of political meetings in the second half of 1971 laid bare the kind of interdependence both parties were now ready to cultivate. Chancellor Brand, by his own admission, had come to "look differently" at Kosygin's suggestion two years earlier that the countries create a joint commission to coordinate economic cooperation and trade; he was now ready to support it.[137] In the summer the tradesman Wolff von Amerongen, in Moscow in his capacity as president of the German Chamber of Commerce, echoed the long-standing Soviet wish to transform what had been, up to that point, discreet, individualized trade deals into a form of routinized exchange.[138] "Most of the leading West German enterprises and even entire industries do not have essentially stable ties with Soviet foreign trade organizations," noted Wolff von Amerongen.[139] They hoped, in the name of the West German business community, to create "a solid, long-term basis for trade and economic

---

[134] Ibid. One of the insistent messages Patolichev was conveying that day was that France had, in the last recent long-term agreement, compromised to full liberalization by 1974.
[135] Ibid., l. 5.   [136] Ibid.
[137] RGANI, f. 3, op. 72, d. 476, l. 181. In talks with Brezhnev on September 17, 1971.
[138] RGAE, f. 413, op. 31, d. 4407, ll. 38–41.   [139] Ibid., l. 39.

relations between the Soviet Union and West Germany."[140] The politics for it was in place, and as the Soviets saw it, "the improvement of political relations between both governments creates a congenial atmosphere for the development of business cooperation, and the development of business cooperation in turn helps with the further improvement of political relations."[141] So was the energy infrastructure. And most importantly, so was the debt relationship. This last was what Patolichev explained the Soviets wanted to fix above all. The gas-for-pipe deal had established a bottom-line lending interest that suited the Soviets in their endeavor to put trade in frictionless motion, and those conditions "should not be the exception, but the rule."[142]

At around the same time, Brezhnev was advised to bring up during his meeting at the end of September with Brandt a couple of old standbys of party doctrine, followed by a plea to intensify the most successful substantiation of that doctrine. The party line was one and the same for Brezhnev as it was for Patolichev and everyone down the line: "It should be noted directly," he was advised, "that in this area [of trade and economic relations] our capabilities are quite broad and promising. Our countries are not competitors here, but fortuitously complement one another. In addition, we do not start from scratch. We have a certain experience of doing business in a mutually beneficial way. There is a great interest from both Soviet organizations and enterprises as well as from the West German business community in raising cooperation to a higher level."[143] Specialization through trade and the international use of comparative advantage was a deeply ingrained ideology of economic governance, voiced at every opportunity.[144] Large projects, however,

---

[140] Ibid., l. 38. The reader, perhaps Andrei Gromyko, to whom this diplomatic memo was circulated, underlined this part of the document alone. This is unsurprising, given how it expressed a notion the Soviets had been seeding in their partners a very long time.

[141] Ibid., l. 22, in a meeting between Soviet trade apparatchiks and a West German parliamentary delegation in September 1971, in ibid., ll. 19–23. "Political and foreign trade problems are intertwined," is how Patolichev put it to Ranier Barzel in December, in ibid., ll. 1–2. "In some cases economic relations lead to better political relations between countries, and in other cases it's the opposite." To which Barzel responded, perhaps wearily, that they already spoke last time they met about the interdependence between politics and economics.

[142] Ibid., l. 5, in a meeting with another parliamentary delegation in December, in ibid., ll. 1–8.

[143] RGANI, f. 80, op. 1, d. 570, l. 143. The memo is dated September 12, 1971. Brezhnev studiously brought all this up with Brandt a week later during their several meetings. See RGANI, f. 3, op. 72, d. 476, l. 186.

[144] Here once again Western imaginings of purported Marxist doctrine fly in the face of actual Soviet practice. There was no meaningful internal discussion over economic engagement with the outside world, nor an about face on the issue from Stalin to Khrushchev, only greater opportunity and structural connectivity. This does not

had lent a new, welcome dimension to this doctrine that had so far been lacking: temporal stability. So despite the fact that one agreement had already been signed, and another had already been resolved, it is no surprise that Brezhnev was advised to raise the prospect of more with Brandt: "The most prospective and promising would be the implementation of large-scale projects and transactions with the fullest possible use of the industrial and economic potential of our countries," Brezhnev was advised to note. "In this respect, an example would be the conclusion of a contract for the supply of Soviet natural gas in exchange for wide-diameter pipe."[145] What Brezhnev actually told Brandt a week later, besides everything else, was this: "Economic relations represent a strong lever for deepening general relations between states. It is well known that deep political relations can be established only between countries that have close economic, technological, and trade relations with each other."[146]

The near horizon, however, was blurring for these erstwhile partners. The first gas deal had been struck in the context of what would, in hindsight, turn out to be mild uncertainties relating to the deutsche mark revaluation and the sheer newness of the infrastructural bond.[147] It was a cooperative market-making endeavor smoothed by the still operative settlement in energy of the 1930s that had kept the price of oil stable and, working in tandem with Bretton Woods control, allowed for a general price stability in more or less crisis-free economic environments. When both parties had played their tug of war over pricing and finance, the newfangledness of the situation was at least encased in a world with a built-in measure of certainty. Just two years later in 1971, this world was vanishing in real time, leaving behind a lingering evocation of the world that still was, that could be again. Just two years later, the price of oil had gone up almost 50 percent, and perhaps Ruhrgas came to regret its insistence on linking the price of gas so narrowly to the price of heating oil, because the roles were now reversed. It was the Soviets' turn to discourse about the workings of a market whose indicators were natural

---

preclude that academics or otherwise politically inconsequential Marxists in the Soviet Union might have thought different; whatever the case, the doctrine the state labored under was Ricardian from the beginning, as documented in Sanchez-Sibony, *Red Globalization*, and "Global Money and Bolshevik Authority: The NEP as the First Socialist Project," *Slavic Review* 78:3 (2019): 694–716.

[145] RGANI, f. 80, op. 1, d. 570, l. 144.

[146] RGANI, f. 3, op. 72, d. 476, l. 186. Brezhnev found it "not bad" if they could gradually pull the CMEA into these relations but considered this "the next phase."

[147] A revaluation had seemed unlikely in 1968 even in the eyes of West German bankers, as per head of Bank für Gemeinwirtschaft's Walter Hesselbach's opinion expressed to Soviet bankers in RGAE, f. 7590, op. 17, d. 268, ll. 20–22.

gas's energy source competitors, while the Germans argued that the high prices in oil and oil products of the moment "should not be the basis of a contract for the next 20–25 years."[148] Schelberger now claimed, incredibly given his arguments two years earlier, that gas prices were falling. By rights Ruhrgas should have been asking for a lower price, "but in an effort to come to an agreement more quickly, the firm is ready to confirm the price of the main contract."[149] And as far as the heating oil went, it was now being overproduced in West Germany, so surely prices would fall – never mind that 50 percent increase in the price of its basic raw material.

The West Germans were as market-directed as they had ever been, as the Soviets were. And the market was their arbiter. The Soviets had come equipped with what they no doubt conceived as the authoritative technology for negotiations of this kind: the Platts Oilgram Price Report. It was from this source, rather than their vast experience selling large quantities of oil, that they could make the claim of the 50 percent increase in the first place. And the report further augured that the increase would reach anywhere from 58 to 65 percent by 1975. The price of heating oil, based on the report's quote of Rotterdam FOB (Free on Board, or at cost before shipping) prices, was likewise expected to increase 60–80 percent by 1975.[150] In view of this reversal, the Germans were now the ones arguing for the complexity of the market. And as the negotiations deepened, German demands for gas volume multiplied beyond the capacity of the pipeline laid through Czechoslovakia, leading the Soviets to study the possibility of compounding the infrastructural bond by laying even more pipe, which, inasmuch as Ruhrgas now had the ambition of bringing Soviet gas to the north of the country, had the potential to bring East Germany into the technopolitical project in turn.[151] As infrastructure building worked on time to delay repayments, finance worked to bring flows of revenue forward, creating in the process new reserves of internationally circulating money the Soviets could command. As energy proliferated, so did finance, even in teeth of an energy crisis that would cripple industrial society. If the promise of Soviet demand for steel had transformed struggling German steelmakers into the midwives of a nascent pan-European political economy, helping to bring elites from both polities to the table, the temporal transformations that were brought into being produced at length financiers rather than industrial workers.

But market thinking and claim-making also moderated demands coming from the Soviets, which amounted to a 20–25 percent increase on the agreed gas price of 1969 – which over the course of negotiations

---

[148] RGAE, f. 413, op. 31, d. 4407, l. 50.   [149] Ibid., l. 51.   [150] Ibid.
[151] Ibid., l. 55.

they took down to 15 percent before settling on 13.6 percent, – even as the Germans continued to bristle at the poor market-sense the Soviets repeatedly displayed.[152] Prisoners to sociopolitical undercurrents they could neither grasp nor fit within the principles of their economistic framing, the Soviets now expressed a "readiness to consider the possibility of linking the base price to various economic factors and development of prices for the kinds of fuel that compete with gas" that they had earlier disputed. The market was here a claim mechanism based on power struggles over labor, spatial mobility, commodity materiality, and political control that appeared at the negotiating table in numerical abstract form. It is only the mathematical tendencies over which these erstwhile Marxists ever felt the need to claim expertise; in other words, it is this abstract form that dominated their political imagination.[153] And the incessant hammer continued to temper a Soviet ideational firmness: "The Soviet experts' price proposal is based on the actual situation in energy markets and corresponds to the trends in this market."[154]

Oil prices went on to clock a four-fold increase in 1974. Market forecasting could not and did not predict how Soviet material relationships would change. But none of this curbed the drive to use the oil crisis to affirm market principles, of which the oil crisis became, impossibly, the textbook example.[155] The market stood: a mirage in the haze. The market had won, and the Soviet Union was its standard-bearer.

---

[152] Ibid., ll. 52–56.

[153] Econometrically inclined economists who could offer the state precise analyses of markets had edged out more broad-minded Marxist economists as consultants to power decades earlier, in Stalinist times. See Kyung Deok Roh, *Stalin's Economic Advisors. The Varga Institute and the Making of Soviet Foreign Policy* (New York: I. B. Tauris, 2018). A strikingly similar progression occurred in the intellectual development of advisory networks of Western left parties and the transformation of economic expertise, as argued in Stephanie M. Mudge, *Leftism Reinvented. Western Parties from Socialism to Neoliberalism* (Cambridge: Harvard University Press, 2018).

[154] RGAE, f. 413, op. 31, d. 4407, l. 52, repeated almost word for word a day later, in l. 53.

[155] Timothy Mitchell, "The Work of Economics: How a Discipline Makes Its World," *European Journal of Sociology* 46:2 (2005): 297–320. Jenny Andersson has shown that oil companies were engaged in the political, economic, and moral renovation of their social role from as early as 1967, with a particular emphasis on producing a new common sense organized around the idea of virtuous market relations. To this end, effectively the production of new visions of capitalism, they created think tanks and expertise that only expanded in size and influence over the following decades. Jenny Andersson, "Ghost in the Shell: The Scenario Tool and the World Making of Royal Dutch Shell," *Business History Review* 94:4 (2020): 729–751.

5 France
The Travails of Institutionalization

France was the norm; France was the mean; France was the standard. Although Western historiography tends to see the normative West as American by and large, Eleonory Gilburd has rightly emphasized that the Soviet Union's "West" was more a pan-European affair than an Anglo-American one, with France a chief cultural node. In more institutional terms, the Franco-Soviet long-term agreement for cultural exchange of 1956, she shows, became the template for an explosion of similar agreements over the next decade.[1] This chapter will show a similar leadership in the institutionalization of economic cooperation as well.[2] And then there is the chart below (see Figure 5.1), which shows that numerically speaking, France was indeed the standard. Another way of saying that is that France was not a trendsetter. Soviet trade with France grew at the same rate from 1955 as Soviet trade with the First World – or the industrially developed capitalist countries, in Soviet parlance. France confirms one argument clearly: Soviet trade did not begin with its need for grain at the end of Khrushchev's tenure. The grain crisis reshuffled the Soviet Union's partners for two years, represented in the chart below as a short-term deviation from the mean – itself a general experience for most of the West.[3] Then trade resumed as it had been, following the fast pace it set with France. And neither was trade or rapprochement for the Soviets an outcome of détente; it clearly anteceded it. Rapprochement

---

[1] Eleonory Gilburd, *To See Paris and Die. The Soviet Lives of Western Culture* (Cambridge: Harvard University Press, 2018).

[2] Invoked in Mikhail Lipkin, *Sovetskii Soiuz i integratsionnye protsessy v Evrope: seredina 1940-kh – Konets 1960-kh godov* [The Soviet Union and the Integration Processes in Europe: the mid-1940s – the End of the 1960s] (Moscow: Ruskii fond sodeistviia obrazovaniiu i nauke, 2016), which notes the closeness of the relationship as well as the fact that France led other capitalist countries in the number and assortment of meetings with the Soviets.

[3] The fall in turnover is all due to a fall in imports from France that year, part of which was also about paying off the trade deficit the Soviets had developed with France over the previous year, as reported in RGAE, f. 413, op. 31, d. 299, l. 18.

Figure 5.1 Trade growth (1955 = 100)[6]

and the diffusion of concentrated US power was part and parcel of the politics of Soviet trade and world market-making.

This is why the Soviet embassy in Paris expressed a certain disappointment in a spring 1964 comprehensive annual report to its ministry and the Central Committee back in Moscow. Despite there being many issues of international politics in which France and the USSR "either generally coincide or converge on certain aspects," the report noted, France's "ruling circles" showed "neither initiative nor a willingness to promote Franco-Soviet relations internationally and to seek common points of contact where the two countries could cooperate and act together to defuse international tensions."[4] But that chart does not lie. And that is because, as the Soviets understood it, these same ruling circles "did not offer any significant resistance" when it came to commerce. In fact, "under pressure from the country's business circles, which consistently expressed a desire to develop trade and economic ties with the Soviet Union as a serious and reliable partner, the French government was forced to pay attention to the development of [economic] relations."[5]

---

[4] G. Zh. Mullek, Z. K. Vodop'ianova, T. V. Domracheva and T. G. Zazerskaia, eds., *Ot Atlantiki do Urala. Sovetsko-frantsuzskie otnosheniia, 1956–1973. Dokumenty* (Moscow: Mezhdunarodnyi fond "Demokratiia," 2015): 211.

[5] Ibid.

[6] Constructed from the the *Vneshniaia torgovlia SSSR za… Statisticheskii obzor* series for each year published in Moscow by *Vneshtorgizdat*.

This was the consequence of another reality of 1960s international political economy the embassy reported on and which weight was increasingly felt as the decade wore on: "France faces the constant threat of competition from its adversaries, not only in Western Europe but also in other parts of the world, and French industry needs to make especially great efforts to counter economic competition from the United States, which the French consider to be the most dangerous to them."[7] This international competition, more or less new under the sun in the 1960s, and steadily intensifying, was the purpose and outcome of Bretton Woods – in its aim to make national economies legible to one another and their products amenable to numerical contrast and international circulation – and also an important reason for its demise. It was of a piece with the saturation of domestic markets the Soviets kept witnessing throughout Western Europe, and benefiting from. As we saw, this same dynamic lead German steel conglomerates to push for a gas deal with the Soviets. And so it was with the French, the Soviets observed:

The problem of sales of industrial goods and equipment, as well as agricultural products, continues to be quite acute; there is still a threat of a decline in production growth in many industries, and there is a continuous increase in prices... The active steps recently taken by the French government to seek new markets for goods and sources of raw materials, primarily in Asia, Latin America, and the Middle East, cannot produce rapid positive results because, as the influential bourgeois newspaper Le Monde stressed, developing markets in these areas takes a long time, and it takes a long time for France to 'adapt' to these markets.[8]

As a trade report that same spring noted, it was not just the volume of trade with France that embodied the Western mean; it was also its structure. Unlike with Great Britain, where Sterling-denominated trade encompassed an economic geography larger than the UK itself, trade with France balanced – if not strictly year to year, then in cycles of several years. The Soviets sent natural resources – anthracite coal, oil products, manganese and chrome ore, asbestos, timber. The quantities did not amount to a large Soviet role in French trade generally, but they were important suppliers in those resources they did supply, anywhere from 15 to 40 percent of French consumption. The French paid for this in machinery and equipment for the chemical, paper, food, construction, and electronic industries.[9]

---

[7] *Ot Atlantiki do Urala*, 208.   [8] Ibid.
[9] RGAE, f. 413, op. 31, d. 299, ll. 18–20. As with exports, the Soviets were important consumers in some sectors, for example in French electronics, where they were one of

So volume and structure. Finally, there was Franco-Soviet trade development. Here too, the relationship with France followed possibilities as they became available in a way that was more or less normative to Soviet economic exchange with the West. As a matter of state management this began with France in 1951, with an agreement for commercial exchange and the establishment of trade representation in the Soviet embassy in Paris. Two years later they negotiated another agreement for the use of trade lists, that technology of exchange that did so much to introduce Soviet commodities and production to the West. The strict balancing of exchange necessary through the 1950s loosened up in 1960 – a year and a half after the French franc became convertible – with the negotiation of a payments agreement that transitioned their trade to settlements in francs and other convertible currencies. And from 1963, perhaps uncharacteristically late, the two countries began basing their exchange on three-year agreements.[10]

We have seen that the timing of events involving the material relationship with France does not support the idea that the Soviets were forced into trade by the 1963 grain crisis, or that the politics of trade followed up on the diplomatic relationship and the advent of détente. The 1964 trade report clarifies another sticky temporal point that has been used by scholars to make Brezhnev's politics of international cooperation different and somehow more practical than those of Khrushchev: The drive to change the structure of Soviet exports away from natural resources and toward machinery also predates Brezhnev's rise to power. It was always there, part of the same notions of the benefits and political meaning of foreign trade that had always been central to the Soviet ideological outlook on the world. Exporting manufactures rather than natural resources was not only good for the national economy, it was also an important marker of the country's status within the hierarchy that was the world economy writ large. And here they expressed a certain anxiety. French participation in the Common Market meant that the Soviets would be unable to compete fairly in this fight for status. Up to that point, the report noted, this had not been a problem, "inasmuch as Soviet exports to France have so far been dominated by fuel, raw materials, and semi-finished products imported duty-free or duty-exempt. In the future, as exports from the USSR of machinery and equipment, chemical products, and industrial consumer goods increase, our interests will be affected more and more."[11] This was the future the

---

the main clients in the world, as per another April 1964 report from the Ministry of Foreign Affairs, in *Ot Atlantiki do Urala*, 223.

[10] RGAE, f. 413, op. 31, d. 299, l. 19.   [11] RGAE, f. 413, op. 31, d. 299, ll. 19–20.

Soviets envisaged, and the one they wanted to discuss with Minister of Economy and Finance – and future president – Valéry Giscard d'Estaing at the beginning of the year.[12] If the end of Bretton Woods and the consequent advent of financialization ultimately had to do with changing the relationship between production and circulation on the one hand, and time on the other, then an argument can be made that 1964 was a year pregnant with the beginning of the end. Consider the three main issues on the Franco-Soviet agenda: 1. the conclusion of five-year trade agreement that would supersede, and cut short, the earlier three-year agreement – and would be timed to the rhythms of the Soviet Union's five-year plans; 2. the request, not then conceded, that France provide credit longer than five years, and; 3. the ever-increasing inclusion of machinery and equipment in French imports from the Soviet Union.[13]

Of these issues, the adaptation of Franco-Soviet economic relations to the institutionalized cycles of the Soviet five-year plan was pioneering and a clear victory for French corporate lobbying, which had been pushing for just such an arrangement, even if it meant rewriting the labored three-year agreement signed just the year before.[14] French business had met the Soviet Central Committee's decision at the end of 1963 to further develop the chemical industry with mouthwatering anticipation. So much so that the French chemical industry had prevailed on the French government to urge importers of timber to switch their purchases from Sweden to the Soviet Union, this as a means of finding balancing incoming resources for what they hoped would soon be a binge of outbound Soviet orders of equipment for its nascent chemical industry.[15] The Soviet embassy in Paris further reported that "a number of French chemical trusts, especially those associated with France's largest private business bank, Paribas (*Banque de Paris et des Pays-Bas*), have proposed specific measures to increase, in practice, the terms of credit to 8–10 years by bypassing legal lending practices in France."[16] This was a stopgap solution to deal with the fact that the industrial and financial lobbying had failed to move the French government on the issue of credit. The state in time offered another of its own: a 330-million-ruble

---

[12] D'Estaing's January 28, 1964 discussion with Foreign Trade Minister Nikolai Patolichev is in RGAE, f. 413, op. 31, d. 116, ll. 13–18.

[13] RGAE, f. 413, op. 31, d. 299, l. 20. This had explicitly been laid down by Patolichev in his talks with d'Estaing, RGAE, f. 413, op. 31, d. 116, l. 18.

[14] The pioneering quality of this coordination was substantiated in discussions with the British Board of Trade, which followed up on Soviet premier Alexei Kosygin's 1967 offer to sign such an agreement and found that the Soviets had a well-established practice with France and Finland, in RGAE, f. 413, op. 31, d. 1677, ll. 46–49.

[15] *Ot Atlantiki do Urala*, 223.   [16] Ibid., 207.

credit line for orders of French industrial goods to go along with the new five-year trade plan.[17]

This resulted from the meeting between Foreign Trade Minister Nikolai Patolichev and d'Estaing, in which the Soviet minister made finance the main item of discussion. And there was also the fact that at that very moment at the beginning of 1964, France's industrial competitor across the channel, Great Britain, was making its big move against the institutionalized practices of the Berne Union and was expanding its financial offerings to the socialist world in volume and time. Now was the time for everyone – French "business circles," French bankers, and their Soviet allies – to strike as one. The opening salvo sounded like the refrain the Soviets would use time and again, like a talisman against the exclusions of the past. The old trade lists were well and good, Patolichev began, "they are a sufficient basis for the expansion of trade. But real results on trade this year and in future years will depend on how favorable conditions will be for the operation of trade from both sides, Soviet foreign trade organizations and French firms."[18] Conditions, particularly when designated as favorable, meant always one thing: finance. Patolichev meant to change the temporal relationship between East and West, a point he made clear with the two most promising vehicles that had so far presented themselves: Italian energy demand and (unrelatedly for the moment) British finance. Time was the connective tissue. Patolichev wanted d'Estaing to know that they had signed an agreement with ENI for deliveries of oil all the way to – "and including" – 1970. And that any moment now they would be signing a game-changing agreement with large British banks for long-term credit. They could be doing all of this with France too, Patolichev told the French minister, "if French firms were able to offer acceptable, that is, no worse than firms in other countries, terms of its delivery, including payment conditions."[19] In fact they could decide the issue right there and then, that very morning; if France took "a sober and businesslike approach to the development of trade, like Italy and England are doing," he continued, "then results would be good." Patolichev was striking while the iron was hot. And what he did at the highest level, his lieutenants echoed down the minis-

---

[17] RGAE, f. 413, op. 31, d. 568, l. 27. The line was available until the end of 1966, and credit was repayable seven years after delivery, which put France at least within competitive reach of the British offer from almost a year earlier, even if ultimately the deal was reached on an exceptional basis, rather than as institutionalized practice.

[18] RGAE, f. 413, op. 31, d. 116, l. 17.   [19] Ibid.

terial ladder.[20] This included the rather unexpected – and somewhat uncharacteristic – pressure evident in Patolichev's interaction. In talks that same day with the Trade and Finance Ministry's foreign economic relations department head, Aleksei N. Manzhulo countered the French official's objection to changing the credit practices of the past with the warning that unless a renegotiation of credit conditions is on the table – which is to say the negotiations of new long-term credit arrangements – there would be no negotiation later that year for the new, five-year-plan-straddling long-term trade plan the French wanted.[21]

France did not share this Soviet vision of the future, not yet. Balance – punctual, uncomplicated, non-dependent – was for France the present and the future. And as long as they were careful to balance, the "problem" of credit would not arise, d'Estaing responded. It was the height of Bretton Woods, and "to say it plainly," they ultimately could not go beyond the current practice of five years of repayment after delivery, with an extra two-year maximum wait from signing the contract to delivery, which, d'Estaing noted, was standard for domestic credit as well as credit to all developed countries.[22] Patolichev persevered: The five-year credit had had its day, and had played an important role in the development of exports, but now countries were moving on to long-term loans, "up to fifteen years, for example, in England."[23] He suggested that the French think about it, but, shrewdly, he wanted to see this reflected in the joint statement. He wanted it to convey that, before the start of negotiations on the long-term trade agreement, they had agreed "to conduct negotiations between the banks of both countries in order to identify opportunities to improve credit conditions for Soviet buyers of French equipment."[24] An official statement like that might just be enough to aid in the creation of the competitive market environment the Soviets ultimately sought through finance.

Even if the French government did not rework the country's laws on finance to meet the British challenge, it was, as its British counterpart, still susceptible to lobbying from French firms themselves. In 1965 pressure from French companies prevailed on the state to allow Soviet

---

[20] The leaders agreed that after lunch French delegation members would meet with their respective counterparts at the Ministry of Foreign Trade and talk about more concrete matters. They were met with an insistence on credit, for example in ibid., ll. 10–12.

[21] Besides that financial condition, the Soviets also mentioned the increase of Soviet machinery and equipment exports as a condition. RGAE, f. 413, op. 31, d. 299, ll. 3–4.

[22] RGAE, f. 413, op. 31, d. 116, ll. 15–16. D'Estaing further noted that longer credit had been given to some developing countries, but the volume of credit was consequently limited and anyway it was arranged as a replacement for aid.

[23] Ibid., l. 15.   [24] Ibid.

foreign trade associations to be considered "private persons," a designation that allowed French banks to offer "buyers' loans," which at least
allowed firms to offer direct credit to the different departments of the
Soviet Ministry of Foreign Trade – their all-union associations.[25] The
wheel was turning.

****

If the French state was unwilling to move on finance, it was from the
start instrumental in the Soviets' second demand: raising the volume of
Soviet industrial exports. This perhaps came easier to French state
initiative. While, as French officials kept pointing out to the Soviets,
financial conventions had been arrived at as part of an international
consensus, organizing industry in the name of commercial expansion
had been the core of French political economy since the war, and
particularly since the 1958 Rueff Plan, which introduced France into
the Common Market by liberalizing its international trade, implementing
a measure of austerity and, most importantly for the competitiveness of
French production, devaluing the French franc by 17 percent. Timed to
the arrival of convertibility across the main currencies and coupled with a
robust industrial policy, the stabilization plan underwrote the greatest
economic expansion in French history. While France had certainly been
part of the postwar miracle growth before 1960, it had been somewhat
eclipsed by Italy and Germany. The 1960s would be something else
altogether. French economic growth surpassed that of all other advanced
economies except Japan. Or put another way, if French per capita
income had been almost a quarter below that of Great Britain in 1950,
a quarter century later it was almost a quarter richer.[26]

The core of this expansion was international trade. By 1964 France
had become the fourth largest exporter in the world.[27] The Soviets were
witnesses, instigators, and beneficiaries of the national coordination that
produced that French iteration of the postwar miracle. Among the Soviet
Union's Western European partners, the French were the only ones to
take seriously the Soviets' insistent demand to import Soviet industrial
goods. And although this demand had been made before, the year

---

[25] These loans could not be extended to the Soviet Bank for Foreign Trade (VTB), even if,
the Soviets were told, French firms were hard at work lobbying the French government
to do so. RGAE, f. 413, op. 31, d. 1158, l. 77.

[26] William James Williams, "What's in a Name? French Industrial Policy, 1950–1975," in
Christian Grabas and Alexander Nützenadel, eds., *Industrial Policy in Europe after 1945.
Wealth, Power and Economic Development in the Cold War* (London: Palgrave Macmillan,
2014): 67–69.

[27] Robert Gildea, *France since 1945* (Oxford: Oxford University Press, 1996): 100.

1964 proved to be, as in other matters of trade and finance, a seminal year. In April a large French delegation from the Ministry of Industry went to Moscow to work the issue out.[28] The French government, always in the service of its export ambitions for the chemical industry, served the Soviet state as coordinator, agent, and something like a consultant. Its first piece of advice: It was important to "1) improve the maintenance and spare parts supply [of exported machine tools], and there should be a spare parts warehouse; and 2) expand the gamut of machine tools sold."[29] It furthermore did a measure of market analysis for the Soviets, providing a list of Soviet machine tools that might find customers in France. The list is telling, and it gives the lie to the idea that all Soviet technology was uselessly and hopelessly behind the times, uncompetitive. Soviet technology is often described as if it was in a constant state of catching up to the West, a metonym for wealth or per capita income. But the list the French came up with reminds us that we might just as usefully look to demography to judge the technological needs of any particular nation, and that our references for modernity and social development appeared only yesterday. It confirms historian David Edgerton's argument that while we use the word "technology" to connote invention and innovation, attending to technology-in-use changes our sense of technological time and scrambles our perceptions of what makes societies modern.[30] For it transpired that the French delegation, in looking sincerely at Soviet machinery and technology that might find use in France, suggested an array of imports from tractors and other agricultural machine tools to any number of large and small technologies involved in construction, drilling, and tunneling.

Because for all its empire, excellence in arms manufacturing and history of scientific prowess, France was still under construction. Unlike some of the industrialized northern countries, France's demographics shared something with Europe's peripheries in the South and East: Half of all its people were still rural dwellers.[31] Meanwhile the Soviet Union's richest areas too, its European regions, had yet to be built. Despite what may seem from a historiography that has paid so much attention to the Stalinist 1930s and its so-called industrialization drive, the real industrialization of the Soviet Union and its associated rural-urban migration is by and

---

[28] RGAE, f. 413, op. 31, d. 299, ll. 37–38 and ll. 52–56.   [29] Ibid., l. 53.

[30] David Edgerton, *The Shock of the Old. Technology and Global History since 1900* (Oxford: Oxford University Press, 2006).

[31] Martha Lampland reminds us that in Hungary, one of the more advanced of the socialist bloc countries, the main implement for harvests as late as 1964 was the scythe, Martha Lampland, *The Object of Labor. Commodification in Socialist Hungary* (Chicago: The University of Chicago Press, 1995): 200.

large a post–World War II story.[32] And here we find another unspectacular truth of the relation between economic and technological history: The great miracle growth and social transformation both countries experienced more or less concurrently in the 1950s and 60s was the outcome, not of the integration of the latest productive technology, but rather of the mass incorporation into economic life of technologies of the late nineteenth century's second Industrial Revolution.[33] It was not semiconductors, mainframe computing, or satellites that were transforming the everyday life of Europeans and their national economies, but rather the internal combustion engine, electricity and the electric generator, and chemical fertilizer. This is all to say that the technologies that were allowing both the Soviets and the French to improve agricultural productivity while encouraging the connected depopulation of rural areas were, in the last instance, interchangeable. As Robert Gildea has pointed out, in France "the great discovery of the immediate post-war years was the tractor. In 1946 there were 20,000 tractors in France; in 1964 over a million, equipping over half of French farms."[34] If those numbers are accurate, the foreign trade compendiums of the USSR tell us that about 2 percent of those French postwar tractors were Soviet; over the next five years, with the help of French state-industry coordination, the Soviets more than tripled the number of their tractors in use in the French countryside.[35]

This is not to argue that the Soviet Union revolutionized the French countryside, or the country's construction industry. The aim is much more modest; simply, it explains the chart above (see Figure 5.2), showing that France was the most receptive and constant Western partner when it came to responding to Soviets' demands to increase their industrial imports. These imports plateaued in the late 1960s in the 6–8 percent range of all Soviet exports to France – all the way to the second

---

[32] Focused on the migration side of that equation, Lewis Siegelbaum speculated that part of the reason grand narratives of the Soviet Union often fail to incorporate this vast postwar transformation has to do with the way post-Stalin history is associated with stagnation and stability, in contrast to the mobilizational Stalinist state, an ultimately misleading contrast. In "People on the Move during the 'Era of Stagnation:' The Rural Exodus in the RSFSR during the 1960s–1980s," in Dina Fainberg and Artemy Kalinovsky, eds., *Reconsidering Stagnation in the Brezhnev Era. Ideology and Exchange* (Lanham: Lexington Books, 2016).

[33] This argument made for the 1920s–1950s period of US economic growth in Robert J. Gordon, *The Rise and Fall of American Growth. The US Standard of Living since the Civil War* (Princeton: Princeton University Press, 2016) is even more on point when it comes to Europe and its postwar growth.

[34] Gildea, *France since 1945*, 102.

[35] Calculated from the the *Vneshniaia torgovlia SSSR za… Statisticheskii obzor* series of foreign trade compendiums for the postwar years to 1969.

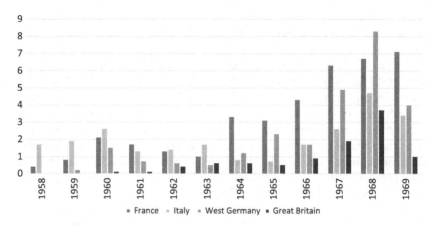

Figure 5.2 Imports of Soviet industrial goods as percentage of total Soviet imports[36]

oil crisis in the late 1970s, which radically transformed again the Soviet Union's international relationships.[37] Given the rapid growth of trade at that time, and in particular the growth of energy exports, this low percentage figure, while not a distinct success, continued to seem to the Soviet leadership like a down payment on an imminent future in which the Soviets could claim a rough industrial and technological parity.[38] That 7 percent was not the goal, but it seemed a promise that animated another quasi ritualistic utterance of commercial interlocution with the Soviets for the next decade: the need to expand Soviet industrial imports even more. In its moment of historical economic expansion, France found room for Soviet machinery, demonstrating the extent to which transformation is capacious of productive diversity. When the expansion and transformation ended a decade later, so too did this particular French indulgence. As it happened, the Soviets did finally lay claim to

---

[36] Constructed from the *Vneshniaia torgovlia SSSR za... Statisticheskii obzor* series for each year published in Moscow by *Vneshtorgizdat*.

[37] In 1970, almost one-fourth of West German imports from the USSR were industrial, but this is likely related to the pipeline projects both countries undertook at the time. And unlike the French, the Germans failed to institutionalize the kind of coordination that delivered a steady stream of such imports, making 1970 an odd year out.

[38] The French officials back in 1964, when Soviet industrial imports amounted to about ten million, had envisaged imports of about sixty million francs by the late 1960s. While they did not reach the goal on schedule, they easily surpassed those numbers only a few years later. See RGAE, f. 413, op. 31, d. 299, ll. 41–45. The slight overestimation shows the real effort the French state expended and contrasts with the chronic underestimations of Soviet energy exports routinely assumed in similar circumstances.

a raised socioeconomic status of approximate similarity with the West in the late 1970s; however the nature of that claim would not be industrial, but financial – and dead blind.

Back in April 1964, the Soviets told the officials from the French Ministry of Industry that they would rely on the ministry to recommend and organize French firms and organizations for the Soviets to meet. They would link their import operations to the exports of their industrial equipment, they warned. This was a warning they offered everywhere in the industrialized world, but only the French seemed to have taken it to heart. That year, the Soviets were met with any number of offers from the French private sector to help with the task. The import/export Groupe CIFAL and seven other firms offered that year to organize a society dedicated to the import of Soviet machines and equipment and organize up to USD$4 million of such imports over the next two years – with the caveat that they be simultaneously taken up as commercial, technical, and financial consultants in the coming expansion of French industrial exports to the Soviet Union.[39]

While everyone sought to position themselves over the coming Soviet shopping spree for its petrochemical industry, then, a set of distinct approaches started to differentiate themselves throughout Europe. The British, with a less competitive set of industrial offerings, relied on finance to do much of the lifting. The Germans relied for the stupendous growth in bilateral trade on unplanned, spectacular projects like the gas pipeline – rather as the Italians did. The French, on the other hand, opted for an early embrace of the cyclical rhythms of the plan. They actively sought out five-year term agreements that would maximize their sales and embed them in Soviet economic development plans, while on the flip side they institutionalized the steady import of Soviet industrial products that year after year rose as fast as Franco-Soviet general trade, even after Soviet energy started streaming into the country's national economy expanding mutual commerce by leaps and bounds.

****

From the late 1940s, European industrialists and import/export entrepreneurs had been the actors spearheading Europe's commercial outreach to the Soviet Union.[40] Their corresponding national state officials had followed in their wake, Cold War politics permitting, and buried

---

[39] RGAE, f. 413, op. 31, d. 116, ll. 21–23.
[40] As documented throughout Oscar Sanchez-Sibony, *Red Globalization. The Political Economy of the Soviet Cold War from Stalin to Khrushchev* (Cambridge: Cambridge University Press, 2014).

deep inside some of those pioneering delegations one might have found the occasional banker. This is why the technologies of exchange used and the deals realized under this regime took the form they did: negotiated annual lists of commodities, trade balances... in a word, planned barter. Finance was atrophied for the simple reason that monetary authority could not be exercised in a world in which money was not to be found in the quantities necessary to take command of the allocation of the tasks societies undertook through their labor: Economists call this investment. In this environment, investment decisions were taken first by states, and later by states in consultation with the industrialists that managed and governed over the social undertakings resulting from these political allocations. As US dollars filled European coffers and then overflowed them from 1960, money and its managers began to acquire a steadily increasing degree of social power. As they did so, their proposals in Moscow increased in number, value, and independence. They began to decide those sociopolitical tasks. By the mid-1960s, the Soviets themselves were routinely demanding that bankers be an integral part of the largest project-oriented negotiations. And slowly, as the decade progressed, they would come to replace industrialists and state officials as agents of the material and infrastructural connections ushering the Soviet Union and its commodities into European economic life.

This social elevation of financiers was promoted by the very industrialists and entrepreneurs whose importance to Moscow steadily attenuated. By 1964 these actors had come to understand how much more attractive their proposals were for the Soviets if they brought with them ready finance or, better yet, a banker to speak to the all-important (for the Soviets) credit side of the offer. A French export agent for the pulp and paper industry, for example, came to Moscow in February 1964 armed with credit on hand from Paribas for a compensation deal avant la lettre: A loan of up to ten years at a 5.5 percent rate of interest would pay for the import of equipment for a paper mill, 30 percent of which could be paid back in paper from the resultant Soviet mill. In time the Soviets would come to grasp the extent to which compensation deals had the effect of circumventing restrictions on international credit, lengthening repayments in time. That winter, all they managed to do was to point, not to the competitive level of the technology proposed, but, as they almost always did, to the competitive level of the "conditions of payment."[41] When the winter thawed that year, another export agent who had had long dealings with the Soviets brought with him a banker from Bank

[41] RGAE, f. 413, op. 31, d. 116, ll. 19–20.

Lyonnais, precisely as a way to mitigate the relentless refrain the paper agent was subjected to a few months earlier about more competitive payment conditions. For the Soviets, hearing that the period of repayment could not be longer than the equipment's amortization (its schedule of repayments) was not good enough in a world in which the British had upended the norms of international credit and in which "even West German firms" could offer better than five years.[42] But that was as good an offer as a French firm could make until the government allowed a different set of debt-making practices. So it might have been helpful to have a banker on hand to tell the Soviets, as the Bank Lyonnais banker did, that they had organized a consortium with other banks to offer the Soviets the lowest interest rates in Europe, as low as 2–2.5 percent below that of other countries.[43]

Even intermediaries with long-standing relations with the Soviets, like Groupe CIFAL, understood that their continued relevance in the French-Soviet relationship depended on the extent to which they could prearrange competitive financing. When the import/export firm's President Detoeuf went to Moscow in June 1966 to finally submit "concrete conditions" on a complete factory to produce powder milk, these conditions consisted mainly in better financing.[44] But there was a strange inversion here. The Soviets had already reached an understanding with state-owned bank Société Générale, so in order to entice the Soviets to switch the financing to CIFAL's preferred bank, the National Bank for Trade and Industry (BNCI), the firm offered a discount on the equipment that was to be understood as a discount on the interest rate offered.[45] Rather than one contract, the Soviets were supposed to sign two separate contracts: one for the equipment and another for the loan. This seemed to bring a small ray of hope that they might be able to bring the interest rate down on a separate negotiating process with BNCI, but that hope was soon dashed: They were free to "conduct whatever negotiations" they pleased, the interest rate would ultimately be the same 5.95 percent as any other contract with France. Four of the main national banks were, after all, state banks.

The financiers might have been introduced into Moscow offices by entrepreneurs and industrialists, but they soon proved to the Soviets they could be useful agents on their own. That Bank Lyonnais banker, for one, told the Soviets something else. He wanted them to know that his bank had lobbied the French government to lift the five-year lending limit, and had warned his superiors that otherwise it would not be worth going to Moscow to talk to the Soviets. He was there also to intermediate.

---

[42] Ibid., ll. 71–74.   [43] Ibid.   [44] RGAE, f. 413, op. 31, d. 1158, ll. 76–79.
[45] Ibid., l. 78.

The French government had told the bank that if the Soviets would draw up a list with a finalized set of technical specifications regarding the specific purchases they would make with a long-term loan, a deal for a long-term loan would be decided positively and quickly. He was ready to take the list back to Paris that very day.[46]

As we have seen, the French government balked at changing the rules governing export credits but consented to subsidizing a long-term loan that might at least help its firms contest the Soviet petrochemical bounty with their British competitors. Paribas had been the chosen medium for this financial initiative, and a year later, Paribas bankers revealed to the Soviets that they had in fact lobbied the government assiduously to bring it to fruition.[47] As with the British loan, the Soviets had not drawn its full extent, and the Western press was, a year hence, criticizing France for granting a generous loan that was not even "producing results."[48] Meanwhile, as we have seen in a previous chapter, the Soviets were speaking ill of French firms and the way they had increased prices when they thought the Soviets were bound into purchasing from France. French firms had become in Soviet discourse an object lesson in market pedagogy.[49] Long-term loans were good, a step in the right direction, but nationally bound as they still were, they did not of themselves make markets. At any rate, those lessons had not stayed in London; Soviet complaints had gotten back to France and to Paribas. The bankers had grown alarmed at the fact that their initial success was, a year later, being criticized from all corners. It was 1965 and Paribas too had come to Moscow, alone, to advocate for French industry.

Bankers were gaining confidence in their tentative role as intermediators for industry, a role they had not really exercised before. As the French pulp industry licked its wounds after the Soviets spurned French paper and pulp mill equipment, the bankers were busy coming up with the next scheme. They were back in Foreign Trade Ministry offices next spring, 1966, to "continue the exchange of views" begun the year before on "the new forms of cooperation between France and the Soviet Union."[50] This was not tactful language; it was descriptive. What the Paribas banker had in mind was an uncertain attempt at a kind of exchange that would soon be called compensation trade and become a consistent Soviet request through the 1970s – with moderate success. The compensation object was the complete paper mill the French would produce on a turnkey basis, 30 percent of which was to be paid back in paper exports from the mill itself. In other words, two years hence, and

---

[46] RGAE, f. 413, op. 31, d. 299, ll. 62–65.   [47] RGAE, f. 413, op. 31, d. 632, ll. 80–82.
[48] Ibid., l. 81.   [49] Used to teach British business and state officials in chapter 2.
[50] The meeting dates from March 17, 1966, in RGAE, f. 413, op. 31, d. 1158, ll. 19–25.

the French were at it again. But what was important here was what was being innovated. It certainly was not the kind of paper-industry equipment on offer, or the fact that it was meant to be a complete set. This kind of exchange had already reached legendary heights with the Fiat offer the year before – an exchange that would go down into legend and was the apogee of a certain Bretton Woods practice which room for further development seemed to be expiring. The clue, of course, was that the man sitting across the negotiating table was no paper-industry titan, but rather a banker. What was being innovated here, was a certain form of finance that lengthened repayment periods and was making compensation trade possible by the middle of the 1960s. It was Italy's gas-for-pipes proposal, still up in the air as of that spring, that was its model, although it is unclear the Soviets were categorizing both proposals together, as the name of the category, "compensation," was not yet in widespread use.

The sales pitch shows something else bankers knew that analysts of the Soviet Union had a harder time grasping – a difficulty that continues in much of the historical analysis of the socialist bloc done today. The Paribas banker was not offering a chance at import substitution. Import substitution is of course a default category of political economy linked to communism in Cold War analysis to invoke state failure; no, he was inviting the Soviets to participate in the international paper market. This proposition at export-led industrialization was enframed in market language. There was a great opening at the moment for sales of paper and pulp, as "the current offer of pulp does not meet existing demand."[51] The current volume of Soviet international sales was low, especially in capitalist countries, the French banker noted before asserting that it would not be difficult to sell in markets that offered the best prices. These was all fairly standard discourse, without much transcendence, commonplace in Soviet offices. But Paribas bankers had not had a decade-long relationship with the Soviets for nothing. What they proposed next was a sales pitch closer to Soviet desire: a viable, steady, and enduring connection to world markets. "At the moment, buyers of Soviet pulp are promoting their purchases from the Soviet Union as a minor addition to the large volumes they buy on the world market," the French banker observed, "but if large quantities of Soviet pulp are offered, then a continuous contact will be created between supplier and consumer, and for the consumer, purchase of Soviet pulp will constitute the bulk of its program."[52]

---

[51] Ibid., l. 20.   [52] Ibid.

Then the sales pitch took a turn. The French did not offer a continuous relationship on the basis of market-making through finance, as the Soviets had construed British proposals. In France it seemed that even the bankers still thought of organizing such relationships through institutions. Here was an agent of capital proposing precisely the kind of sabotage the economist Thorstein Veblen had characterized at the beginning of the twentieth century as an essential element of agential behavior under the capitalist social form.[53] It was predictable enough that Adam Smith had captured the practice centuries earlier when he famously declared that "people of the same trade seldom meet together, even for merriment and diversion, but the conversation ends in a conspiracy against the publick, or in some contrivance to raise prices."[54] The Paribas banker proposed just such a conspiracy: Once the Soviets were selling large quantities of pulp, he suggested, perhaps an organization could be formed that could "regulate the market for pulp, keep prices at a certain level and dictate terms."[55] The banker calculated that the Soviet Union would have to create large reserves of pulp as well as pulp productive potential – all of it with French exports of turnkey factories – to spearhead such an organization. Besides guarantees over the quality of the product and its market competitiveness, the French banker wanted two other sets of guarantees. First that the price of the paper and pulp be below market prices, inasmuch as the French would presumably be buying "continuously and in big volumes."[56] And second, that the pricing politics in the sale of the pulp through the prospective cartel organization and the established organizations of Soviet foreign trade be executed in unison in order to avoid competitive pricing dynamics. Connectedly, the French banker demanded that the Soviets be proscribed from signing a similar agreement on pulp with other Western countries.[57] What was going on here?

It is interesting to speculate what might have prompted this proposition to reorganize the global paper and pulp industry. First and foremost, whatever else might happen, the bank wanted to enter into a long-term, compensation-based agreement with the Soviets, and it wanted to finance as many complete sets of factories under such arrangement as the Soviets would take. French finance still very much worked within a national frame. Second, there was a recognition of the immense potential for that industry that the Soviets represented, especially as the Soviets

---

[53] Thorstein Veblen, *The Engineers and the Price System.*

[54] Adam Smith, *An Inquiry Into the Nature and Causes of the Wealth of Nations* (Oxford: Oxford University Press, 1976): 145.

[55] RGAE, f. 413, op. 31, d. 1158, l. 20.   [56] Ibid., l. 21.   [57] Ibid., ll. 21–22.

were already globally significant exporters of paper's primary component, timber, and we have seen, leading suppliers to France in particular. What the French were suggesting in effect was a geographical relocation of the industry closer to its natural resources. In the absence of the possibility of ownership of the resultant production – therefore in the absence of the possibility of foreign direct investment in the socialist world – the French wanted a measure of political control over the commodity's circulation and marketing. But a more speculative and intriguing motivation arises from the earlier October 1965 discussion, in which Paribas bankers explained to the Soviets that French paper mills found prices for Soviet pulp much too high.[58] The French paper and pulp industry was fragmented, the banker had explained then, and so firms could not individually make the kinds of bulk purchases executed in West Germany and England. Here was an industry in which France did not have the kind of scale necessary to survive in the increasingly competitive late 1960s. The French pulp market, the bankers had argued, offered the prospect of steady, increasing business, rather than the large but sudden, discontinuous bulk orders of their competitors elsewhere in Europe. Six months later, French finance had come to Moscow to see about institutionalizing a relationship that might protect the French paper and pulp industry from the novelty of international market competition. In a liberalizing world, French financiers in their national role sought a regulatory solution for an industry in which the national organization was not compatible with a future of international competition slowly sharpening into view.

The response may well represent the Soviet Union's truest face, tendering an answer redolent with caution born of an insistent sense of impotence in the face of such an almighty abstraction as the world market. It would have flummoxed many a Western analyst then, and perhaps today; non-market solutions that might have the effect of disorganizing the monopolistic capital of "the West" writ large seems like precisely the kind of Marxist thing Soviet political economy was about for wide swaths of scholars then, and still too many now: anti-West and anti-capitalist. If only there was evidence for it. To be sure the Soviets welcomed all of the proposals having to do with the organization of the nascent compensation trade the French bank was proposing. As the Soviet interlocutor that day repeated the offer to make sure he understood it correctly, he highlighted its novel qualities: No advance payments would be necessary, as the deal would be paid back in pulp

---

[58] RGAE, f. 413, op. 31, d. 632, ll. 80–81.

production; and peculiarly, the French firms involved were yet to be decided upon. The deal would be wholly organized through financiers in the first instance.[59] The answer to the much more involved pitch on the pulp cartel must have been as disappointing to the French bankers as it might be disconcerting to anyone still clinging to the idea that Cold War political binaries must organize Soviet political economy: "The most difficult issue will be that of the monopoly on the world market," the Soviet deputy minister du jour responded. "The Soviet Union cannot make its entire pulp exports dependent on some group of sellers of this pulp on the world market."[60] The same practiced impulse that led them to spread out their consumers and suppliers in a wide, competitive network, led them also to cast their net wide for agents as a matter of instinct. When it came to such large, ineffable arenas as "world markets," the Soviets held a greater hope for managing their interests through the known dynamics of capitalist competition than the unfamiliar, untested accretion of power that might obtain from monopolistic institution building. The underdog attitude: At a certain scale, the Soviets never overcame it.

★★★★★★★★★★

Over several decades now, Cold War historians of France have established the extent to which the country struggled to make room for itself for independent maneuvering.[61] Dependent at the outset on the goodwill of the United States, it sought under the decade-long presidency of conservative nationalist Charles de Gaulle from 1959 to come out from under the shadow of American power. This was also the Soviet assessment in real time. Expressed in a Marxist vocabulary, the Communist Party's International Department understood de Gaulle's "ambition to ensure the independence of the country within the Western camp" to be the foundation of his politics. The department reported that "changes in the overall balance of economic and political forces in the capitalist camp, the strengthening of the positions of France, on the one hand, and of West Germany on the other, create in Europe the basis for growing contradictions and push France into an active struggle for a leading role in Europe. France's political clashes with other Western powers continue to be based on its opposition to the Atlanticist, integrationist course of the United

---

[59] Ibid., l. 23.   [60] Ibid., l. 24.

[61] The literature is vast; the thirteen essays in Christian Nuenlist, Anna Locher, and Garret Martin, eds., *Globalizing de Gaulle. International Perspectives on French Foreign Policies, 1958–1969* (Lanham: Lexington Books, 2010) give a useful overview of the many facets of French Cold War foreign policy during this period.

States, which seeks to maintain the dominant position of the United States in the Western camp."[62]

This push for greater independence passed through the ongoing export boom, which the French state promoted in a much more hands-on manner than other European states. This is what a state delegation was doing in Moscow in May 1966; Eighteen months after signing the five-year trade plan, they were there to check up on its fulfillment. The French were there to check up on all the major deals that had not quite come together: the paper mills, the steel mill in Egypt, electric locomotives from Renault, the credit outstanding. And they wanted to add more to the protocol they had agreed to for that year. They were met by Patolichev at his most pedagogical: "Naturally, our all-union associations buy and will continue to buy equipment from the firm that offers the best conditions both technically and commercially." The usual, followed by the dissembling: "We have no power that could force our associations to buy equipment from companies that do not offer competitive offers." And a final proclamation that was as true as it was aspirational: "We have developed such offers and we have entered the world market with them."[63] The world economy as final arbiter.

A similar dynamic would play out down the bureaucratic ladder. The French search for independence made explicit its technological dimension. But what they rendered in a technopolitical language, the Soviets countered with the language of commercial politics, a language that drew directly from classical political economy. Take this exchange between the general director of Chantiers de L'Atlantique, one of France's leading shipyards, and Deputy Minister of Foreign Trade Nikolai D. Komarov. The French director wanted to talk with the Soviets on two issues: "French exports and technical independence."[64] His sales pitch was clothed in Cold War garb, which is to say, in keeping with French aspirations to chart an independent path within the Cold War. In this, the director's pitch gained in authority, echoing as it did the political basis of the kind of partnership both countries were groping toward. It began with alarm at the advance of American preponderance, as European markets were "increasingly being conquered by US firms through the use of a higher technical level of production and the development of technical thought," he opined. "We are forced to observe our dependence on American licenses in many fields of production," he continued, "with the exception of nuclear energy, shipbuilding, diesel engineering, oil refining, and color television." The general director

---

[62] *Ot Atlantiki do Urala*, 330.   [63] RGAE, f. 413, op. 31, d. 1158, ll. 47–48.
[64] RGAE, f. 413, op. 31, d. 1158, l. 50.

finished with an appeal: "Without the help of the USSR, we cannot end this dependence."[65] What the good director meant was that the development and improvement of autochthonous technologies and technological processes "require markets, and especially in the USSR."[66] This, he further expounded, was not just for the good of France, but for all of Europe, "which future, in my opinion (…), depends on its own progress in the technical level of production, which will ensure its economic independence. But to achieve this, your country's help is necessary. Otherwise, we can only talk about the patronage of the United States." The end point of this geopolitical imaginary was commercial, "export orders."

Perhaps the director might have found a more amenable audience at the offices of the KGB, where this kind of thinking was more familiar. But the KGB did not set the course of the Soviet Union's political economy. That course had by the second half of the 1960s been well represented in the daily speech and practice at the offices of the ministries that mediated foreign capital. And the Ministry of Foreign Trade was just such a one. In the face of geopolitical discourse, the Soviets were unyielding in their pedagogy of classical economics. The purchases the Soviets had made should be enough for such a big country, and "naturally, we also had the advantage of using the international division of labor," Komarov replied. All French firms needed to do was to "make competitive offers both technically and commercially, which is the only basis for realizing concrete deals."[67] The Soviets were unyielding, but not, it would seem, impervious to flattery. The idea that they were a large enough market that they could build for their partners a national industry is one they came in time to appropriate. To the suggestion from French Minister of Economy and Finance Michel Debré later that year that trade growth should be based on long-term contracts with companies that could consequently orient themselves and grow on the basis of those exports, Patolichev came to boast that the Finnish shipbuilding industry had been built on just such demand from the Soviets, so much so that even Sweden was making orders from Finland.[68]

As usual, French companies came to Moscow in the wake of that state delegation to work out concrete terms. Renault followed just weeks after to propose the automation of Soviet automobile factories. The Fiat deal explored the year before had been made public in 1966, and it had "wounded French national pride" that the Italian upstarts had gotten

---

[65] Ibid.   [66] Ibid., ll. 50–51.   [67] Ibid., l. 52.
[68] Ibid., ll. 140–144, in a meeting on November 18, 1966.

the prize, explained Managing Director Michel Maison.[69] As ever, however, the Italians had also shown the path forward, and that path passed through finance. Renault had not yet learned that lesson. Maison was there to discuss the upgrading of the Moskvich 408, which production the Soviet leadership had ordered to expand to meet the demand for passenger cars in the Soviet Union.[70] Having received the decree in 1965, the Ministry of Automobile Production soon realized the myriad problems that would have to be resolved, and so the Soviets had turned abroad instead. It was, then, no wonder that Maison had arrived ready to discuss the engineering challenge. But what had been discussed as a problem of engineering by both the industrial ministries of the Soviet Union and their partner in France, the Ministry of Foreign Trade quickly turned it into one of finance. "Before answering all the questions," the foreign trade officials cut in, they had to return to the question of finance:

French lending conditions are inferior to those offered by other countries, in particular England and Italy, in terms of the size of the guarantee payment, terms, interest rate, insurance fees, etc. Another obstacle for placing orders in France is also the fact that bank credit is granted only if the contract amount reaches five million US dollars or more. Opportunities for the development of business relations between all-union associations and the firm Renault will expand significantly if French banks will grant credit for all contracts on the delivery of equipment and technical documentation on conditions not worse than conditions provided by other countries.[71]

Maison had come somewhat unprepared, and could only affirm that Renault's dealings with the Soviets had the direct support of de Gaulle. When he came back three months later, the Soviets met him with disappointment at the fact that the interim letter Renault had sent did not indicate the terms of the credit.[72] This time Maison the industrialist was ready to play financier. The credit conditions would be the same Fiat had signed with the Soviets. Fiat, in fact, was in for $20–25 million on a deal that could go for as much as $100 million to be paid back in ten years. The Soviets had forced their hand, making international what Renault and de Gaulle had wanted to keep national; the Soviets could negotiate independently for each segment of the deal to upgrade the production of the Moskvich-408, but Renault was happy to put it together for a 2–3 percent commission on those international elem-

---

[69] Ibid., ll. 54–59. This first meeting took place on May 26, 1966.
[70] Siegelbaum, *Cars for Comrades*, 84–87.   [71] RGAE, f. 413, op. 31, d. 1158, l. 57.
[72] Ibid., ll. 118–120, on September 21, 1966.

ents.[73] The deal moved quickly from there, but always under the shadow of a higher power: "Soviet foreign trade associations know the equipment market very well," the Soviets warned. "We expect that Renault's proposals will be based on world market prices and other real supply conditions."[74] Perhaps it was this invocation of the market panopticon, and almost surely the best financial terms to have come out of France helped, whatever the case this erstwhile partnership had worked out beyond anybody's expectations. Many doubted that the minimal volumes of exchange discussed in 1966 would even be reached, they reminisced two years later. By the end of 1968, that volume would be exceeded three times over, and Renault would be lobbying the French administration to extend the loans past their deadline at the end of the year, and beyond their volumes.[75]

As Renault had followed the trail of Italian carmakers, so would other leaders of French industry follow Italian industrial trailblazers. After Italy tried and failed on another push in late 1966 to close the gas-for-pipes deal – but before Bavarian public servants made an official overture for a deal on February 1967 – the French commercial attaché in Moscow ushered Gaz de France into Soviet offices to join in the bidding.[76] It was perhaps this sudden rush of interest, which included Austria, that further expanded Soviet ambitions beyond anything Italy had initially proposed, making Italy's June 1967 round of proposals a dead letter. Meanwhile, Compagnie française de pétroles (CFP, rebranded Total in the 1980s) had been buying Soviet crude from the Italians for years – not least for their branches in Italy itself. At end of 1967, they also finally decided to obviate their Italian middlemen and establish a direct link with Moscow.[77]

But now the Renault deal itself had become a basic reference point for French industry to improve upon. When Paribas came that February to follow up on Gaz de France on financing the pipeline construction – and the financing for a prospective hotel for foreigners in Moscow – with its offer of a five-year credit line at 5.25 percent interest rate, or a seven-year one at 5.95 percent, the Soviets refused to countenance lending

[73] Ibid., l. 119. In a historical ellipse, Renault, which had already been one of the inspirations in the development of the Moskvich line in the 1940s, took ownership over part of the car's former production plant in 2014.
[74] Ibid., l. 120.
[75] As reported by Renault's deputy director in Moscow on December 3, 1968, RGAE, f. 413, op. 31, d. 2348, ll. 62–64. Orders of 540 million francs (about USD110 million) had already been delivered, and new ones for about half that again were being signed by the end of 1968. Loan extensions were required for orders expected beyond those.
[76] RGAE, f. 413, op. 31, d. 1729, ll. 136–137, in a meeting on January 25, 1967.
[77] Ibid., ll. 6–7.

conditions that were worse than those they had attained with Renault.[78] The Soviets even invited Paribas to participate in a whole range of ongoing negotiations for color television technology, hydrocracking for the production of oil fuels, equipment for the production of refrigerators and shoes, and more – always with Renault as reference. In fact the Soviets encouraged the French bank to do more than this: "In accordance with the protocol of October 28, 1966, on the negotiations between the Soviet trade and economic delegation and the French delegation, we are continuing to examine improving the conditions of long-term lending so that they would not be worse than those agreed for the Renault deal. Paribas could take an active part in this work," they suggested.[79] The invitation was limited, but in the larger European canvas upon which the Soviet Union advanced its project, the invitation was really for the larger Soviet mission to change the global role and reach of finance, a project that still had to be advanced, as late as 1967, under nationally segmented auspices.

Paribas had laid out the lay of the financial territory as it stood in early 1967, limits the Soviets would come to breach with the construction of infrastructure that would redraw the European energy landscape. Paribas touted its experience in financing two transnational pipelines. In this protean moment, their view was that participating countries, including the Soviet Union, Hungary, Czechoslovakia, Austria, Italy, "and possibly France," should create a consortium for the construction of the pipeline:

According to the Paribas's preliminary estimates, the cost will be about 1,500 million dollars, of which about half is the cost of pipes and equipment. The consortium should provide financing for 40–45 percent of the cost of the pipeline construction, i.e., about $600 million. The global financial market can provide no more than $1.2 billion a year for all projects. These 600 million dollars will have to be obtained by issuing international bonds for the corresponding amounts over several years. At the same time, all countries must conclude a multilateral agreement under which the USSR must guarantee the supply of certain annual quantities of gas (...). The quantity of gas supplied annually must provide the currency necessary to pay for the pipe and equipment loans and the interest on the loans, as well as to pay for the international loans and the interest on those, which are usually issued for 3 years.[80]

In time, the pipeline deal, and all the deals, both in energy and industry, that were built either directly on it or on the flow of energy and debt it put in motion, would overcome all of these estimates and limitations. But it would not be Paribas or the state to which it belonged that would lead that charge.

---

[78] Ibid., ll. 106–110, in a meeting on February 23. 1967.   [79] Ibid., l. 109.
[80] Ibid., l. 107.

****

Société Le Nickel was born of French imperialism. Its main nickel deposits were in New Caledonia, a series of islands in the South Pacific. A few years after its establishment, it was taken over by the French branch of the Rothschild family, which expanded the company into the junior partner of what became essentially an international duopoly with the Canadian INCO (International Nickel Company). Between the two, they produced almost two-thirds of global nickel production. Only the Soviet Union produced in similarly outsized volumes, just over 15 percent of world production by the end of the 1960s.[81] Like most commodity markets since the 1930s, nickel was not ordered around anything like supply and demand. Much like oil, the politics of the industry were directed at managing scarcity and maintaining price stability, based around the management of stocks of nickel. And like oil, the global governance of nickel production had little use for Soviet meddling; the Soviets were brought in as suppliers only when stocks needed shoring up in order to uphold the price.[82] This, at least, was the dispensation until the late 1960s. Petroleum, it turns out, was not the only commodity which governance was upended at this moment, suggesting a story of systematic proportions, rather than one internal only to the global organization of energy. What kept irrupting in Moscow, goading the Soviets into a historically situated set of international relations, was a system.[83]

Two-thirds of the nickel consumed today goes into the production of steel and steel alloys, a percentage that was only slightly lower half a century ago. One of New Caledonia's main costumers in the 1960s were the rapidly expanding steel mills of Japan, even as others around the Global South and the industrialized world likewise expanded.[84] This

---

[81] Guy di Méo, "Le nickel dans le monde," *Travaux de l'Institut de Géographie de Reims*, vol. 12 (1972): 15–30. Cuba, with a third again of Soviet production, took a distant but still important fourth place in world production after Canada, France-New Caledonia, and the Soviet Union.

[82] See Ibid., p. 20. This process sometimes involved INCO's buying nickel at official prices only to turn around and resell it at a lower price, a practice that no doubt met with no opposition from the Soviets, who were otherwise usually weary of resales and often explicitly included interdictions of the practice in their contracts.

[83] A lucid explanation for cotton in the socialist world is Jan Zofka, "Chairman Cotton: Socialist Bulgaria's Cotton Trade with African Countries during the Early Cold War (1946–1970)," *Journal of Global History* (2022). See also Berthold Unfried, "Friendship and Education, Coffee and Weapons: Exchanges between Socialist Ethiopia and the German Democratic Republic," *Northeast African Studies* 16:1 (2016): 15–38.

[84] Consumption demand in Japan increased around 15 percent annually from 1950 to 1970, more or less equaling the increase in the Global South. The expansion of demand in Europe was at half that rate, from a much higher base, Mohammed R. Rafati, "An Econometric Model of the World Nickel Industry," Kiel Working Paper 160, Kiel

acceleration was met with an immense increase in global production capacity, more than tripling it in two decades from 1950. But more importantly, it was met with a diversification of production; INCO's hegemonic position inevitably eroded, eroding with it its ability to govern the commodity. The term "erode," however rarely does justice to the notion of governance; it is true that political authority can "erode" over time, but the consequences are never of the steady geometric kind it suggests. Political erosion tends to create a crisis point, after which developments accelerate in the manner of an uncontrolled fissile reaction. This was the case in the governance of the price of nickel starting from 1965. It had remained steady through much of the postwar period, increasing some 20 percent over fifteen years. And then it nearly doubled in the second half of the 1960s, continuing to increase in the 1970s in tandem with other commodities. By the end of the 1970s, and after several crises of overproduction, INCO's share of global capacity had been cut by half, while its ability to control the price had disappeared altogether.[85]

It was in the midst of this competitive, expansionist frenzy that Le Nickel first approached the Soviets. It did so within the loosely connected and well-established discursive framing of French Cold War objectives. Le Nickel operated, the firm's director said, within an American hegemony from which it wanted to break free. Its aim of widening its commercial relations was being threatened by its US partners as well as rival INCO, which had warned the French firm to stay away from the socialist world or else.[86] Despite these warnings, Le Nickel wanted to buy 9,000 tons of nickel over three years from the Soviets and, unlike INCO, it would not resell to other firms to manage official prices. What is more, it wanted to become an agent of Soviet nickel, for a "small commission." As the Soviets were not bound by the networked practices of global price management that governed Le Nickel's nickel deliveries, it would help the Soviets sell their nickel at non-official, "black market" prices and, what is more, would provide the Soviets regular and detailed information on the nickel market.[87] But it was when the Soviets asked how the international price of nickel might be raised that Le Nickel explained its ultimate goal. What is interesting is that this goal was an echo of the goals the other fading set of monopolists in the petroleum

Institute of World Economics, Kiel, Germany, 1982. www.econstor.eu/bitstream/10419/52654/1/673097064.pdf.

[85] J. H. Bradbury, "International Movements and Crises in Resource Oriented Companies: The Case of Inco in the Nickel Sector," *Economic Geography* 61:2 (1985): 129–143.

[86] RGAE, f. 413, op. 31, d. 2348, l. 75, on December 18, 1962.   [87] Ibid., l. 76.

industry were concurrently busy in bringing about. "The company has long been in favor of raising prices as soon as possible," the French director explained, "because [we] want to cover the cost of investment in the expansion of nickel production, which recently amounted to $150 million US dollars."[88] The expansion and competition that prevailed everywhere at the time had lost for the duopoly the power to govern the price. The organization of control that had served both companies during the years of Bretton Woods was now constraining the expansion they needed to keep up with the diversification of production and circulation of nickel. More unforgivably, they were missing out on clear and present profit. They were losing market share and felt increasingly under threat; the politics of expansion, overproduction, and bust in the industry, new under the sun of the late 1960s, required a new approach to corporate management and market governance. The Soviets, having spent decades in the administration of self-sufficiency and autarky in these particular sets of commodities encouraged by both Bretton Woods and geological lottery, were now being asked to add their significant commodity reserves to the task of reconfiguring this global industry. The organizing, flattening principle of US dollar accumulation, not the French political goal of European independence from US technological hegemony, translated and leveled these endeavors into an easy numerical object. Helping in this political task meant greater purchase in a world organized by the US dollar – the world as it existed under capitalism, not as it might be made to exist beyond it. In nickel as in oil.

The plan and the US dollar, sometimes collaboratively and sometimes independently, continued to organize decision-making in Moscow. And that balance moved in a definite direction. Italy pursued its politics of energy through novel infrastructural sorties in energy provision and within the limits of what Italy could capitalize; Great Britain translated its much deeper capital markets into its own approach to industrial politics with the socialist world. France followed more deliberately, trying to institutionalize relationships that were quickly being overtaken by energy and finance. It was 1969, and the French deliberated. Banks were arriving both independently and by the hand of the experienced import/export firms that had managed Bretton Woods exchanges through the licensing system. But French financiers continued busying themselves with lobbying the de Gaulle administration. As late as 1969 French trade with the socialist bloc was still financed indirectly, crediting French companies that exported to the Soviet Union. An import/export firm ushered a director

---

[88] Ibid., l. 77. The corresponding argument for the oil industry is in Timothy Mitchell, *Carbon Democracy. Political Power in the Age of Oil* (New York: Verso, 2011), chapter 6.

from Crédit Lyonnais so he might tell the Soviets that they would all be fighting together that year for a change in French regulations that would allow French banks to lend directly to Soviet banks. This change in French financial politics would be fought at the Franco-Soviet Committee on Cooperation that had been set up a few years before to discuss short-, medium-, and long-term exchange planning. They were late, they knew; "England, Italy, and West Germany already provide such loans."[89] Not all French banks agreed with Crédit Lyonnais's position, as the change would mean that the risk of bank-to-bank loans would be fully borne by French banks. The Renault deal had pushed credit boundaries but had not innovated this kind of loan with the Soviets, as those loans had still been provided only indirectly through French suppliers; but they had innovated it in a more recent deal in Hungary. And Yugoslavia too had already received bank-to-bank loans. It was a matter of time. And they did not need the Soviets to tell them that time had been working against French purpose. The Soviets said it anyway; it was by then political doctrine: "In some deals, such as those with Renault and shipbuilding companies, the terms of credit have been improved, but in other deals they have remained the same, and it is primarily French firms that suffer, for this reason their competitiveness is lower than that of firms in some other countries."[90] Finance was the vector the Soviets had chosen to rev up competition. And while they could count on French banks as partners for certain forms of financial liberalization, French bankers also felt limited in other forms. At least Crédit Lyonnais thought so: "As for the role of banks, in France they serve firms, unlike in West Germany, where they run firms."[91]

Crédit Lyonnais was optimistic that the upcoming Franco-Soviet committee meeting would help nudge the financial politics of de Gaulle's government. Their optimism was based on the fact that the discussion would revolve around French participation in the gas deal, which was quickly becoming a pan-European affair. The dynamic was similar to that of the nickel and oil industries. French gas consumption had expanded on supplies from the Netherlands and Algeria, and the state-owned Gaz de France was looking to diversify and grow within a context of rapid expansion. The geography of its energy provision made its timetable different from that of other European countries. They would not need to ramp up production, it seemed then, until 1972–1973. But the prospective infrastructural project in Europe was tipping their hand, and as with changes in

---

[89] RGAE, f. 413, op. 31, d. 2348, l. 65, the meeting dates from December 4, 1968.
[90] Ibid.   [91] Ibid., l. 67.

financial politics, the French remained slow and indecisive. By March 1969 they had yet to confirm their participation, Patolichev complained to the French ambassador in Moscow.[92] As it happened, the Franco-Soviet committee meeting came and went, and the Soviets would have to make the gas project the main point of contention in a much more important platform: the renewal of the five-year trade plan covering the first half of the 1970s.

When negotiations began that April, the discussion whirled around three objects: trade liberalization, finance, and energy. The Soviets wanted liberal outcomes, that is, full participation in the markets the US dollar was beginning to organize; the French state wanted control in a world on the cusp of a vast reorganization. That at least was the order of business when Patolichev met with French Minister of Economy and Finance François-Xavier Ortoli that month on renewing the five-year trade agreement for the first half of the 1970s. After the perquisite complaints about the slow pace in the liberalization of socialist goods, Patolichev followed with the perquisite demand to liberalize French finance so that "French firms might be competitive with firms from other Western countries."[93] The French state was most interested in intensifying the deliveries of complete factories, and Patolichev wanted to make sure that this was done on what was quickly crystalizing as a compensation strategy. Under compensation, financing would have to be offered for long periods, and repayments on that financing would be carried out in goods from the factories French firms would build on Soviet soil. It is important to note that this was not an import substitution strategy, as socialist trade policies are usually described. The idea was not to replace production that would otherwise have to be imported; both Patolichev and the French understood that the idea was to build export markets for Soviet production and increase long-term trade in the future. It was a growthist approach to trade; both sides were engaged in building future interdependence, not future Soviet autarky.[94]

One way to increase exchange, the French suggested, was by having the Soviets sell them more oil. The document shows this to be quick as a whisper, and of rare directness. The response was predictable, lengthy, and redolent with wounded pride. No, they would not expand trade on petroleum exports. Were they not both of them "highly developed industrial powers?" The expansion of trade among such as them should be based on exchange of industrial goods and manufactures. But while the French bought $2.5 billion-worth of machinery annually from abroad,

---

[92] RGAE, f. 413, op. 31, d. 3020, ll. 28–29.   [93] Ibid., ll. 31–35.   [94] Ibid., l. 32.

only five million rubles-worth was Soviet, even though the Soviets bought 175 million rubles-worth of French machinery annually. Surely "French suppliers would not suffer too much if France could buy from us 100 million rubles of machinery and equipment," they groused.[95] The French did make a good faith effort at this, as we have seen, but it never became a mainstay of the relationship. Neither did petroleum, which stayed level in volume more or less, except briefly between 1971 and 1973, when it suddenly spiked just before the energy crisis, a volume that would not be matched again until the end of that decade. The value of this volume of oil, however, would afford the Soviets much more social purchase in France throughout the decade.[96]

The French understood the Soviets' fixation on finance, but unlike the British or, at length, the Germans, they were unwilling to indulge it. There was, partly, a conjunctural problem in 1969. That year saw a readjustment in European money values that revalued some currencies and devalued others by the end of the year; uncertainty made money tight. Through the 1960s France had undergone a comparative turnover in its industries and labor. The class of workers that had been created in the first and second industrializations had reached the apogee of its power by the mid-1950s. It was their labor that had made the postwar economic miracle possible. With continued strike action and struggle through the 1960s, culminating in 1968, they had won for themselves a material share of that miracle.[97] The French state had reached the conclusion that the continued worker demand for higher wages was dissipating the great boost in competitiveness it had fashioned out of the austerities of the Rueff Plan of 1958. Currency devaluation, not financial liberalization, would be the French state's choice for a path back to international competitiveness. But that was in the future – in August, it turned out. In the spring of 1969, they were refusing to accommodate Soviet demands for better credit. But they had not turned a deaf ear to the joint and cooperative lobbying of Soviet officials and French financiers. As Crédit Lyonnais had hoped a few months earlier,

---

[95] Ibid., ll. 34–35.

[96] By way of reference, as per the *Vneshniaia torgovlia SSSR za… Statisticheskii obzor* series for the respective years, 1972 and 1975 recorded similar exports in the volume of oil to France, just over three million, but its value had grown by four. This shows that despite existing contracts, the Soviets were able to keep up with the rise in prices of oil that had been induced cooperatively between Western companies and OPEC countries. Or perhaps it shows that France had failed to navigate the crisis with sagacity and commit the Soviets to long-term deliveries earlier, at lower prices.

[97] An excellent analysis of the transformations of the French working class is in Gérard Noiriel, *Une histoire populaire de la France. De la guerre de Cent Ans à nos jours* (Marseilles: Agone, 2018): chapter 15.

the French state announced that they would no longer oblige banks to offer loans only to the French firms exporting to the Soviet Union. They would now be allowed to offer credit directly to the Soviet Bank for Foreign Trade (Vneshtorgbank, or VTB, still very much in business in the twenty-first century).[98] The French state had finally come around to a point of view financiers all over Europe had held for a long time; the Soviet Union was creditable.

So in both liberalization and finance, the French continued to make small steps forward and asking for time. In all three of the issues that took center stage in 1969 – liberalization, finance, and energy – the dynamic element was the Soviet Union. When it came to gas, France seemed to freeze in real time. By 1969, the Austrians were already receiving gas and seeking increased volumes; negotiations were now moving rapidly with Germans and Italians. In each of those negotiations, the Soviets heard that the French government had expressed interest in joining the project. What the French government had not done is express its interest directly to the Soviets. But when the Soviets finally resolved to establish a direct conversation, they found the French government could not really make up its mind on the matter. After a series of ultimatums – "we need to know the position of France before resolving the issue with West Germany" – France finally committed to participate.[99] The Soviets needed to know what French gas consumption would be so as to know how wide pipes should be. But the French government could not decide on a number, or when they wanted gas deliveries to begin, perhaps by 1974/75, perhaps as late as 1980. The French continued to hedge well past the resolution of the issue with West Germany.[100]

"The French side should not get the impression that the Soviet Union is trying to sell its gas to France at any cost [*vo chto by to ni stalo*]," Osipov, who headed all pipe-for-gas negotiations throughout Europe, told a French dignitary in yet another delaying exercise in September 1969.[101] It was true, however, that France, unlike Austria, did not need gas with any particular urgency. They were well supplied through the 1970s by the Netherlands to the north, Algeria to the south, as well as by their own gas reserves. Their first and second reaction was to argue for the creation of institutions that would handle the construction and governance of the pipeline. Although happy to indulge the French government in similar forms of

[98] RGAE, f. 413, op. 31, d. 3020, l. 33.   [99] RGAE, f. 413, op. 31, d. 3020, ll. 53.
[100] Meetings on gas occurred throughout 1969, but both parties did not really sit down to more technical negotiations until 1970. The following is based on meetings through 1969 recorded in RGAE, f. 413, op. 31, d. 3020, ll. 52–55, 72–78, 80–85, 104–106.
[101] Ibid., l. 75.

institutionalization to raise trade volumes and handle other politically sensitive problems, here the Soviets remained steadfast. Construction would be left to each individual country to arrange.[102] Just as the Soviets waived away this French concern, so did the French waive away Soviet preoccupation with credit – "it will not cause much difficulty."[103]

The French government was waiting for West Germany; only after the ink dried on that deal with the Soviets at the end of 1969 did it move forward. France had no immediate need for gas, but neither did it wish to be left out of one of the most important infrastructure constructions of the next decade. The Soviets surmised something else: The French were delaying the deal in order to turn around and "put pressure on the Dutch on the question of prices."[104] Only in October did the French Ministry of the Economy finally allow Gaz de France to meet with Soiuznefeksport in order to negotiate the details.[105] But four days later there was little to show for it; they did not meet again until January, when five more days of intense negotiations brought little forward movement.[106] Efforts between the two energy administrations in February and May went similarly nowhere.[107] By July 1970 the Soviets' patience had run out. A meeting at the end of that month between Osipov and Director of Foreign Economic Relations in the Ministry of the Economy and Finance Jean Chappelle broke down the numerous obstacles to the inclusion of France in the gas deal, most of which were of a French persuasion and came down to price.[108] The French wanted a price well below that reached by West Germany, Austria, and even Italy. The country was further away, which increased costs, said Chappelle. It would be well supplied for the next half-decade and could afford to wait, said Chappelle. And what is more, France was much more oriented toward fuel oil than Italy and West Germany, said Chappelle. What this meant was that there was a greater degree of competition to natural gas in France in the form of fuel oil.[109] Chappelle also let the Soviets know, almost casually, that they had made a deal with the Dutch for better gas prices – the strategic delay the Soviets had suspected had worked after all.[110] After more than a year of haggling, the shared aspirations of an independent Cold War Europe that had been invoked in some

---

[102] Ibid., l. 55.   [103] Ibid., l. 78.   [104] RGAE, f. 413, op. 31, d. 3680, l. 52.
[105] RGAE, f. 413, op. 31, d. 3020, ll. 113–117.   [106] Ibid., ll. 123–127.
[107] RGAE, f. 413, op. 31, d. 3680, ll. 56–58 and ll. 50–53 respectively.
[108] Ibid., ll. 29–34.
[109] Ibid. l. 58. Gaz de France had in fact told the Soviets in February that in France gas was only allowed in regions in which fuel oil was not in competition.
[110] Ibid., l. 30. Or more specifically, the Dutch were now willing to sell them higher calorie gas at the same price as they had been selling lower quality gas. This, they argued, more

of the dealmaking of the mid-1960s had long been forgotten.[111] In their stead, both parties had done their best to imagine a plausible market within which to frame a price. But markets are not always as straightforward as our everyday speech today makes us think they are, or that is at least what Franco-Soviet inability to agree on a basic set of market coordinates suggests. The Soviets were done waiting; blueprints for the pipeline were being drawn, and they needed to know how much gas they needed to pump. They gave the French two weeks to make up their minds.

The deadline came and went without an agreement, and that was that. France, alone in Europe, failed to secure what should have been easy, competitively price red gas. But the story has an epilogue. Almost a year later, in May 1971, after all the initial deals started to spring new ones as if through spontaneous reproduction, France once again revived the 2.5 bcm-a-year deal the Soviets had first heard about from Italy a half-decade earlier. They were again following Italian tracks, but this time quite directly. Italy had just made a deal for 6 bcm of annual gas imports from Holland, and the French wanted to divert 2.5 bcm from there, for which the Italians would be compensated with an equal volume from the Soviet Union that France would pay for. They were even willing to pay the Italian price for it.[112] But 1971 was not 1969. The price of most of the oil the French imported from the Middle East and North Africa had already increased by 45–65 percent, and the Soviets were already making deals with West Germany for more gas at a 15 percent mark-up. The French were essentially trying to backdate the purchase of gas by appropriating a contract negotiated more than a year earlier. Both parties ended up reaching a preliminary agreement, and quickly at that, a rather unsurprising outcome when viewed in the general tenor in which this narrative has viewed it: Soviet eagerness matched to French lethargy. Once the latter element disappeared, everything was speed. The Soviets achieved some of their goals in this deal. They received $250 million from France for purchases of pipe construction equipment, and received it somewhat speculatively. The French allowed the Soviets to

---

or less would cover French demand for high-calorie gas, which was the type the Soviets sold. What is more, they argued that, unlike its neighbors, France used those two types of gas, and building an infrastructure for Soviet gas would be costly.

[111] In ibid., l. 58. There is here a slight contrast with Algeria, which apparently had received a very generous price from France for its gas as part of an effort to aid the development of Algerian industry. Gaz de France was arguing to take that price off the table as part of the market-making efforts both countries were making, as it was a politicized price, and to use only Dutch prices.

[112] RGAE, f. 413, op. 31, d. 4448, ll. 56–58, the meeting dates from May 6, 1971. The issue was first broached at a lower level on April 6, 1971, although the Soviet head of the department for the export of raw materials that received the request seemed not to have understood what it entailed, in ibid., ll. 64–67.

draw from this credit before they had a chance to commit the Italians to the exchange, an arrangement pushed by the exporting firms in France.[113] At length, Italy refused to participate, leaving France with a large credit line to the Soviets, but without gas. Italy was itself asking the Soviets for more gas and refused to reach an agreement with France.[114] The Soviets, meanwhile, were quickly reaching pipeline capacity, leading to a scramble among European countries for what capacity was left. Time was speeding up, and only the Soviets seemed to be keeping up. France had been steadfast in its caution to open new flows of energy and finance with the Soviets. And it continued to choose to ride the currents opened by others.

★★★★★★★★★★

Innovations in finance would not come from France. Revenant Minister of Economy and Finance and future president d'Estaing made clear in July 1971 – if clarity was needed after all these years – that "the main purpose of the loan agreement signed with the USSR is to finance the supply of French equipment."[115] Perhaps he felt he needed to reaffirm this basic tenet of French financial politics because an ever-increasing number of cases were emerging in which French deals required partial supplies from non-French companies.[116] The French leadership was still living in a Bretton Woods mindscape that was increasingly divorced from the interconnections of global economic life. The French government's approach to financing its relationship with the Soviet Union – and its own industry – had not moved from the arrangements they had made in 1964 in response to the gauntlet thrown by the British that year. With every new long-term trade agreement timed to the Soviet five-year plan, the French government still led by making a pool of credit available for borrowing. Except whereas the problem then was the bad press of a generous credit arrangement the Soviets failed to exhaust, the problem now was that the pool dried up in the first years of the arrangement. D'Estaing had to be called into action to lengthen its deadline and cover the actual period of the plan, and to periodically increase the volume of capital available.[117]

France followed, but this still meant a liberalization of trade and finance the French government continued to reluctantly enable. The

---

[113] Ibid., l. 34.   [114] RGAE, f. 413, op. 31, d. 5199, ll. 51–53.
[115] RGAE, f. 413, op. 31, d. 4448, l. 46.
[116] This was the immediate context of this unprompted reaffirmation. It concerned equipment for a complete paper mill in Ust-Ilimsk, which needed boilers and pulp bleaching equipment not produced in France.
[117] Ibid., l. 45.

face of that liberalization was the Soviet Union. Complaints about the slow pace of trade liberalization only intensified over time; although they had always been there in the big meetings, they seemed over time to be triggered more readily. In 1967, for example, Deputy Foreign Trade Minister Manzhulo called the French embassy's economic advisor to express outrage at what seemed to be a step back on France's promise of liberalization toward the socialist world. Recent actions by the French government, Manzhulo fumed, "in no way correspond to the spirit of the relationship between the Soviet Union and France," especially given that they were expecting the next meeting with then Minister of Economy and Finance Debré to usher a full liberalization of Soviet imports to France. It all turned out to be about sunflower oil. Soviet sunflower oil, along with that of Bulgaria and Romania, had just been slapped with a tariff. "This measure surprised us very much and we do not understand it; such a discriminatory and demonstrative gesture distresses us and it is not clear why the French authorities needed it, especially since we have not sold sunflower oil to France this year," Manzhulo continued. "We do not impose our products, but when there is a demand and there are buyers, we would like to have the same conditions as other suppliers (...). And by the way, our sunflower oil is of very high quality, it has a high fat content and a very pleasant taste and aroma."[118]

There was performance here too, surely. But even if sunflower oil was not a Soviet export, the distress may have come from genuine surprise as well. Soviet sensitivity to trade discrimination was real enough, played out internally within the Ministry of Foreign Trade. A report earlier that year from the Soviet trade representation in France on the liberalization of imports from the socialist bloc had been skeptical about France's promises of liberalization. The French had liberalized 177 products, of which only 21 pertained to Soviet exports amounting to about 1 percent of its export revenues from France – zinc, looms, woodworking and electric welding equipment, and even kvass extract, among others.[119] There was much work to be done; some 80 percent of socialist imports passed through the licensing system, despite the fact that 38 percent of that, in terms of Soviet revenues, was freely traded in other European countries. In this, the socialist world took a semi-peripheral position; they were at least not part of the list of forty-nine countries that received "less favorable treatment" – which included Latin America and much of Asia, including Japan.[120] The department for trade with Western countries brooked no such positivity. The trade representative's report had

[118] RGAE, f. 413, op. 31, d. 1729, ll. 12–13.   [119] RGAE, f. 413, op. 31, d. 1975, ll. 1–7.
[120] Ibid., l. 6.

"serious distortions on the issue it deals with and therefore does not reflect the real situation in the field of contingent exports and the licensing of Soviet exports to France."[121] It ran contrary to reports on the subject from the previous three years. And it lumped within the "licensing regime" products that were in effect automatically licensed for import, as opposed to others such as oil that were licensed rather more strictly. Perhaps the trade representation saw sluggishness where other departments observed progress, but whatever the internal disagreements on the matter, the Soviet performative politics of trade continued to be based on outrage wherever and whenever expected market norms could be argued to have been breached within the late 1960s context of gradual market formations.

A French state delegation gave another set of coordinates in 1968 for thinking about France's efforts at liberalization. Since 1966, France had reduced the list of socialist products whose imports into France were restricted from 600 to 100. France had responsibilities to their partners in the Common Market, and sometimes, as in the sunflower oil trifle, had to defer to those politics; to these they offered a compensation of stereotypical proportions: They stood their ground against the Common Market on horse meat, whose imports from Eastern Europe were now growing fast.[122] Of course this did little to assuage Soviet pressure, which continued in meetings high and low. Soviet arguments could have come straight from the pages of the British liberal standard *The Economist*: "Comrade Manzhulo dwelled on the negative influence that the presence of restrictions on the import of a number of Soviet goods has on the development of mutual trade," went one such complaint to a French embassy advisor in October 1970. "These restrictions restrain the expansion of activities of Soviet foreign trade organizations on the French market and their commercial initiative because they create an environment of uncertainty in the possibility to complete certain transactions. Under such conditions, Soviet trade organs prefer to act more actively in the markets of those countries where such restrictions have already been removed."[123] The driver was international competition, as Manzhulo suggested. No doubt national firms also informed the French state regularly on these matters. And that sense-making was certainly enhanced by the insistence and invariability of market discourse that

---

[121] Ibid., ll. 25–26.   [122] RGAE, f. 413, op. 31, d. 2348, ll. 2–3.
[123] RGAE, f. 413, op. 31, d. 3680, ll. 10–11. The threat of going elsewhere was old hat, but the argument of market restrictions as confidence sapping was new at the ministry, as far as I can tell, confidence being a mainstay category of liberal argument vis-à-vis the economy.

the Soviets made foundational to their performative trade politics around liberalization.

French dignitaries high and low tired of these repetitions, ineffectually repeating that "they understood the Soviet point of view."[124] Another response to these Soviet complaints was the organization of a plethora of working groups and other forms of institutionalized arrangements, carried out by both French public and private entities. As we saw already with Paribas's bold proposal to regulate the paper industry through the development of large Soviet capacity and reserves, the Soviet Union was often the last rock of refuge for firms and even industries that were seeking a place to shelter from the rapid development of competition in the late 1960s. In 1967, for example, a French petroleum distributer proposed that the Soviets create a mixed enterprise in France that could eventually merge with the French firm.[125] No longer able to compete on price, the French distributer offered its ownership of valuable licenses to import foreign oil into France in exchange for a partnership that would render ready access to a seemingly inexhaustible supply of cheap Soviet oil. But like the rock in Nina Simone's "Sinnerman," the Soviets gave no shelter. The issue in the oil industry was not international competition, but rather consolidation. Of some ninety-two independent oil refiners and distributors in 1928, only eight to ten remained by the late 1960s.[126] The rest had been bought over the years by "large oil monopolies," the firm informed the Soviets. These pleas fell on deaf ears; monopoly capital worked on the kind of economic and political scale the Soviets needed for the realization of their global political economic project.

In other words, whether the initiative came from the private or public realm, institutionalization was the peculiarly French course of cooperation in political economy. This was not in contrast to some opposite entrepreneurial approach; the oil partnership was an entrepreneurial accretion, after all. Institutions could take a corporate form, or they could be a form of interstate cooperation. It is only that what the Soviets tried to render through finance what British, Germans and Italians tried to limit through dealmaking, and what the Austrians tried to forestall by keeping the exchange technologies of Bretton Woods. The French, in turn, sought to institutionalize. Economy and Finance

---

[124] As d'Estaing did in a meeting in October 1969, RGAE, f. 413, op. 31, d. 3020, ll. 107–110, though instances are too numerous to cite without trying the reader's patience (even more).

[125] The Soviets also quickly shut down the company's first request to lower the price of their oil. RGAE, f. 413, op. 31, d. 1973, ll. 4–6.

[126] Ibid., ll. 7–8.

Minister Debré brought yet another such proposition at the beginning of 1968. He offered to invite ten large French trade firms into an association with the Soviets to spearhead Soviet imports into France of consumer and industrial goods. Not to monopolize Soviet imports, he quickly qualified. He knew the Soviets preferred to keep their marketing partner options open. They could still make as many private deals with individual firms as they saw fit. He simply wanted to institutionalize a steady and growing exchange that would allow France to grow exports in return.[127] The fate of this proposal over the next year is instructive. By March the association was given a name, Kometorg, which a month later was renamed Franktorg.[128] It was to be led jointly by trading firms J.A. Goldschmidt and CIFAL, but its structure remained nebulous and undefined. The initiative met with something bordering indifference from the Soviets. They liked anything that might promote Soviet manufactures abroad, but they did not see how an association that might end up monopolizing Soviet exports to France would improve on the direct and diverse, market-making relationships they maintained with French firms. To be fair, neither did anybody else. And sure enough, a year later the ambitious plan to have Franktorg promote Soviet manufactures in France had devolved into the establishment of a Soviet shop in Paris, "The Russia House." Excitement over the mission had likewise waned. Goldschmidt could no longer get a meeting with any of the deputy foreign trade ministers, and anyway was in Moscow in January 1969 to convey that after the invasion of Czechoslovakia and the tightening of the credit markets, a store of the sort "would hardly be profitable."[129]

France had other institutional commitments that at times seemed to conflict with those they were pursuing with the Soviets, especially in the form of the European Economic Community. But Debré was probably right to tell them that their "worry for the influence of the Common Market was excessive." No, the Common Market was not behind the sudden restrictions on imports of anthracite coal, he explained in reaction to Patolichev's off-hand accusations. It was linked to a strictly internal problem in the French coal mining sector. And the Common Market ultimately helped France's economy grow, he argued, which helped its relations with the Soviets.[130] Then again, if the Soviets seemed on edge, there was a good reason for that too. The 1970 deadline for the final consolidation of the Common Market was around the corner.

---

[127] RGAE, f. 413, op. 31, d. 2348, ll. 1–5, in a meeting on January 9, 1968.
[128] Ibid., l. 14 and ll. 37–38 respectively. [129] RGAE, f. 413, op. 31, d. 3020, ll. 2–3.
[130] RGAE, f. 413, op. 31, d. 2348, ll. 3–4.

Debré was mainly in Moscow to convey that the French government had recently reached the decision to maintain the bilateral structures that organized Franco-Soviet relations. This would be the official position France would defend when the issue came under discussion with its European partners in 1969. In fact, Debré made clear that France would not simply maintain bilateralism; the French government wanted to deepen the institutionalization of the relationship with the creation of an array of state-to-state institutions and practices. The goal was to have Franco-Soviet economic relations take "first place of all Common Market countries, and not third, as at present." To this end "new instruments for promoting trade between our two countries have now been created or are being established, including: a Franco-Soviet Chamber of Commerce; mixed working groups by industrial sector; 'liberalization' of Soviet imports to France; a new association of French firms."[131] As it did with cultural relations in the 1950s, France would continue to create new templates for state-to-state dialogue and dealings with the Soviets that others would imitate.[132] It was the first European country to see one of its enterprises, in this case the Franco-Soviet Chamber of Commerce, establish a permanent representative office in Moscow in January 1968.[133] A flood of requests for permanent offices followed. They proved themselves over time, or at least until the 1980s, but France never did take first place. A different organizational form, it seems, did even better.

A propos of which, Paribas followed Debré to discuss finance for two deals, the paper mills and French participation in the gas-for-pipe deal. Inasmuch as Paribas offered an interesting alternative financing option on each, the Soviets had the chance to make clear the parameters of what they wanted from financiers. It was certainly not the seven-year standard financing Paribas offered for the paper mills; Soviet purchases of paper mills had all been planned out through 1970, and although they were happy to lock in procurements from 1971, they would not countenance conditions that were equivalent to those they used to get in 1965. For the Soviets, planning ahead was fine, but unless banks offered a priori better

---

[131] RGAE, f. 413, op. 31, d. 2348, l. 5. This was quite the volte-face from just a few years earlier, when France insisted that the Soviets deal with the European Commission over tariffs, in RGAE, f. 413, op. 31, d. 116, ll. 13–14.

[132] As Kansikas notes, the long-term economic cooperation agreement "was in fact seen as a model for other members," Suvi Kansikas, *Socialist Countries Face the European Community. Soviet-Bloc Controversies over East-West Trade* (Frankfurt: Peter Lang, 2014), 70.

[133] RGAE, f. 413, op. 31, d. 2348, l. 51.

conditions, they were not going to waste a chance to use these large scale, USD300 million acquisitions as exercises in market-promotion. Finance, as far as the Soviets were concerned, had to be in a constant treadmill of self-improvement, overcoming itself with every new offer. The French paper mill offer did have an internationalization element the bank's president had been astute enough to foreground in his talks with Sveshnikov at Vneshtorgbank. Paribas would lend the credit, and the Soviets would be free to buy the paper mill equipment in France or some third country; either way payments would be done in sale of paper products in France.[134] The French banker presented the same deal later that day at the Ministry of Foreign Trade, where Deputy Minister Komarov quickly seized on that quality: "We are interested in whether the bank will finance deliveries of equipment from other countries."[135] If the finance was not going to break any temporal norms, perhaps it could disrupt spatial ones.

Paribas was not in a position to spearhead any break with Bretton Woods norms, but it did make another interesting – and similarly futile – proposal with regard to French involvement in the gas deal: It offered to organize the credit through an issue of bonds on the world market in the name of a prospective international organ that would build the pipeline – a kind of consortium made up of the USSR, the Western users of the pipe and banks. The "foundation" of this organ would be the bond itself.[136] What is interesting here is that Paribas knew what the Soviets were ultimately after and tried to sell precisely that quality of the debt that they knew would appeal to the bank's socialist partners. The terms, were, otherwise, unexceptional, but the success of the bond would not just facilitate the pipeline's financing, it would also "help the USSR act independently in the international market for long-term capital."[137] The Soviets promised to discuss the proposal internally, but gave the French bankers no hope for it, as they could not then, on the second year of negotiations with Italy and Austria, push this alternative on them. And at any rate, the market was never likely to offer better terms than those they expected from state-supported negotiations; these proposals were ultimately too expensive. But they would, they promised, "remember them."[138]

The French insisted on initiatives of the sort, to increasing disinterest from the Soviets. When three French banks suggested in October 1969 developing a joint venture to study French markets for the Soviets

---

[134] RGAE, f. 7590, op. 17, d. 267, ll. 105–107.
[135] RGAE, f. 413, op. 31, d. 2348, l. 11.   [136] Ibid., ll. 9–13, on January 30, 1968.
[137] RGAE, f. 7590, op. 17, d. 267, l. 106.   [138] Ibid., l. 107.

and promote bilateral trade, Deputy Minister Komarov told them that there were "already a number of organizations engaged in the study and expansion of Soviet-French trade and economic relations, including the Large and Small Committees, sectoral working groups within the framework of these committees, and the Franco-Soviet Chamber of Commerce. Therefore, it is hardly necessary to create another organization with the same tasks."[139] Meanwhile, earlier that summer French businessman and fellow traveler Jean-Baptiste Doumeng, the "Red Millionaire" who made his money trading agricultural produce and materiel with the Soviet bloc, had looked to establish a working group with the Soviets to promote Soviet tractors and equipment in French farms. Even his initiative met a rather cool reception.[140] Instituting working groups that would meet regularly to discuss trade and finance had been fruitful for the Soviets at the height of Bretton Woods and the technologies it purveyed, such as trade lists and trade plans. They were still, in many ways, the backbone of the economic relations the Soviet Union maintained with its Western neighbors. What they were not, however, was the future the Soviets envisaged.

****

France makes for an interesting contrast with its Western neighbors in terms of European national political economies and the connected realm of East–West relations. The country's predilections reveal much about the Soviet Union's own predilections. This story of France's relative inertia when it came to change was just that, relative. Bretton Woods as a system governing the beginning of our current globalized era had, after all, allowed France an export-led economic expansion like it had never known before, and would never see again. The institutions of dialogue and bureaucratized cooperation that some scholars have seen as the crucial innovation and the reason for the success of Bretton Woods were the kind the French government doubled down on during this period of change.[141] France did not lead in the reorganization of energy and finance in the continent, but it was compelled to follow. In time, the gas-for-pipe project opened new forms of cooperation between East and

---

[139] RGAE, f. 413, op. 31, d. 3020, ll. 111–112.   [140] Ibid., ll. 63–65.

[141] And the main difference with the failures of the 1930s. This constitutes much of the main body of work of Barry Eichengreen, in particular, *The European Economy Since 1945. Coordinated Capitalism and Beyond* (Princeton: Princeton University Press, 2007). France clearly led in instituting the coordination of trade with the Soviet five-year plan, which the French government fought for in the face of the 1970 deadline for the Common Commercial Policy of the EEC.

West that proved more amenable to the kind of procedural, institutional-ized dialogue over economic exchange the French state preferred. The Soviets called it compensation trade, and Siberia became its playground.

In contrast to the gas deal, the French government did not dither on the five-year cooperation agreement, which it signed swiftly at the end of May 1969 after much of the ground had been cleared by the Large and Small Committees it had innovated with the Soviets. Financial prece-dents elsewhere had created, by the end of the 1960s, new baselines for Soviet demands. Conditions that the Soviets had celebrated five years earlier as historic, they now described during lead up negotiations to that agreement as "the establishment of strict (*zhestkoi*) lending proced-ures."[142] But new financial normative baselines did not derail the rela-tionship. The Soviets wanted a new temporal relationship with the West, and the French offered one that was not financial, but rather project-based. It originated in large part in the new possibilities the gas-for-pipe deal inaugurated, both as a model and in the creditability it wrought for the Soviets. Patolichev was explicit about it. The new five-year plan created a new party line on the development of new geographical fron-tiers consisting mainly of vast mineral deposits in Siberia, as well as Kazakhstan and Ukraine; they would be open to Western cooperative agreements.[143] The stress was on the "development of cooperation with France on a long-term basis," and the best – and mostly solitary – example was the gas pipe already under construction.[144] France had made clear that they would not open the spigots of finance to balance the torrents of energy about to flow West; instead, and unlike its Western neighbors, it would manage credit emanating from both banks and the state in strict relation to the projects inscribed within the Soviet five-year plan. Except the definition of "long-term" had changed. It now no longer meant five to seven years, but rather ten to twenty years; the gas pipe had shown this to be possible. These were projects larger and more complex than any that had been built at the height of Bretton Woods, larger in fact than could be built by any one national enterprise, as the Fiat factory had been. The development of Udokan's copper deposits alone, French Foreign Affairs Minister Maurice Schumann admitted, were beyond

---

[142] RGAE, f. 413, op. 31, d. 3020, l. 51.   [143] RGAE, f. 413, op. 31, d. 3680, l. 9.

[144] The quote is from a meeting between Manzhulo and an adviser of the French embassy in October 27, 1970, Ibid., ll. 10–12. Patolichev, in his meeting with the French ambassador three days later, introduced it in much the same way, speaking of the gas project they had with Italy, West Germany and Austria as well as a timber deal they made with Japan, in ibid., ll. 6–9.

"the economic and financial capabilities of France."[145] Just as the Soviets were beginning to explore consortium-based projects in the Global South, so would the West begin to organize international consortiums to help develop new geographical frontiers within the Soviet Union. French predilections were fair enough, and plenty profitable on both sides, but the Soviets would keep pushing the boundaries of Bretton Woods that had served France so well. And France followed.

---

[145] In talks on October 13, 1969 with Patolichev, in RGAE, f. 413, op. 31, d. 3020, ll. 100–103.

Coda
Italy, Cold War Straggler

In the frustrating months that inaugurated the year 1968, two new insistent demands made their first appearance in the routine negotiations between Italy and the Soviet Union. The Soviets pleaded for greater purchases of more industrial goods. They had done this before; far from an innovation of the government of General Secretary Leonid Brezhnev, this had always been Soviet policy. But this moment at the end of the 1960s brought a new insistence on the part of the Brezhnev government. Unlike elsewhere in Europe, in Italy this insistence fell on deaf ears. The Italian government for its part began to stump for its small and medium enterprises to join this profitable trade. The Soviets met this with a certain political blindness, responding almost by rote that they did not care who was offering what, but only that the deal was profitable in itself.[1] Over time, the Soviet Union would learn to accommodate this Western political concern as part of its commercial diplomacy; and in turn, the Italians quickly learned to make trade with their small and medium sized companies attractive by offering the Soviets special credit.[2] Both novelties are a reminder that this was still the heyday of Keynesian governance, which is to say, that trade deals were still financed if they "increase employment and stimulate the further development of Italian industry," as Italian Trade Minister Tolloy explained.[3] Or on the other end, as Soviet foreign trade officials still understood it, "granting loans is the business of government bodies and companies offering equipment for delivery, if they want to have orders for the delivery of complete equipment."[4]

The Austrians overtook the Italians. Rather than fighting the Soviets on price – a fight which at the beginning of 1968 had moved the Italians three dollars per 1,000 cubic meters up from the original offer more than

[1] RGAE, f. 413, op. 31, d. 1699, l. 94.
[2] Suggestions for this came as early as January 1968. RGAE, f. 413, op. 31, d. 2316, ll. 26–27.
[3] RGAE, f. 413, op. 31, d. 1699, l. 92.   [4] Ibid., l. 93.

215

a year earlier, and the Soviets two dollars down – the Austrians had quickly accepted the price the Italians had rejected a year before. For the Soviets, the most important failsafe against any price injustice was the addition of a clause in the contract that would trigger renegotiations should the international price of gas fluctuate up or down. The Austrians agreed to make price readjustments operative after the end of the first seven-year contract.[5] For the first contract, the Austrians had agreed to a price of $14.10 per 1,000 cubic meters, at a moment when the Italians were summarily rejecting a $12.1 offer. The board of directors of Austria's state oil and gas company ÖMV, apparently unlike that of Italy's state energy company ENI, was satisfied that the price was competitive against offers from Algeria and the Netherlands.[6] Upon this development, and after a year of moribund negotiations, ENI quickly fell into negotiating a similar line concerning the long-standing Soviet suggestion of price readjustments.[7]

Italian negotiating practices had done better during the first two maverick decades of the country's relationship with the Soviet Union. The Cold War had given Italian firms and their intermittently supportive government a degree of leverage they had exploited quite openly.[8] As Europe-wide markets slowly drew closer to one another, overlapping, integrating, and obviating the Keynesian boundaries of the first two postwar decades, the Soviets began experiencing what they had long worked for and helped construct: competitive offers that looked ever more like market forces.

Market forces, of course, could profit sellers or buyers depending on conditions the Soviets often referred to as "conjunctural" (*kon"iunkturnyi*). The Italians too had changed their predicates. Where a decade earlier they used Cold War discourse to negotiate the Soviets down, by the end of the 1960s they too had learned to use the discourse of market supply. In talks preliminary to the first round of gas negotiations in the fall of 1966, both countries had used benchmark prices around the world to orient the other. But while the Italians had sought those benchmark

[5] Osipov, the Soviet point man for all gas negotiations, did not even wait for official Austrian approval before he was already informing the Italians about it in talks dated January 19, 1968, in RGAE, f. 413, op. 31, d. 2316, ll. 19–21.

[6] Per Högselius, *Red Gas. Russia and the Origins of European Energy Dependence* (Basingstoke: Palgrave Macmillan, 2013), 61–64.

[7] ENI had long insisted on one price for the length of the twenty-year deal. By early 1968, a potential price changes after the first seven-year contract became the basis of further negotiations. See for example RGAE, f. 413, op. 31, d. 2316, ll. 30–33 and ll. 28–29.

[8] For an example Oscar Sanchez-Sibony, *Red Globalization. The Political Economy of the Soviet Cold War from Stalin to Khrushchev* (Cambridge: Cambridge University Press, 2014), 187.

prices in the Americas (Canadian gas cost the United States $8.6 per 1,000 cubic meters, and Mexican gas was only $6.06!) to justify their $8 offer, the Soviets staked out the more pertinent Dutch, Algerian, and Libyan prices, which validated the $14 they asked for.[9] A year later, and with talks in a moribund state, the Italians started more aggressively signaling the many sources of European supply, Dutch, Algerian, Libyan, to which they added possible new gas discoveries in the Adriatic Sea. The Italians argued the tendency was toward lower prices, and they tried to convince the Soviets that the market was changing faster at that moment than ever before. They announced that Italy just agreed to a further 3 bcm annually from Libya; they informed that the Dutch were looking for and finding oil and gas in the North Sea, and that Shell had discovered large fields in the Adriatic Sea that were soon to be exploited. Algeria was close to delivering gas to Sicily, and they had hinted they might sell gas to Italy more cheaply than the gas they delivered to France. And all the while, heating oil waited in the wings, ready to take over whatever geography gas did not reach.[10] The Italians even used the Nederlandse Aardolie Maatschappij (NAM), the Royal Dutch Shell/Esso joint venture established to exploit the Dutch gas fields, as a counterweight to the Soviets; this last approach was especially disingenuous and failed to move the Soviets, especially since the Soviet-ENI deal negotiations had originated in 1966 precisely to counter NAM's near-monopoly position in Italy.[11] The Soviets understood this explicitly, as when Deputy Foreign Trade Minister Nikolai Osipov told ENI representative Pasquale Landolfi that the deal was important for ENI economically and politically, "because it will give ENI the opportunity to free itself from dependence on the Anglo-American monopolies and strengthen its position in negotiations with them."[12] The Italians' use of Algeria to put pressure on the Soviets was equally unconvincing; only years before they had approached the Soviets precisely to weaken

---

[9] In talks between ENI and Soiuznefteeksport on October 12, 1966. RGAE, f. 413, op. 31, d. 1129, ll. 147–149.

[10] RGAE, f. 413, op. 31, d. 1699, ll. 20–22, in a meeting with the Italian ambassador on October 20, 1967. Or in ibid., ll. 4–6, on December 16, 1967. On January 11, 1968, it was ENI's turn, RGAE, f. 413, op. 31, d. 2316, ll. 3–5.

[11] RGAE, f. 413, op. 31, d. 2316, ll. 79–87, Landolfi's most comprehensive attempt came in April 5, 1968, when he informed Osipov that the Anglo-American "monopoly" companies were clearly trying to prevent a Soviet–Italian deal by sweetening NAM's terms. He said that NAM was frontloading the lower prices that they were anyway expecting in the coming years. Interestingly, Landolfi adds that the last time the "monopolies" tried to sabotage Soviet–Italian gas talks was in April 1967, ibid., l. 85. See also Landolfi's June 1968 attempt in ibid., ll. 105–106.

[12] Ibid., l. 85.

possible Algerian positions in Italy.[13] Market discourse had long been the medium the Soviets had used to manage relations with the West. The Italians, for their part, had in the past countered with a politicized discourse of Cold War risk. Now they joined the Soviets in using a naturalized mimicry of stock market analysis: "The exploration of new fields and the increase in industrial gas reserves will have a natural psychological effect toward a downward trend in prices."[14] Even the memory of this leverage began to change its language. As Landolfi explained, forgetting all arguments of US pressure he had so often used, "when the first deal on oil was concluded, it was done so below market prices because you have to pay for entering in a new market."[15]

As the Soviets pivoted to Austria and Germany for a deal on gas, price disputes in other deals with Italy seemed to develop a harder edge as well. While ultimatums were diplomatically insinuated in the gas negotiations, the Soviets had a similar situation with Pirelli, which had been recruited as part of the Fiat deal to provide tire-production technology.[16] With about $3 million separating the two sides in a $50 million deal after almost a year of negotiation, the Soviets were happy to split the difference. Pirelli, possibly piqued by the implication that its dealmakers were frivolous when it came to pricing, countered with an ultimatum to leave negotiations altogether. Once again it was the Italian state apparatus that would intervene to save the deal.[17] Although Italian state officials had done so in the past on their own initiative, the Soviets were learning to add employment concerns and those of the small and medium firms to their rhetorical appeal for help from the state, as in: "In order to develop our trade relations, it would be advisable, in our opinion, for Pirelli to reconsider its position and conclude a contract that will make it possible to give work to a large number of Italian engineering sub-supplying companies."[18]

---

[13] Ibid., ll. 36–37, in which Landolfi informed Osipov that the Italian foreign minister was in Algeria in February 1968, where he was pressured to conclude new deals. By March even the documents themselves express the tedious repetitiveness of Italian invocations of market pressures, as in "again, as in earlier talks, he mentioned the changed situation over the last 8–10 months in the European gas market." Ibid., l. 60.

[14] Ibid., l. 4.

[15] RGAE, f. 413, op. 31, d. 2316, l. 81, in an April 5, 1968 meeting with Osipov. A decade earlier there was no mention of the market, only of the scolding and pressure ENI and Italian officials would have to endure from the US government.

[16] See ibid., ll. 6–8, on the veiled ultimatum, in which ENI announced on January 12, 1968, that the delegation that had just arrived would either find an agreement within the week or "end contract discussions."

[17] Ibid., ll. 9–12.   [18] Ibid., l. 10.

Political risk remained a concern. In 1968 it incorporated the risk of currency fluctuations to its meaning, in addition to more blunt forms of (US) government interventions – which in their turn slowly loomed less and less threateningly. During the great year of global protests, the Soviet state spent its time in fear not of domestic social conflict, but of currency devaluations. To counter that fear, they insisted on including a gold proviso on all new long-term contracts. Currency risks had not been an issue since the prewar days of the gold standard, so it was probably no coincidence that when they resurfaced again the Soviets would go for such an archaic solution. Later, after petrodollars flooded the banking system and banks were released to finance projects on their own, the US dollar would, paradoxically, make gold provisos irrelevant. But this was still a Keynesian world, finance still served national purpose, and the coming devaluation of the dollar threatened commodity exporters as well as the sense of stability that had reigned over the past two decades. The uncertainty added another wrinkle to Soviet–Italian negotiations that already had its share of difficulties while it transitioned into a more socioeconomically integrated environment.

And all the while the drumbeat toward greater liberalization continued, with its usual pattern of hectoring, comparison, and threat, reaching a fever pitch in 1969. Hectoring: Italy had the strictest licensing regime of all Western countries; this decreased the interest of Soviet exporters in Italian markets, especially in machines and equipment. Comparison: "From the first of May England fully liberalized the import of machinery and equipment and the majority of finished products from the USSR. On May 19 we initialed an agreement with France that provides for a meaningful improvement in their import regime of Soviet goods." Threat: Unless Italy liberalized its imports, Soviet trade organizations would be forced to take their trade operations to other countries.[19] Rinse and repeat. With talks for a new long-term agreement coming up, the time for pressure on the Italians was ripe, and as usual, the Soviets used both business and political channels.[20] Their leverage on the European Economic Community was less direct, particularly while they refused to admit the European Commission existed as part of the constellation of international institutions.[21] But still they conveyed

---

[19] RGAE, f. 413, op. 31, d. 2994, ll. 33–35, from a meeting on May 22, 1969, between Deputy Minister Manzhulo and Italian embassy trade advisor Lo Faro.

[20] In ibid., ll. 40–41, or example, in talks with Agnelli's youngest brother Umberto, on Fiat business, on June 27, 1969, as well as in talks with the Italian foreign ministry on February 12 in ibid., ll. 15–19.

[21] Suvi Kansikas, *Socialist Countries Face the European Community. Soviet-Bloc Controversies over East-West Trade* (Frankfurt: Peter Lang, 2014).

their displeasure through national conduits like Italy with the EEC's decision in December 1968 to liberalize imports generally while excepting the Soviet Union.[22] The Italian government, for its part, could only proclaim support for a liberalization effort for Soviet products that seemed to be out of its hands.[23]

The year 1969 was an awkward one for the Italian position in the upcoming negotiations for that new five-year agreement. The country had suddenly developed a trade surplus with the Soviets, which, in the Keynesian world of balance, gave the Soviets an edge in the performance of an ethics discourse of economic exchange. The Communists used this edge in commercial ethics with panache. Under the cover of that deficit, the Soviets pushed a whole set of objectives. At the enterprise level, when the machinery maker Innocenti told the Soviets the machine tools it had bought from them worked badly, the company's management was told there were many other machines the company was buying abroad that could be purchased in the Soviet Union. And may they remind the Italian managers that Soviet organizations buy much more from Innocenti than they supply to the company?[24] The Soviets knew how to leverage their weight in a Bretton Woods world. At the level of the state, they put pressure for industrial exports, reminding the Italians in the same breath that they were satisfying Italian requests to purchase Italian consumer goods like clothes and shoes – the general public may not have understood that this was very much against Soviet trade policy and commercial disposition, but Italian negotiators understood well the ethics of this remonstration.[25] Minister Patolichev, meanwhile, was advising that Italy start negotiating the next long-term agreement within a year to a year and a half after the new agreement went into effect, so as to forestall any great fluctuations in trade such as the one they were experiencing that year – an idea that would also be promoted by the Soviet foreign ministry.[26]

ENI did not need the Soviets to explain the benefits of long-term contracts. In fact they were agents for Soviet interests, with bosses Eugenio Cefis and Raffaele Girotti volunteering to actively lobby the Italian

---

[22] RGAE, f. 413, op. 31, d. 2994, l. 17.
[23] Ibid., ll. 10–11. Italy's admission that much decision-making on trade with Eastern Europe lay with the EEC is in ibid., ll. 18–19.
[24] Ibid., ll. 30–32.   [25] Ibid., l. 16.
[26] Ibid., l. 12. Italy was the Soviet Union's fourth trade partner after England, Japan, and Finland, and the first in the common market area. To maintain that position Italy would need to plan ahead, Patolichev warned. The Soviet ambassador's talking point to the Italian foreign ministry that a stable economic relationship with Italy would be fundamental for relations of all other kinds is in ibid., ll. 15–16.

government on those long-term agreements.[27] The tehnopolitics of the deal meant it was hardly one that concerned Italy as a nation – though it would certainly impact it. Italian business generally likely preferred the largest possible deal: The larger the deal the greater the chances a given Italian firm might sell something to the Soviets. But for ENI this was not a game of probability; the aim was to monopolize the trading relationship and leverage the conglomerate's different components to drum up business for its close partners. This was the case, for example, for Montedison – formed in 1966 after the fusion of two other companies that had long been involved with the Soviets, Montecatini and Edison. Having recently bought a large stake in the newly created company, ENI was now in a privileged position to transmit to the Soviets their expectation that Montedison pick up all Soviet business in Italy related to the chemical industry in any long-term agreement of large capital and energy exchanges, just as they wanted to mobilize increasing sales for Finsider, its pipe-making partner in the steel industry.[28] Any bilateral long-term agreement between the two nations could only strengthen state-owned ENI, its conglomerate business, and those in the government tied to that capitalized behemoth of domestic social power.[29]

ENI was not above making use of that sense of partnership to keep the flow of energy going. Although the company had been failing in securing gas from the Soviets, it had been wildly successful in securing oil. When the Soviets informed ENI it would not be able to supply the five million tons agreed upon for 1970, it was again telling that ENI no longer made use of the Cold War rhetoric that had availed it at the beginning of the relationship. Instead, the appeal was on the grounds of Italy's own domestic situation: "ENI's leadership has maintained for many years that the USSR is a reliable source of [oil] supply. Certain circles in Italy are interested in showing that this is not so."[30] The appeal to loyalty worked enough to soften the cut. Ambassador Sensi was, after all, not wrong in his remark, in a meeting in September 1969, that "despite the fact that over the last five years several governments succeeded each other, the line of cooperation with the Soviet Union remained unchanged." The Soviet memorandum of that meeting

---

[27] Ibid., l. 38.   [28] Ibid., ll. 21–24.
[29] For a look into ENI's sociopolitical role during Italy's economic miracle as a tool for the Christian Democrats, see Francesca Carnevali, "State Enterprise and Italy's 'Economic Miracle': The Ente Nazionale Idrocarburi, 1945–1962," *Enterprise & Society* 1:2 (2000): 249–278.
[30] The Soviets were offering ENI three million tons of crude oil rather than the five million contracted. They told the Soviets they had been quiet about this possible breach of contract so as not to give fodder to their mutual enemies in Italy, but that rumors were flying. In the end the Soviets found other ways to cut back on oil exports, by half a million tons in crude and oil products for 1970, and another million in 1971. RGAE, f. 413, op. 31, d. 2994, l. 56.

continued: "Sensi then observed that over the last five years in his post as ambassador in Moscow, four different ministers of foreign trade have taken their turn."[31]

The ethical discourse that had grown around commercial practices enframed by the unyielding balances of the Bretton Woods regime reproduced an unchanging set of concerns for as long as the regime was operative. Patolichev's policy line regarding Italy revolved around liberalization, increasing exports of machinery and equipment, tariff levels – which is to say, Italy's role as lobbyist within the EEC – and strategies for increasing overall turnover. Patolichev preferred that these be covered by the experts in the upcoming long-term trade agreement negotiations, relegating these issues to technocratic maneuvering. And he was clear about what the main Soviet concern was. As Kuz'min conveyed it, they were "worried about the financial side of trade, since it is unrealistic to count on a further increase in the export of raw materials from the USSR. Much will depend on the Italian side, which should offer us the same conditions of trade as it offers its Western partners. That decision cannot but affect our plans for further purchases in Italy."[32] ENI had been the quintessential partner for breaking the confines of Cold War politics and the limits of the Bretton Woods regime. As ENI and its government clung to the instruments of Italy's postwar social peace, it had come to rely on its partnership with the Soviets. The Soviets were happy to oblige but were also looking to elevate banks and financiers as a new set of partners in their drive to intensify the regime's ties to international capital.

And gas was its prophet. There was one task pending between the two political entities, as political entities, before a new long-term agreement could be fully envisioned. The Italians had mistakenly thought time was on their side. The Soviets had used time more wisely, stitching together from national fragments a bare European tapestry of market competition. Patterns of exchange around energy and finance were slowly standardized around supranational criteria made internationally translatable through continuous reference. This new makeshift market had hardened Soviet positions on the price and financing of gas and had stalled Soviet-ENI negotiations for years. After having done so much to disrupt old patterns and practices of energy exchange, ENI had failed, in the context of an embryonic politics of the market at the end of the decade, to

---

[31] Ibid., l. 60. This was by way of introducing the latest foreign trade minister, Riccardo Misasi, who was only thirty-seven but could be relied upon to follow the long-established policy line.

[32] Ibid., ll. 63–64.

establish itself as a hub for the flow of Soviet energy into Western Europe. It is usual among Cold War historians to see no relevant link between the Cold War and the Bretton Woods regime, or to see the former enabling and subsuming the latter. Made relevant by its maverick Cold War disposition, ENI's enduring inertia at the end of the Bretton Woods regime turned out to be the opposite of creative destruction. This is to say, the sudden rearrangements of Bretton Woods made Cold War discourse superfluous. Might we learn something if we read this back to the origins of both?

The Soviets had more or less frozen negotiations with Italy since Austria and Germany entered the picture at the beginning of 1967. A resolution by the Italian government that spring endorsing ENI's negotiations with the Soviets did nothing to move them forward, as a final failed round in the summer made abundantly clear. A flurry of diplomatic activity tried to jumpstart and simultaneously close the deal at the beginning of 1968. Ambassador Sensi made clear that all decisions at this point were Cefis' to make, even if the rest of the Italian state machinery would be involved in the diplomatic protocols around the signing of the deal.[33] In the spring of 1968, ENI changed its positions; for the following year and a half the Soviets would insistently argue that while they had tried to meet the Italians half way, the latter had moved the goal posts.[34] Cefis admitted as much, conveying through Landolfi in April that as of today "he cannot buy the gas at the price ENI had offered before."[35] Cefis explained his toing and froing inconsistently and without much credibility. Enemies of the deal, both internal and external, would have his head if he gave in too much on price to the Soviets, he would say. Or it was the Anglo-American monopolies trying to block Soviet gas from flowing into Europe – a believable charge a decade earlier that was increasingly difficult to sustain in the wake of Austria and Germany's imminent deal.[36] Or, in the new liturgy of the late 1960s, "you have to pay to enter a new market." Cefis' most dramatic claim was, unusually in the Soviet documentation of such meetings, quoted verbatim:

If I had confirmed the $11 offer six months ago, then now there would be such a press campaign that I could not save myself. I would have been accused of paying the Russians at least two dollars per 1,000 cubic meters over the Dutch offer. And

---

[33] RGAE, f. 413, op. 31, d. 2316, ll. 45–46, 52, 53.

[34] Ibid., ll. 71–73 is the earliest instance of this accusation was, on March 14, 1968, in a meeting between Osipov, who had been put in charge of all gas negotiations, and General Director Angelo Fornara, even if later the Soviets would insist on April as the date.

[35] Ibid., l. 81.

[36] Ibid., l. 89. In Cefis' colorful prattle, "these opponents constantly fired on the deal with the Soviet Union with high-caliber guns."

I would have to seek refuge. Recently, and Mr. Bakhtov knows about this, a campaign was launched in the newspapers against ENI, and for me, every article means that I must go to at least five ministers to give them an explanation. The Dutch offered me $9 and I can't pay more. The question is whether you believe me or not. If you do, then it's up to you to decide.[37]

Belief was immaterial. The Soviets would have none of it. They reminded the Italians simply and correctly for the length of the next year and a half that they always were and always would be for closing the deal, but that ENI baselessly and unexpectedly changed its position.[38] From that moment, the Soviets decided to wait for ENI to decide.

ENI took its time. By 1969 managers were aware that they had lost the initiative to the northern neighbors, but they expected the Soviets would keep their offer standing. The expectation might seem odd, but they could confirm it with every prodding conversation, each of which – on average one every few months – seemed to return a repetition of positions from the moment they were frozen in 1967. New discoveries had been made in the Adriatic Sea, and new deals had opened up for the company in North Africa. It is likely that ENI wanted these opportunities to work themselves out before jumping back into negotiations with the Soviets.[39] Whatever the reasons for ENI's immobility, or its strategy if there was one, documents show that the company's efforts at bringing the Soviets back to the table were cavalier. The best that can be said for them is that they entailed a bet on a generalized decline in gas prices. This had been one in the scattered, incoherent set of arguments Cefis had performed in his spring 1968 trip to Moscow. A year and a half later, ENI's director for foreign relations Giuseppe Ratti both excused and reaffirmed the company's price position – at $9 per 1,000 cubic meters – by saying that the price Cefis had quoted Kosygin then was not so much a commercial proposal as much as an expression of the direction of prices.[40] By October Osipov had had enough. He had the impression, he told Ratti then, that "our friends at ENI don't need negotiations on the purchase of Soviet gas, but 'negotiations about negotiations' (...). If ENI has changed its position and does not want to negotiate on the gas, it should be said directly. We believe that we, as

---

[37] Ibid., l. 91. The Soviets understood the Dutch offer, likely correctly, to be unprofitable and "provocative."

[38] RGAE, f. 413, op. 31, d. 2994, l. 58. The Soviets were, in fact, to be consistent in asking for a price in the $11.10–$12.10 range.

[39] Ibid., l. 12, ll. 23–24, l. 25. Almost a year after the fact, in a meeting in March 1969, Landolfi even threw in the Prague Spring as an explanation for the delay, while adding in the same breath that the deal could be signed at any moment if the right price was reached "without great difficulties." In ibid., l. 26.

[40] Ibid., l. 57.

partners of ENI, have given no reason for such behavior. We do not impose our gas. ENI turned to us with a proposal to buy gas in the Soviet Union. In order to plan some gas quantities for Italy and hold the necessary negotiations with the Czechs on the gas pipeline construction we need clarity on the issue of the contract with ENI. So far, we have taken the words of the ENI representatives seriously. Maybe we were too trusting."[41]

The long-term agreement negotiations were now badly delayed.[42] Everything seemed to hang on a resolution to the "great gas problem," as Landolfi called it.[43] And Soviet patience was coming to an end. The Soviets offered a carrot: Despite Italian capriciousness, which at that point included faints toward changing technical terms already preliminarily agreed to, the Soviets were happy to maintain all initialed agreements from the last two years, which left mostly only finance and price as the two outstanding issues. And they offered the stick, which took the form of a nascent energy market: "We cannot endlessly reserve the previously agreed quantities of gas for ENI, especially when the quantities of pipes that were offered for purchase with gas payment will obviously be available from other countries for the sale of a smaller quantity of gas than we had originally agreed on with ENI."[44] The writing was on the wall, and ENI rediscovered the meaning of alacrity. The company now offered to resolve both the price and the finance simultaneously.

That testy exchange had taken place in mid-October, 1969. The next substantial meeting, a month and a half later in Florence, was a mere few days after Osipov's triumphant agreement with the Germans. This changed environment would quickly produce the results that could have been reached more than two years earlier and would have made of Italy and ENI the main hub and partner for the supply of red gas in Western Europe. But rather than driving the locomotive, the Italians were now running desperately to catch up to the last wagon as the train left the station. The Soviets felt vindicated by the fact that the price of gas had not fallen, generally speaking, and that they had been right in 1968 when Cefis had suddenly decided to lower his price offer.[45] In fact, the prices they negotiated with Austria and Germany were further vindication. But it was the forcible integration of European gas purchases, as mediated and centralized in Moscow, that gave the Soviets the most forceful arguments for their position that

[41] Ibid., ll. 69–70.

[42] Ibid., l. 63. Patolichev seemed slightly annoyed that the Italians had delayed the difficult long-term agreement talks so long that they would end up running into his habitual end-of-the-year talks with Eastern bloc countries.

[43] Ibid., ll. 36–37.   [44] Ibid., l. 70.   [45] Ibid., l. 83.

in December 1969, compared to April 1968, the situation has changed to the advantage of the Soviet side. In April 1968, ENI was the only major consumer of Soviet gas, and today Soviet gas has already been sold to two countries, even as active negotiations are being carried out with a third one. That is, if then ENI had some right to tell Soiuznefteeksport about the need to pay for entry into the market, they have now lost that right. Moreover, the conditions of the deal are no longer as interesting to the Soviet side, since in 1967 ENI wanted to receive 10 billion bcm of gas for Italy, Austria, and France by offering a $500 million credit for the purchase of 1.5 million tons of pipe and equipment, of which Italy could offer 1020 mm diameter pipe with a pressure of 56 atmospheres. But now the Soviet Union has received a credit for $500 million and purchased 520,000 tons of 1220 mm diameter pipe from Austria and 1. 2 million tons of 1420 mm diameter pipe from Germany with a pressure of 75 atmospheres. And we are carrying out negotiations with France for a $200 million credit to purchase more than 500,000 tons of 1220 mm diameter pipe. Thus the Soviet Union will give less than 10 billion bcm a year, and receive 2. 2 million tons of pipe. And the Germans offered credit with a 12-year repayment.[46]

The market they created steeled the Soviets. After half a decade, it took only seven days for the Soviets and Italians to reach an agreement. On the fifth day, Cefis finally took over the negotiations. And on the seventh day, he ended the work which he had made. Cefis caught up with Osipov in Florence on his way back from Sicily, where he had traveled with Patolichev and the rest of the Soviet delegation. The seventh day was a Sunday. And the Soviets rested from all the work they had made. And they saw every thing that they had made, and, behold, it was very good.

[46] Ibid., l. 87.

Bibliography

I Archival Sources

Russian State Archive of Contemporary History (*Rossiiskii gosudarstvennyi arkhiv noveishei istorii*, RGANI).

Fond 3: Politbiuro TsK KPSS (1852–1990).

Fond 5: Apparat TsK KPSS.

Fond 80: Brezhnev, Leonid Il'ich (1906–1982).

Russian State Archive of the Economy (*Rossiiskii gosudarstvennyi arkhiv ekonomiki*, RGAE).

Fond 413: Ministry of Foreign Trade of the USSR (*Ministerstvo vneshnei torgovli SSSR*).

Fond 4372: State Planning Committee of the USSR (*Gosplan SSSR*).

Fond 7590: Bank for Foreign Trade (*Vneshtorgbank*).

II Document Collections and Statistical Publications

Food and Agricultural Organization of the United Nations. *The State of Food and Agriculture 1964* (Rome: FAO, 1963).

Kennedy, John F. *Public Papers of the Presidents of the United States: John F. Kennedy; Containing the Public Messages, Speeches, and Statements of the President, January 20 to November 22, 1963* (Washington, DC: US Government Printing Office, 1964).

Ministerstvo vneshniaia torgovlia. *Vneshniaia torgovlia SSSR za 1956 god. Statisticheskii obzor* (Moscow: Vneshtorgizdat, 1958).

Vneshniaia torgovlia SSSR za 1958 god. Statisticheskii obzor (Moscow: Vneshtorgizdat, 1959).

Vneshniaia torgovlia SSSR za 1918–1940 gg. Statisticheskii obzor (Moscow: Vneshtorgizdat, 1960).

Vneshniaia torgovlia SSSR za 1960 god. Statisticheskii obzor (Moscow: Vneshtorgizdat, 1961).

Vneshniaia torgovlia SSSR za 1962 god. Statisticheskii obzor (Moscow: Vneshtorgizdat, 1963).

Vneshniaia torgovlia SSSR za 1963 god. Statisticheskii obzor (Moscow: Vneshtorgizdat, 1964).

Vneshniaia torgovlia SSSR za 1964 god. Statisticheskii obzor (Moscow: Vneshtorgizdat, 1965).

Vneshniaia torgovlia SSSR za 1965 god. Statisticheskii obzor (Moscow: Izdatel'stvo "Mezhdunarodnye otnosheniia," 1966).

Vneshniaia torgovlia SSSR za 1966 god. Statisticheskii obzor (Moscow: Izdatel'stvo "Mezhdunarodnye otnosheniia," 1967).

Vneshniaia torgovlia SSSR. Statisticheskii sbornik, 1918–1966 (Moscow: Izdatel'stvo "Mezhdunarodnye otnosheniia," 1967).

Vneshniaia torgovlia SSSR za 1970 god. Statisticheskii obzor (Moscow: Izdatel'stvo "Mezhdunarodnye otnosheniia," 1971).

Vneshniaia torgovlia SSSR, 1922–81. Iubileinyi statisticheskii obzor (Moscow: Izdatel'stvo financy i statistika, 1982).

Mullek, G. Zh., Z. K. Vodop'ianova, T. V. Domracheva, and T. G. Zazerskaia, eds. *Ot Atlantiki do Urala. Sovetsko-frantsuzskie otnosheniia, 1956–1973. Dokumenty* (Moscow: Mezhdunarodnyi fond "Demokratiia," 2015).

US Department of State. *Foreign Relations of the United States, 1961–63, Vol. 5, Soviet Union* (Washington, DC: US Government Printing Office, 1998).

III Secondary Sources

Andersson, Jenny. "Ghost in the Shell: The Scenario Tool and the World Making of Royal Dutch Shell," *Business History Review* 94:4 (2020): 729–751.

Andrew, Christopher. *Defend the Realm. The Authorized History of MI5* (New York: Alfred A. Knopf, 2009).

Beckert, Sven, and Seth Rockman, eds. *Slavery's Capitalism. A New History of American Economic Development* (Philadelphia: University of Pennsylvania Press, 2016).

Bell, Daniel. *The Cultural Contradictions of Capitalism* (New York: Basic Books, 1976).

Belykh, A. A. "A Note on the Origins of Input-Output Analysis and the Contribution of the Early Soviet Economists: Chayanov, Bogdanov and Kritsman," *Soviet Studies* 41:3 (1989): 426–429.

Bini, Elisabetta. "A Challenge to Cold War Energy Politics? The US and Italy's Relations with the Soviet Union, 1958–1969," in Jeronim Perović, ed., *Cold War Energy. A Transnational History of Soviet Oil and Gas* (Cham: Palgrave Macmillan, 2017).

Block, Fred. *The Origins of International Disorder. A Study of United States International Monetary Policy from World War II to the Present* (Berkeley: University of California Press, 1977).

Bockman, Johanna. *Markets in the Name of Socialism. The Left-Wing Origins of Neoliberalism* (Stanford: Stanford University Press, 2011).

"Socialist Globalization against Capitalist Neocolonialism: The Economic Ideas behind the New International Economic Order," *Humanity* 6:1 (2015): 109–128.

"Democratic Socialism in Chile and Peru: Revisiting the 'Chicago Boys' as the Origin of Neoliberalism," *Comparative Studies in Society and History* 61:3 (2019): 654–679.

Bösch, Frank. "West Germany, The Soviet Union and the Oil Crises of the 1970s," *Historical Special Research/Historische Sozialforschung* 39:4 (2014): 165–185.

Bradbury, J. H. "International Movements and Crises in Resource Oriented Companies: The Case of Inco in the Nickel Sector," *Economic Geography* 61:2 (1985): 129–143.

Bren, Paulina, and Mary Neuburger, eds. *Communism Unwrapped. Consumption in Cold War Eastern Europe* (Oxford: Oxford University Press, 2012).

Brenner, Robert. *The Economics of Global Turbulence. The Advanced Capitalist Economies from Long Boom to Long Downturn, 1945–2005* (New York: Verso, 2006).

Brown, Kate. "Gridded Lives: Why Kazakhstan and Montana Are Nearly the Same Place," *American Historical Review* 106:1 (2001): 17–48.

Plutopia. Nuclear Families, Atomic Cities, and the Great Soviet and American Plutonium Disasters (Oxford: Oxford University Press, 2013).

Manual for Survival. A Chernobyl Guide to the Future (New York: W. W. Norton, 2019).

Calleo, David P. *The Imperious Economy* (Cambridge: Harvard University Press, 1982).

Cantoni, Roberto. "What's in a Pipe? NATO's Confrontation on the 1962 Large-Diameter Pipe Embargo," *Technology and Culture* 58:1 (2017): 67–96.

Carnevali, Francesca. "State Enterprise and Italy's 'Economic Miracle': The Ente Nazionale Idrocarburi, 1945–1962," *Enterprise & Society* 1:2 (2000): 249–278.

Clark, D. L. "Planning and the Real Origins of Input-Output Analysis," *Journal of Contemporary Asia* 14:4 (1984): 408–429.

Connell, Raewyn, and Nour Dados. "Where in the World Does Neoliberalism Come From? The Market Agenda in Southern Perspective," *Theory and Society* 43:2 (2014): 117–138.

Cooper, Frederic. "Writing the History of Development," *Journal of Modern European History* 8:1 (2010): 5–23.

Copley, Jack. "Why Were Capital Controls Abandoned? The Case of Britain's Abolition of Exchange Controls, 1977–1979," *British Journal of Politics and International Relations* 21:2 (2019): 403–420.

Costabile, Lilia. "Continuity and Change in the International Monetary System: Dollar Standard and Capital Mobility," *Review of Political Economy* 34:3 (2022): 585–597.

Crotty, James. *Keynes against Capitalism. His Economic Case for Liberal Socialism* (London: Routledge, 2019).

Crowley, David, and Susan E. Reid, eds. *Pleasures in Socialism. Leisure and Luxury in the Eastern Bloc* (Evanston: Northwestern University Press, 2010).

Cucu, Alina-Sandra. "Going West: Socialist Flexibility in the Long 1970s," *Journal of Global History* (2023).

de Cecco, Marcello. "International Financial Markets and US Domestic Policy since 1945," *International Affairs* 52:3 (1976): 381–399.

"Origins of the Post-War Payments System," *Cambridge Journal of Economics* 3:1 (1979): 49–61.

"Financial Relations: Between Internationalism and Transnationalism," in Roger Morgan, Jochen Lorentzen, Anna Leander, and Stefano Guizzini, eds., *New Diplomacy in the Post–Cold War World* (New York: St. Martin's Press, 1993).

de Groot Michael. "The Soviet Union, CMEA, and the Energy Crisis of the 1970s," *Journal of Cold War Studies* 22:4 (2020): 4–30.

Demuth, Bathsheba. *Floating Coast. An Environmental History of the Bering Strait* (New York: W. W. Norton, 2019).

di Méo, Guy. "Le nickel dans le monde," *Travaux de l'Institut de Géographie de Reims*, vol. 12 (1972): 15–30.

Dimier, Véronique. *The Invention of a European Development Aid Bureaucracy. Recycling Empire* (Basingstoke: Palgrave Macmillan, 2014).

Dobson, Alan. "When Strategic Foreign Policy Considerations Did Not Trump Economics: British Cold War Policies on East-West Trade," in John Fisher, Effie G. H. Pedalu and Richard Smith, eds., *The Foreign Office, Commerce and British Foreign Policy in the Twentieth Century* (London: Palgrave Macmillan, 2016).

Dohan, Michael R. "Soviet Foreign Trade in the NEP Economy and Soviet Industrialization Strategy" (PhD dissertation, MIT, 1969).

Edgerton, David. "The Decline of Declinism," *Business History Review* 71:2 (1997): 201–206.

The Shock of the Old. Technology and Global History since 1900 (Oxford: Oxford University Press, 2006).

Eichengreen, Barry. *The European Economy since 1945. Coordinated Capitalism and Beyond* (Princeton: Princeton University Press, 2007).

Globalizing Capital. A History of the International Monetary System (Princeton: Princeton University Press, 2008).

Exorbitant Privilege. The Rise and Fall of the Dollar and the Future of the International Monetary System (Oxford: Oxford University Press, 2010).

"Bretton Woods After 50," *Review of Political Economy* 33:4 (2021): 552–569.

Ellman, Michael. "Money, Prices, and Payments in Planned Economies," in Stefano Battilossi, Youssef Cassis and Kazuhiko Yago, eds., *Handbook of the History of Money and Currency* (Singapore: Springer, 2020).

Engerman, David C. *The Price of Aid. The Economic Cold War in India* (Cambridge: Harvard University Press, 2018).

Faudot, Adrien. "The European Payments Union (1950–58): The Post-War Episode of Keynes' Clearing Union," *Review of Political Economy* 32:3 (2020): 371–389.

Fauri, Francesca. "The 'Economic Miracle' and Italy's Chemical Industry, 1950–1965: A Missed Opportunity," *Enterprise & Society* 1:2 (2000): 279–314.

Fava, Valentina. "Between Business Interests and Ideological Marketing: The USSR and the Cold War in Fiat Corporate Strategy, 1957–1972," *Journal of Cold War Studies* 20:4 (2018): 26–64.

Fraser, Nancy. "Legitimation Crisis? On the Political Contradictions of Financialized Capitalism," *Critical Historical Studies* 2:2 (2015): 157–189.

Frieden, Jeffry A. *Global Capitalism. Its Fall and Rise in the Twentieth Century* (New York: W. W. Norton & Company, 2006).

Friedman, Milton. "The Euro-Dollar Market: Some First Principles," *Federal Reserve Bank of St. Louis Review* 53 (July 1971): 16–24.

Gardner, Richard N. *Sterling-Dollar Diplomacy. Anglo-American Collaboration in the Reconstruction of Multilateral Trade* (Oxford: Clarendon Press, 1956).

Gavin, Francis J. *Gold, Dollars, and Power. The Politics of International Monetary Relations, 1958–1971* (Chapel Hill: University of North Carolina Press, 2004).

Gerth, Karl. *Unending Capitalism. How Consumerism Negated China's Communist Revolution* (Cambridge: Cambridge University Press, 2020).

Gilburd, Eleonory. *To See Paris and Die. The Soviet Lives of Western Culture* (Cambridge: Harvard University Press, 2018).

Gildea, Robert. *France since 1945* (Oxford: Oxford University Press, 1996).

Goland, Yurii. "Currency Regulation in the NEP Period," *Europe-Asia Studies* 46:8 (1994): 1251–1296.

Goldman, Marshall. *The Enigma of Soviet Petroleum. Half-Full or Half-Empty?* (London: Allen & Unwin, 1980).

Gordon, Robert J. *The Rise and Fall of American Growth. The US Standard of Living since the Civil War* (Princeton: Princeton University Press, 2016).

Gorin, Zeev. "Socialist Societies and World System Theory: A Critical Survey," *Science & Society* 49:3 (1985): 332–366.

Graeber, David. *Toward an Anthropological Theory of Value* (New York: Palgrave, 2001).

Graf, Rüdiger. *Oil and Sovereignty. Petro-Knowledge and Energy Policy in the United States and Western Europe in the 1970s* (New York: Berghahn Books, 2018).

Grandin, Greg. *The End of the Myth. From the Frontier to the Border Wall in the Mind of America* (New York: Metropolitan Books, 2019).

Gunder Frank, André. "Long Live Transideological Enterprise! The Socialist Economies in the Capitalist International Division of Labor," *Review (Fernand Braudel Center)* 1:1 (1977): 91–140.

Gustafson, Thane. *Crisis Amid Plenty. The Politics of Soviet Energy under Brezhnev and Gorbachev* (Princeton: Princeton University Press, 1989).

Hale-Dorrell, Aaron. *Corn Crusade. Khrushchev's Farming Revolution in the Post-Stalin Soviet Union* (Oxford: Oxford University Press, 2018).

Hamilton, Shane and Sarah Phillips, eds. *The Kitchen Debate and Cold War Consumer Politics. A Brief History with Documents* (Boston: Bedford/St. Martin's, 2014).

Hanieh, Adam. "Petrochemical Empire: The Geo-Politics of Fossil-Fuelled Production," *New Left Review* 130 (July/Aug 2021): 25–51.

Hanson, Philip. *Trade and Technology in Soviet-Western Relations* (London: The Macmillan Press, 1981).

Hardie, Iain and Helen Thompson, "Taking Europe Seriously: European Financialization and US Monetary Power," *Review of International Political Economy* 28:4 (2021): 775–793.

Hardt, John P. and George D. Holliday, "Technology Transfer and Change in the Soviet Economic System," in Frederic A. Fleron, Jr., ed., *Technology and Communist Culture. The Socio-Cultural Impact of Technology Under Socialism* (New York: Praeger, 1977).

Harvey, David. *The Condition of Postmodernity. An Enquiry into the Origins of Cultural Change* (Oxford: Basil Blackwell, 1989).

A Brief History of Neoliberalism (Oxford: Oxford University Press, 2005).

Hatzivassiliou, Evanthis. "Commerce as a British Cold War 'Heresy:' The Intra-NATO Debate on Trade with the Soviet Bloc, 1962–5," in John Fisher, Effie G. H. Pedalu, and Richard Smith, eds., *The Foreign Office, Commerce and British Foreign Policy in the Twentieth Century* (London: Palgrave Macmillan, 2016).

Helleiner, Eric. *States and the Reemergence of Global Finance. From Bretton Woods to the 1990s* (Ithaca: Cornell University Press, 1994).

Forgotten Foundations of Bretton Woods. International Development and the Making of the Postwar Order (Ithaca: Cornell University Press, 2014).

"The Life and Times of Embedded Liberalism: Legacies and Innovations since Bretton Woods," *Review of International Political Economy* 26:6 (2019): 1112–1135.

Hirsch, Francine. *Soviet Judgment at Nuremberg. A New History of the International Military Tribunal after World War II* (Oxford: Oxford University Press, 2020).

Hitchcock, William I. *The Struggle for Europe. The Turbulent History of a Divided Continent, 1945–Present* (New York: Doubleday, 2003).

Hodge, Joseph M. "British Colonial Expertise, Post-Colonial Careering and the Early History of International Development," *Journal of Modern European History* 8:1 (2010): 24–46.

Högselius, Per. *Red Gas. Russia and the Origins of European Energy Dependence* (Basingstoke: Palgrave Macmillan, 2013).

Energy and Geopolitics (London: Routledge, 2019).

Högselius, Per, Anna Åberg and Arne Kaijser, "Natural Gas in Cold War Europe: The Making of a Critical Infrastructure," in Per Högselius, Anique Hommels, Arne Kaijser, and Erik van der Vleuten, eds., *The Making of Europe's Critical Infrastructure. Common Connections and Shared Vulnerabilities* (Basingstoke: Palgrave Macmillan, 2013).

Huber, Matthew T. "Enforcing Scarcity: Oil, Violence, and the Making of the Market," *Annals of the Association of American Geographers*, 101:4 (2011): 816–826.

"Fueling Capitalism: Oil, the Regulation Approach, and the Ecology of Capital," *Economic Geography* 89:2 (2013): 171–194.

Humphrey, Caroline. "Barter and Economic Disintegration," *Man* 20:1 (1985).

Hyman, Louis. *Temp. How American Work, American Business, and the American Dream Became Temporary* (New York: Penguin Books, 2018).

Jackson Ian. *The Economic Cold War. America, Britain and East-West Trade, 1948–63* (New York: Palgrave, 2001).

Jackson, Marvin. "When Is a Price a Price? The Level and Patterns of Prices in the CMEA," *Soviet and Eastern European Foreign Trade* 22:1 (1986): 100–112.

James, Harold. "The Multiple Contexts of Bretton Woods," *Past & Present* 210 (2011): 290–308.

Jentleson, Bruce W. *Pipeline Politics. The Complex Political Economy of East-West Trade* (Ithaca: Cornell University Press, 1986).

Judt, Tony. *Postwar. A History of Europe since 1945* (New York: The Penguin Press, 2005).

Juhasz, Antonia. *The Tyranny of Oil. The World's Most Powerful Industry—and What We Must Do to Stop It* (New York: William Morrow, 2008).

Kansikas, Suvi. *Socialist Countries Face the European Community. Soviet-Bloc Controversies over East-West Trade* (Frankfurt: Peter Lang, 2014).

Kaser, Michael. "Trade Relations: Patterns and Prospects," in Alex Pravda and Peter J. S. Duncan, *Soviet-British Relations since the 1970s* (Cambridge: Cambridge University Press, 1990).

Kenen, Peter B., ed. *Managing the World Economy. Fifty Years after Bretton Woods* (Washington DC: Institute for International Economics, 1994).

Keohane, Robert. *After Hegemony. Cooperation and Discord in the World Political Economy* (Princeton: Princeton University Press, 1984).

Khalili, Laleh. *Sinews of War and Trade. Shipping and Capitalism in the Arabian Peninsula* (New York: Verso, 2020).

Kieninger, Stephan. "Diplomacy beyond Deterrence: Helmut Schmidt and the Economic Dimension of Ostpolitik," *Cold War History* 20:2 (2020): 176–196.

Kindleberger, Charles P. *The World in Depression, 1929–1939* (Berkeley: University of California Press, 1973).

Klinghoffer, Arthur. *The Soviet Union and International Oil Politics* (New York: Columbia University Press, 1977).

Kontorovich, Vladimir. *Reluctant Cold Warriors. Economists and National Security* (Oxford: Oxford University Press, 2019).

Kotkin, Stephen. *Armageddon Averted. The Soviet Collapse, 1970–2000* (Oxford: Oxford University Press, 2001).

Krylova, Anna. "Soviet Modernity: Stephen Kotkin and the Bolshevik Predicament," *Contemporary European History* 23:2 (2014): 167–192.

"Imagining Socialism in the Soviet Century," *Social History* 42:3 (2017): 315–341.

Labban, Mazen. "Oil in Parallax: Scarcity, markets, and the Financialization of Accumulation," *Geoforum* 41:4 (2010): 541–552.

Lampland, Martha. *The Object of Labor. Commodification in Socialist Hungary* (Chicago: The University of Chicago Press, 1995).

Le Billon, Philippe and Alejandro Cervantes, "Oil Prices, Scarcity, and Geographies of War," *Annals of the Association of American Geographers* 99:5 (2009): 836–844.

Lemoine, Francoise. "Trading Prices within the CMEA," *Soviet and Eastern European Foreign Trade* 15:1 (1979): 21–41.

Levinson, Marc. *The Box. How the Shipping Container Made the World Smaller and the World Economy Bigger* (Princeton: Princeton University Press, 2006).

Levy, Jonathan. *Ages of American Capitalism. A History of the United States* (New York: Random House, 2021).

Link, Stefan J. *Forging Global Fordism. Nazi Germany, Soviet Russia, and the Contest over the Industrial Order* (Princeton: Princeton University Press, 2020).

Lipkin, Mikhail. *Sovetskii Soiuz i integratsionnye protsessy v Evrope: seredina 1940-kh – konets 1960-kh godov [The Soviet Union and Integration Processes in*

Europe. mid-1940s – late 1960s] (Moscow: Ruskii fond sodeistviia obrazova-niiu i nauke, 2016).

Lorenzini, Sara. "Comecon and the South in the Years of Détente: A Study on East-South Economic Relations," *European Review of History: Revue européenne d'histoire* 21:2 (2014): 183–199.

Maier, Charles. "The Politics of Productivity: Foundations of American International Economic Policy after World War II," *International Organization* 31:4 (1977): 607–633.

Malanima, Paolo. "The Limiting Factor: Energy, Growth and Divergence, 1820–1913," *The Economic History Review* 73:2 (2020): 486–512.

Malm, Andreas. "Who Lit This Fire? Approaching the History of the Fossil Economy," *Critical Historical Studies* 3:2 (2016): 215–248.

Mark, James and Bogdan C. Iacob, Tobias Rupprecht and Ljubica Spaskovska, 1989. *A Global History of Eastern Europe* (Cambridge: Cambridge University Press, 2019).

Marx, Karl and Frederick Engels, C. J. Arthur, ed., *The German Ideology* (London: Lawrence & Wishart, 1974).

Mayer, Jane. *Dark Money. The Hidden History of the Billionaires behind the Rise of the Radical Right* (New York: Doubleday, 2016).

Mehrling, Perry. "Essential Hybridity: A Money View of FX," *Journal of Comparative Economics* 41:2 (2013): 355–363.

Milward, Alan S. *The Reconstruction of Western Europe, 1945–51* (Berkeley: University of California Press, 1984).

Mirowski, Philip. "Polanyi vs Hayek?" *Globalizations* 15:7 (2018): 894–910.

Mirowski, Philip and Dieter Plehwe, eds. *The Road from Mont Pelerin. The Making of the Neoliberal Thought Collective* (Cambridge: Harvard University Press, 2009).

Mitchell, Timothy. "Metaphors of Power," *Theory and Society* 19:5 (1990): 545–577.

"Fixing the Economy," *Cultural Studies* 12:1 (1998): 82–101.

Rule of Experts. Egypt, Techno-Politics, Modernity (Berkeley: University of California Press, 2002).

"The Work of Economics: How a Discipline Makes Its World," *European Journal of Sociology* 46:2 (2005): 297–320.

"Rethinking Economy," *Geoforum* 39:3 (2008): 1116–1121.

Carbon Democracy. Political Power in the Age of Oil (New York: Verso, 2011).

"Infrastructures Work on Time," in New Silk Roads, *e-flux Architecture* (January 2020).

Mudge, Stephanie M. *Leftism Reinvented. Western Parties from Socialism to Neoliberalism* (Cambridge: Harvard University Press, 2018).

Nealy, James Allen, Jr. "Making Socialism Work: The Shchekino Method and the Drive to Modernize Soviet Industry" (PhD dissertation, Duke University, 2022).

Neveling, Patrick. "The Global Spread of Export Processing Zones and the 1970s as a Decade of Consolidation," in Knud Andersen and Stefan Müller, eds., *Contesting Deregulation. Debates, Practices and Developments in the West since the 1970s* (Oxford: Berghahn Books, 2017), 23–40.

Newnham, Randall. *Deutsche Mark Diplomacy. Positive Economic Sanctions in German-Russian Relations* (University Park: Pennsylvania State University Press, 2002).

Noiriel, Gérard, *Une histoire populaire de la France. De la guerre de Cent Ans à nos jours* (Marseilles: Agone, 2018).

Nove, Alec. *The Soviet Economic System* (London: George Allen & Unwin, 1977).

Nuenlist, Christian, Anna Locher, and Garret Martin, eds., *Globalizing de Gaulle. International Perspectives on French Foreign Policies, 1958–1969* (Lanham: Lexington Books, 2010).

Oberländer, Alexandra. "Hatching Money: The Political Economy of Eggs in the 1960s," *Cahiers du monde russe* 61:1–2 (2020): 231–256.

O'Bryan, Scott. *The Growth Idea. Purpose and Prosperity in Postwar Japan* (Honolulu: University of Hawai'i Press, 2009).

Offner, Amy C. *Sorting Out the Mixed Economy. The Rise and Fall of Welfare and Developmental States in the Americas* (Princeton: Princeton University Press, 2019).

Ogle, Vanessa. "Archipelago Capitalism: Tax Havens, Offshore Money, and the State, 1950s–1970s," *American Historical Review* 122:5 (2017): 1431–1458.

"'Funk Money': The End of Empires, the Expansion of Tax Havens, and Decolonization as an Economic and Financial Event," *Past & Present* 249 (2020): 213–249.

Ortiz, Roberto J. "Oil-Fueled Accumulation in Late Capitalism: Energy, Uneven Development, and Climate Crisis," *Critical Historical Studies* 7:2 (2020): 205–240.

Painter, David S. "The Marshall Plan and Oil," *Cold War* 9:2 (2009): 159–175.

Palen, Marc-William. "Marx and Manchester: The Evolution of the Socialist Internationalist Free-Trade Tradition, c. 1846–1946," *The International History Review* 43:2 (2021): 381–398.

Pechatnov, Vladimir O. "The Soviet Union and the Bretton Woods Conference," in Giles Scott-Smith and J. Simon Rofe, eds., *Global Perspectives on the Bretton Woods Conference and the Post-War World Order* (London: Palgrave Macmillan, 2017).

Phillips-Fein, Kim. *Fear City. New York's Fiscal Crisis and the Rise of Austerity Politics* (New York: Metropolitan Books, 2017).

Piketty, Thomas. *Capital in the 21st Century* (Cambridge: Harvard University Press, 2014).

Pistor, Katharina. "From Territorial to Monetary Sovereignty," *Theoretical Inquiries in Law* 18:2 (2017): 491–517.

Pivovarov, N. Iu. "Zernovoi krizis 1963 g. v SSSR i vneshnetorgovye kollizii ego razresheniia [The Grain Crisis of 1963 in the Soviet Union and Foreign Trade Collisions of Its Resolution]," *Gumanitarnye nauki v Sibiri* 26:1 (2019): 28–33.

Polanyi, Karl. *The Great Transformation. The Political and Economic Origins of Our Time* (Boston: Beacon Press, 1944).

Rafati, Mohammed R. "An Econometric Model of the World Nickel Industry," *Kiel Working Paper 160*, Kiel Institute of World Economics, Kiel, Germany, 1982.

Rogers, Douglas. "Petrobarter: Oil, Inequality, and the Political Imagination in and after the Cold War," *Current Anthropology* 55:2 (2014): 131–153.

The Depths of Russia. Oil, Power, and Culture after Socialism (Ithaca: Cornell University Press, 2015).

Roh, Kyung Deok. *Stalin's Economic Advisors. The Varga Institute and the Making of Soviet Foreign Policy* (New York: I. B. Tauris, 2018).

Sampson, Anthony. *The Seven Sisters. The Great Oil Companies and the World They Made* (New York: Viking Press, 1975).

Sanchez-Sibony, Oscar. "Soviet Industry in the World Spotlight: The Domestic Dilemmas of Soviet Foreign Economic Relations, 1955–1965," *Europe-Asia Studies* 62:9 (2010): 1555–1578.

Red Globalization. The Political Economy of the Soviet Cold War from Stalin to Khrushchev (Cambridge: Cambridge University press, 2014).

"Economic Growth in the Governance of the Cold War Divide: Mikoyan's Encounter with Japan, Summer 1961," *Journal of Cold War Studies* 20:2 (2018): 129–154.

"Global Money and Bolshevik Authority: The NEP as the First Socialist Project," *Slavic Review* 78:3 (2019): 694–716.

"Cuba, Soviet Oil, and the Sanctions That Never Were: An Archival Investigation of Socialist Relations," *Journal of Latin American Studies* 54:4 (2022): 593–616.

Sargent, Daniel. *A Superpower Transformed. The Remaking of American Foreign Relations in the 1970s* (New York: Oxford University Press, 2015).

Sarotte, M. E. *Dealing with the Devil. East Germany, Détente, and Ostpolitik, 1969–1973* (Chapel Hill: The University of North Carolina Press, 2001).

Scott-Smith, Giles and J. Simon Rofe, eds. *Global Perspectives on the Bretton Woods Conference and the Post-War World Order* (Cham: Palgrave Macmillan, 2017).

Shutzer, Matthew. "Oil, Money and Decolonization in South Asia," *Past & Present* 258 (2023): 212–245.

Siefert, Marsha, ed. *Labor in State-Socialist Europe, 1945–1989. Contributions to a History of Work* (Budapest: Central European University Press, 2020).

Siegelbaum, Lewis H. *Cars for Comrades. The Life of the Soviet Automobile* (Ithaca: Cornell University Press, 2008).

ed. *The Socialist Car. Automobility in the Eastern Bloc* (Ithaca: Cornell University Press, 2011).

"People on the Move during the 'Era of Stagnation:' The Rural Exodus in the RSFSR during the 1960s–1980s," in Dina Fainberg and Artemy Kalinovsky, eds., *Reconsidering Stagnation in the Brezhnev Era. Ideology and Exchange* (Lanham: Lexington Books, 2016).

Spaulding, Robert Mark. *Osthandel and Ostpolitik. German Foreign Trade Policies in Eastern Europe from Bismarck to Adenauer* (Providence: Berghahn Books, 1997).

Speich, Daniel. "The Use of Global Abstractions: National Income Accounting in the Period of Imperial Decline," *Journal of Global History* 6:1 (2011): 7–28.

Stanek, Łukasz. "Buildings for Dollars and Oil: East German and Romanian Construction Companies in Cold War Iraq," *Contemporary European History* 30:4 (2021): 544–561.

Stent, Angela. *From Embargo to Ostpolitik. The Political Economy of West German-Soviet Relations 1955–1980* (Cambridge: Cambridge University Press, 1981).

Stephanson, Anders. "Cold War Degree Zero," in Joel Isaac and Duncan Bell, *Uncertain Empire. American History and the Idea of the Cold War* (Oxford: Oxford University Press, 2012).

Stokes, Raymond G. *Opting for Oil. The Political Economy of Technological Change in the West German Chemical Industry, 1945–1961* (Cambridge: Cambridge University Press, 1994).

Stone, Randall W. *Satellites and Commissars. Strategy and Conflict in the Politics of Soviet-Bloc Trade* (Princeton: Princeton University Press, 1996).

Stone Sweet, Alec, Wayne Sandholtz and Neil Fligstein, eds. *The Institutionalization of Europe* (Oxford: Oxford University Press, 2001).

Taubman, William. *Khrushchev. The Man and His Era* (New York: W. W. Norton, 2003).

Thornton, Christy. *Revolution in Development. Mexico and the Governance of the Global Economy* (Berkeley: University of California Press, 2021).

Tobin, James. "Commercial Banks as Creators of Money," in Deane Carson, ed., *Banking and Monetary Studies* (Homewood, IL, 1963).

Tooze, Adam. "Reassessing the Moral Economy of Post-war Reconstruction: The Terms of the West German Settlement in 1952," *Past & Present* 210 (2011): 47–70.

Crashed. How a Decade of Financial Crises Changed the World (New York: Penguin Books, 2018).

Toye, John and Richard Toye. "The Origins and Interpretation of the Prebisch-Singer Thesis," *History of Political Economy* 35:3 (2003): 437–467.

Unfried, Berthold. "Friendship and Education, Coffee and Weapons: Exchanges between Socialist Ethiopia and the German Democratic Republic," *Northeast African Studies* 16:1 (2016): 15–38.

Veblen, Thorstein. *The Engineers and the Price System* (New York: B. W. Huebsch, 1921).

Verdery, Katherine. *What Was Socialism, and What Comes Next?* (Princeton: Princeton University Press, 1996).

Vernengo, Matías. "The Consolidation of Dollar Hegemony after the Collapse of Bretton Woods: Bringing Power Back in," *Review of Political Economy* 33:4 (2021): 529–551.

Vitalis, Robert. *America's Kingdom. Mythmaking on the Saudi Oil Frontier* (Stanford: Stanford University Press, 2007).

Oilcraft. The Myths of Scarcity and Security That Haunt US Energy Policy (Stanford: Stanford University Press, 2020).

von Dannenberg, Julia. *The Foundations of Ostpolitik. The Making of the Moscow Treaty between West Germany and the USSR* (Oxford: Oxford University Press, 2008).

Wacquant, Loïc. "Three Steps to a Historical Anthropology of Actually Existing Neoliberalism," *Social Anthropology/Anthropologie Sociale* 20:1 (2012): 66–79.

Wallerstein, Immanuel. *The Capitalist World-Economy* (Cambridge: Cambridge University Press, 1979).

Williams, William James. "What's in a Name? French Industrial Policy, 1950–1975," in Christian Grabas and Alexander Nützenadel, eds., *Industrial Policy in Europe after 1945. Wealth, Power and Economic Development in the Cold War* (London: Palgrave Macmillan, 2014).

Yergin, Daniel. *The Prize. The Epic Quest for Oil, Money and Power* (New York: Simon & Schuster, 1991).

Zofka, Jan. "Chairman Cotton: Socialist Bulgaria's Cotton Trade with African Countries during the Early Cold War (1946–1970)," *Journal of Global History* 17:3 (2022): 438-456.

Zubok, Vladislav. *A Failed Empire. The Soviet Union in the Cold War from Stalin to Gorbachev* (Chapel Hill: The University of North Carolina Press, 2007).

Index

n = footnote; italicised number = figure

Printed in the United States
by Baker & Taylor Publisher Services